The Ethnic Restaurateur

The Ethnic Restaurateur

BY KRISHNENDU RAY

Bloomsbury Academic
An imprint of Bloomsbury Publishing Plc

B L O O M S B U R Y

LONDON • OXFORD • NEW YORK • NEW DELHI • SYDNEY

Bloomsbury Academic
An imprint of Bloomsbury Publishing Plc

50 Bedford Square
London
WC1B 3DP
UK

1385 Broadway
New York
NY 10018
USA

www.bloomsbury.com

Bloomsbury and the Diana logo are trademarks of Bloomsbury Publishing Plc

First published 2016
Reprinted 2016

British Library Cataloguing-in-Publication Data
A catalogue record for this book is available from the British Library.

ISBN: HB: 978-0-8578-5835-1
PB: 978-0-8578-5836-8
ePDF: 978-1-4725-2024-1
ePub: 978-0-8578-5837-5

Library of Congress Cataloging-in-Publication Data
A catalog record for this book is available from the Library of Congress.

Typeset by RefineCatch Limited, Bungay, Suffolk
Printed and bound in Great Britain

To Maa and my Pishis

Contents

List of Figures

List of Tables

Acknowledgments

I have benefited immensely from criticism and encouragement over the years from a number of sources: first and foremost my doctoral students Sierra Burnett Clark and Jackie Rohel, who also conducted some of the best interviews on which this book is based; Anne McBride, with whom I contested many of the enclosed arguments; Hi'ilei Hobart and Christy Spackman, who steered me in various productive theoretical directions; graduate students in the Food Studies Doctoral Seminar at CUNY—in a course taught by Barbara Katz-Rothman and Jon Deutsch—where I first presented the idea in any coherent form; numerous Masters students on whom I tried out some of my arguments; my colleagues Amy Bentley and Jennifer Berg; audiences at annual meetings of the American Sociological Association and the Association for the Study of Food and Society, where I presented early versions of the chapters; and my confederates in The BAWG, Julie Elman, Toral G. Gajarawala, Maggie Gray, Thuy Linh Tu, and Jessamyn Hatcher. Of course, I have often ignored their very good advice and have said what I needed to say in my own way. Feedback from two anonymous reviewers, twice, over a two-year period, was central to re-working the manuscript for coherence and clarity. Vanina Leschziner's insistence that I make clearer the distinction between popularity and prestige of various cuisines forced me to wrestle down Chapter 3 in a more competent way. Josée Johnston and Shyon Baumann's *Foodies* was essential to my articulation of the difference between their story and mine. Paul Freedman has been a remarkable senior colleague who has encouraged me and provided numerous opportunities to think big which have forced me out of the narrow ethnic corner of the field. Thanks to Jo, Piya, and Dan Bender for giving me the space and time, and providing me with the material and emotional frame of mind in Toronto to finish the writing. Most importantly I owe an immense debt of gratitude to the many named and unnamed immigrant restaurateurs who took time off from their very busy schedules to talk to us through the duration of the project.

Preface

As the Grains You Eat, So Will Be the Mind

I had never cooked a meal when I came to the United States in 1988 as a young adult. I had made omelets, taught by a Boy Scouts' Camp Counselor in Jamshedpur. I had brewed tea a handful of times. That's it. That kind of experience with cooking is not an exception. A recent OECD study, released in March 2014, shows Indian men coming pretty close to last in global terms of sharing domestic care-giving work (Rana 2014). In my case, cooking is what mothers, aunts, grandmothers, and servants did. Even if I appreciated the eternal recurrence of delectables, I did not think much about the everyday improvisation of cooking and cleaning. Now I cook often, write about food, and teach it. That was a transformation wrought not by a conscious, thinking, and virtuous subject but by the force of circumstances and the absence of servants and women. My turn to food studies was catalyzed by the realization—forced by immigration—not only that I did not know how to cook, but that I had never thought about it. It was that lack of consciousness about everyday skills of sustenance, in spite of the apparently progressive Marxist politics that I had adopted in high school and college, that cried out for attention. In some ways, progressive, public politics covered over my domestic ineptitude. More than twenty years of cooking, cleaning, and material and affective care-giving was left unaccounted for either in the economic calculations or the narrative of my self. That debt seems to have lingered somewhere, to bubble and burst into recompense in a whole new life. Perhaps we can call it a *hauntology*, after a famous philosopher (Derrida 2006).

I did not think my way out of that ineptitude. Instead, the process should be described as first finding my way through doing what needed to be done, and then the slow, fragmentary, recuperation of that process in thought. I cooked because I had to cook. I thought about it because I had developed an unavoidable habit of doing so. Furthermore, my hands had to be forced to surrender the license of living without a care. I was obviously not the first man to realize that fact, but migration was central to that epistemological recognition, which would shape my subsequent trajectory. Yet it was also retrospective distance rather than proximity that produced insight. In this preface I tell you why I turned to cooking, to the surprise of my family and friends. What that did to my thinking? And how might that in turn contribute to the fields of food studies, sociology, and immigration studies?

My turn to cooking came in graduate school, amidst the heavy theorizing and philosophical engagement that is typical at that age and in such institutions. For a long time I could not reconcile the mundane doing and the high thinking. How could I connect a series of "mere household events, the common, the low, and the familiar" (Das, Jackson, Kleinman, and Singh 2014), with the philosophical strategy of distancing myself from everyday experience? What could be the relationship between the sovereign subject of philosophy and the fragile subject of everyday life, with his craving for the ordinary pleasures of good taste? That is the ground between preparing and eating food, and studying it, as I have come to see after the thoughtful work of Veena Das and her colleagues. For Das it was unclear "what could ever be of philosophical interest in the trivial details of the insecurities of everyday life" (2014: 279). In Michael Jackson's apposite but unintended response, "philosophy saves us from drowning by providing us with the means of regaining our sense of comprehension, composure, and command in a world of confusing and confounding experience" (Das *et al.* 2014: 28). There was this developing chiasmus between the necessity of doing and thinking. Yet, I soon learned that the sharpest retort to old-fashioned theorizing had already been pre-emptively delivered by the seventeenth-century nun and Hispanic Baroque scholar Sor Juana Iñes de la Cruz, who in responding to the chastisement of a powerful bishop noted, "If Aristotle had cooked, he would have written a great deal more" (de la Cruz 2009: 75). Here she was transforming the long-resonant anger given voice in the Indian monk Sumangalamata's ancient poetic outburst, "A woman well set free! How free I am, How wonderfully free, from kitchen drudgery . . . Free too of that unscrupulous man" (Tharu and Lalita 1991: 69). De la Cruz was articulating a subtle theory of knowledge while making room for the care-giver's ways of knowing the world in the kitchen, the parlor and the nursery, *and* thinking and writing about it.

In *What is Called Thinking* (1976), Martin Heidegger attacks the assumed theoretical distinction between the sensible and the intelligible. He is central to the genealogy of major continental thinkers who have made a big difference in re-conceptualizing doing and thinking in the second half of the twentieth century i.e., Pierre Bourdieu, Michel Foucault, Jacques Derrida, Jürgen Habermas, and Richard Rorty.[1] No matter the limits of Heideggerian thinking, some of which will be addressed below, the revolution wrought by his conceptualization is crucial to reimagining everyday practice. First he re-positions and re-valorizes un-theorized, everyday coping skills, over mindful thinking (Harman 2009). Mindful thinking had received all the credit in Western philosophizing since Plato. Heidegger's contribution is the understanding that this ontology of being-in-the-world need not be represented in the mind. It is lived first, thought about later. "The pathbreaking achievement of *Being and Time* consists in Heidegger's decisive argumentative step towards overcoming the philosophy of consciousness" (Habermas 1989: 438). Heidegger's insight can be sharpened by the old pragmatist contention—of Peirce, James, and Dewey—that practice trumps philosophical postulation. That is something that Pierre Bourdieu recognized with telling brilliance in *Outline of a Theory of Practice* (1977), in which he noted that the symbolically structured environment exerts pervasive pedagogic pressure driven by practical mastery that never attains the level of discourse. The child develops whole techniques of the body through mimicking adult gestures and postures, "a way of walking, a tilt of the head, facial expressions, ways of sitting and of using implements, always associated with a tone of voice, a style of speech, and . . . a certain subjective experience" (1977: 87). While practical embodied principles are beyond the grasp of consciousness, they can instill "a whole cosmology, an ethic, a metaphysic, a political philosophy, through injunctions as insignificant as 'stand up straight' or 'don't hold your knife in the left hand'" (1977: 94). When I recoil from a cold glass of water with ice, which is the American norm, I am deploying the embodied understanding of Ayurveda even when I explicitly disavow it. The body sometimes lives in a world that the mind cannot yet think, the tongue articulate, or the fingers inscribe.

Feminist critics such as Hélène Cixous, among others, have long insisted that "écriture feminine" can happen and has happened only in areas un-subordinated to philosophic-theoretical domination by the "conventional man" (Cixous, Cohen and Cohen 1976; DeVault 1991; Charles and Kerr 1988; Murcott 2000; Cairns, Johnston, and Bauman 2010). As Deborah Lupton notes, "food and eating, are commonly regarded as the preserve of the embodied self rather than the disembodied, philosophizing mind. Like food and eating practices, the emotions are traditionally linked with the feminine, with the disempowered and marginalized" (1996: 31). Nevertheless, more than books it was the everyday feminism of colleagues at work, at home, and in the Graduate Student Organization—some of whom were nominally conservative—who were pushing, nudging, and elbowing my perspective into place. Practical everyday feminism was also important before I left India, but there I was surrounded by middle-class feminists who, of necessity, were seeking to break away from domestic bonds and could afford to displace care-work to servants. For Indian feminists in my cohort, domestic care-giving was not the site of positive engagement, so I was never forced to learn that lesson. Instead middle-class American feminism, built in a world without servants in the second half of the twentieth century, was essential to prying open what had already been thought and theorized by women under the double burden of care-giving and conceptualization. With some research—as I show in the first chapter—it was quickly becoming apparent to me that once we take care-giving into the public domain, immigrant men and women have disproportionately cooked, cleaned, and picked up after Americans, since we have records of immigrants writing home and the first official count of occupations and birthplace in the 1850 Census (see Figures 1.1–1.4). The evidence is overwhelming in terms of the association between subjection, care-giving, and cooking that is nevertheless rarely reflected in conscious philosophy.

As in the case of Luce Giard (the exemplary collaborator with Michel de Certeau), I picked up cooking in spite of my thinking. Cooking in general is not considered conducive to thinking. Although the registers of gender are different here and the difference is important, her experience with cooking has echoes that illuminate mine. She writes, "As a child, I refused to surrender to my mother's suggestions to come and learn how to cook by her side. I refused this women's work because no one ever offered it to my brother" (1998: 151–2). But one day in a small apartment she needed to cook so that she could "escape from the noise and crowds of college cafeterias and from the shuttling back and forth to face preordained menus" (1998: 152). From those groping initial gestures she realized, to her surprise, that although she thought that she had never learned or observed anything, "having obstinately wanted to escape from the contagion of a young girl's education and because I had always preferred my room, my books, and my silent games to the kitchen where my mother busied herself, yet, my childhood gaze had seen and memorized certain gestures, and my sense memory had kept track of certain tastes, smells, and colors" (1998: 153). She had to admit that this woman's knowledge had crept into her, "slipping past my mind's surveillance" as she discovered, bit by bit, the pleasures of cooking and eating good meals. What is surprising is that in my case, even as a boy, I had not escaped the example of women's everyday work that surrounded me.

To eat good Indian food I had to cook, because when I left India I left the company of women and servants who could cook Indian food. With cooking I learned the use of tools that never alienated themselves into distant technology. In cooking I began to feel through food and touch other living things in their dying throes, by gutting fish, stuffing chicken, mashing potatoes, kneading dough. Cooking can be humbling because it forces us to consider the connection between death and sustenance. Through cooking I acquired allies in graduate school who both aided me in my academic project and gave me a value that exceeded my worth in ideas, words, and critique. I gave them something to eat. In exchange, cooking gave a certain zest and confidence to my critique of culture and hierarchy because I could cook (appropriating the tools of my gendered and class other), a decidedly common activity, badly at first, but better with each passing day.

Soon it was assumed that I *would* cook. Yet, the strictures of a good liberal arts education kept these two things separate. I had learned to cook in spite of my gender, my class, and in spite of my mind. The future was still ahead in which I could cook and think without apology. That came slowly because there were no available models for it in my social world. As Ann Romines (1997: 87) noted in her study of Methodist cookbooks in Texas, it was a great relief when "I realized that I needn't be torn between two communities—one for scholarship, one for cooking." The limits of my horizon, thrown as I was into an already given, already constituted world, slowly opened up to my inquiry with the aid of others. I am bringing together here the two habits of thinking and doing. My posture towards cooking and the new gestures I have learned have allowed me to remake the world I live in. Cooking and tasting opened new possibilities in at least two directions.

First, they provided the foundations of an alternative relational aesthetic experience of *rasa*, used in Indian performance art, that "necessitates and is only completed by the beholder's presence" (Fisher 1999: 38), which circumvents the dominant Kantian aesthetic formula of distanced consideration. Rasa ruptures the habits of Enlightenment rationality in the conception of shared beauty and good taste (Fisher 1999: 38). To see is to separate the object from the subject, reason from feeling, emotion, which of course is the Kantian project of saving beauty from Humean feeling and opinion by developing rational criteria of judgment by eliminating flavor and taste. We need to pay attention to other theorizations of taste. We need a lot more of the mouth, the tongue, the nose. We need the intermingling of the subject and the object, and of the context, company, and performance. Eating is about socially constructed taste. Taste is about the aesthetics of pleasure. It is preceded by the ethics of feeding. Both ethics and aesthetics are relationships between feeder, partaker, and audience. That is the frame for the pleasures of good food, emotion, affect, company, and context. As Richard Schechner noted,

> Rasa is sensuous, proximate, experiential. Rasa is aromatic. Rasa fills space, joining the outside to the inside. Food is actively taken into the body, becomes part of the body, works from the inside. What was outside is transformed into what is inside. An aesthetic founded on rasa is fundamentally different than one founded on the "theatron," the rationally ordered, analytically distanced panoptic . . . Theory is cognate with "theorem," "theater," "theorist," and such, all from the Greek thea, "a sight" . . . This binding of "knowing" to "seeing" is the root metaphor/master narrative of Western thought (2007: 13).

Yet, to consider good food as something amenable to rasa aesthetics, it is necessary to undermine the usual transcendental claims made in the name of rasa, by philosophically oriented male Indian theorists, as something divine. It is necessary to yoke rasa to the pragmatists' claim that the aesthetically valuable is and can be continuous with this-worldly life of everyday emotions heightened and focused by a form (Schechner 2007; Shusterman 2003; Ghosh 2003; Higgins 2007).

Second, cooking opened up another dimension for me. It showed me how the terms of exchange between domains of cultural activity, art, and everyday cooking can shift dramatically with displacement and re-emplacement—that is, migration, in my case—a fact unaccounted for in Bourdieu's analysis of taste and hierarchy. Transplantation can sharpen perception and cognition by redeploying old concepts in new contexts. Cooking in a different context allowed me to circumvent both the straitjacket of Eurocentric aesthetic theory and the subjection to transcendental Brahmanism. Food studies, for me, emerges in the breach, in the rift, between Western high aestheticism and Brahmanic divination, between measured discourse and unmeasured everyday practice, between explicit and implicit knowledge, between life and thing, object and subject, doing and thinking.

Charles Malamoud picks a pebble on the crowded shores of Vedic texts and rituals, an alternative way of being in the world, to throw light on a religion and system of thinking. He picks the Sanskrit phrase *lokapakti* in the Satapatha Brahmana, translating it as "cooking the world." At the heart of every Brahmanic rite, according to Malamoud, is cooking the world. Every rite hinges on a sacrifice, and every sacrificial operation employs a derivative of one of the roots signifying cook, "*pac* or *sra* (or one of their partial synonyms, such as *us*, *ghr*, *tap*, or *dah*)" (Malamoud 1996: 36–7). That is a powerful, almost magical claim, declaring an unwillingness to place everything under the aegis of Western logic, intelligibility, and translatability. Furthermore, it contends that to live properly is to cook the world just right. The objective of cooking is to conjoin the moral and material properties of the food, the cook, and the eater (Achaya 1994: 64). It clarifies much, about both the ancient Vedic tradition and its contemporary Indic appropriation.

No one connects the Vedic cosmology of food to the current tradition more cogently than R. S. Khare, who, with Mary Douglas, co-chaired the International Commission for the Anthropology of Food from 1978 to 1985, urging various national committees to undertake research on food consumption. Khare extrapolates from his dense ethnographic research on the cosmologies and everyday practices of the Kanyakubja Brahmans of the Avadh region in the state of Uttar Pradesh in India (1976a, b; 1992; Khare and Rao 1986). His is a theory of essential and stable differences between the West and India, which violates current orthodoxies of hybridity and eternal change, so central to both postmodern Western experience and theorizations about food. Furthermore, he invests in a Hindu essence—in terms of both everyday experience and a cosmology—that yokes food to the self, soul (atman), and the universe (brahmand). Sustaining the body sustains the universe, because the pursuit of dharma in daily life maintains the cosmic balance, and good food is essential to good karma. Thus one of the oldest Indic texts, called the *Taitirriya Upanishad* (presumed to be compiled sometime between 700 and 600 BCE), suggests that the essential spiritual principle of the universe can be put in the following words:

> Having performed austerity, he understood that Brahma[n] is food. For truly, indeed, beings here are born from food, when born they live by food, on deceasing they enter into food; mankind is food for death; he is nourished and nourishes: I, who am food, eat the eater of food! I have overcome the whole world (Dimock 1995: 28).

What Khare finds distinctive about the Hindu view is this seamless conjoining of nutrient, taste, morals, aesthetics, medicine, body, other beings, plants, animals, minerals, and the universe. The creator of the Hindu universe is after all a yogi, a conjoiner. Khare presumes a Heideggerian *riss*[2] between severed dualistic categories where he contends that the Hindu conception of food "affords the Indianist a cultural lens to see beyond such basic dichotomies of his analysis as the ideal and the practical; self, body and the other; and abstract and concrete" (Khare 1992: 1). He continues, "food becomes simultaneously a moral and material essence" where the central discourse on food is "ontological and experiential" (1992: 7). He builds on "the popular Hindu intuition concerning the absence of opposition between spirit and matter" and promulgates the "interdependence between body, food and mind" (1992: 33). The "Hindu system treats language and discourse as a function of self (and its *manas*), while this 'mind' depends on food (*anna*) and breath (*prana*)" (1992: 39). Breath, by means of food, yields intellect, which in turn works through the five sensory organs. That is both an obvious empirical fact and a subtle spiritual claim. Not only is the bodily substance made of food but so is the moral code, which could be critically accentuated. "Just as butter is formed by churning milk, so the mind is formed by churning food. It is *annamaya*—comprised of grains. *Jainsa khave anna, vainsa hove manna*—as the grains you eat so will be the mind" (Parry 1985: 613). Purandaradasa, a medieval Hindu saint (1480–1564 CE), employs a battery of semiotic switches which tellingly illuminate the Indic relationship across the dualist divide between the self and the divine, morality and aesthetics, cooking and eating, and essence and experience, when he states ecstatically:

> For the milk-made delicacy of Rama's Name, the sugar is Krishna's Name, and the Name of the Lord Vitthala, the ghee; mix, put it into your mouth and

> see the taste! Take the wheat of Ego, put it into the milk of dispassion and pound it into a soft flour and prepare it into fine vermicelli, boil it, and put it into a vessel of your heart, fill it with water of feeling and cook it with your intellect; take it on a plate and eat; and when you get a belching, think of the Lord Purandara Vitthala, who is of the form of joy (translated in Raghavan 1966: 128–9).

It is the joyous belching as spiritual intellection that denotes a different dialect, different from the one to which modern subjects have become habituated. Dialect is about essential difference, not just different registers for the same people. This mixing of metaphors of devotion and diet is not the Hinduism of statecraft and caste-making, but the domain of everyday worship, especially illustrative of female attention to domestic goddesses and the mundane materiality of care-work (Newark Museum 1995). It is the twined vernacularity of labor and care that is signified in the alliterative Bengali listing of everyday work and worship in *batna-bata* (grinding spices), *kutno-kaata* (cutting vegetables), *ranna-banna* (cooking and cleaning), *jhat-daowa* (dusting and sweeping), *pujor-jhogaar* (collecting the flower, water, fruits for worship), *bashon-maja* (doing dishes), *kaapar-kaacha* (laundry), etc. It is important to underline the difference here between a critical, care-based, pragmatic, everyday form of Hinduism that can be recuperated against the violent, caste-based, nation-making Hinduism that is in power in India today. The latter violates everything that is good and sustainable about small-scale worship and care. The work of sustaining the body, especially others' bodies, is equal to divine worship in some branches of everyday Hinduism, and one could live with that form of religiosity. It is the toil that makes the real difference, not the philosophizing, not the bombastic cultural claims on behalf of national Hinduism. There is much worth recuperating in the Hinduism of care-work against the Hinduism of state-craft. Looking back through the thoughtless rituals that I sat through and the mundane nourishment that made me, it was everyday worship, and food offered and cooked by mothers, aunts, grandmothers, and servants, that was central to my being in a world already there, but covered over in language, text, feeling, and theory. For me, bodily displacement, expatriation, was essential to making the obvious visible and in opening up a space to inhabit where I could both practice cooking and theorize it.

Ritual and everyday food is the riss—the thing that separates and pulls us in a conflictual relationship—not only between gods, men, and priests, or between men and women, servants and masters, but also between one being and another. It is the hinge of an assemblage. This project not only develops that post-Heideggerian (and as I learned, Indic) insight, but in doing so goes past his subject-oriented philosophy. Heidegger's thinking re-opens the intellect to the non-theoretical, pre-reflective knowledge of carpenters, cooks, poets, and philosophers. He does that by re-valorizing implicit, everyday forms of knowing that are not easily amenable to explication. Or to put it in Michael Polanyi's terms, "we know more than we can tell," especially in cooking, decorating, and even thinking (1966: 4). This everyday background of doing is as invisible to the intentional mind "as the eye which sees is invisible to itself" (Searle 1983: 157). Yet Heidegger limits his attention to human beings, and his beings never eat. His brilliant retort to Descartes, "I am, therefore I think," does undermine the fully conscious subject, but it is still subjectivity that interests him. Objects are secondary and derived (Garcia 2014). In contrast, the philosopher Raymond Boisvert's (2014) retort is penetratingly obvious: "I eat, therefore I think." We are finally turning the corner from the anthropocentric anti-materialism that has dominated much of modern Western philosophy and opening up new possibilities of considering cooking and thinking.

Thus the other analytic of my conception is an object-oriented philosophy that has been consolidated lately, in one instance, by Jane Bennett in *Vibrant Matter: A Political Ecology of Things* (2010). She re-animates the object world by invoking the spirit of traditional philosophers such as Baruch Spinoza and Gilles Deleuze, to posit a "world populated by animate things rather than passive objects" (2010: vii). Her guiding question is: "How would political responses to public problems change were we to take seriously the vitality of (nonhuman) bodies? By 'vitality' I mean the capacity of things—edibles, commodities, storms, metals—not only to impede or block the will and designs of humans but also to act as quasi agents or forces with trajectories, propensities, or tendencies of their own" (2010: viii). So we can say that the humanist subject (after Foucault and Derrida) is not only a Eurocentric one, hell-bent on subjecting the world to its own image, but that all subject-oriented philosophies have sustained the obviously improbable fantasy that we are really in charge of the world (of objects, including other bodies) and should be in charge. Here demystification, that venerable trope of critical theory, is the obstacle to seeing that human agency is not at the heart of the matter. The object has returned to view in the academic humanities. Things have begun to matter, and food is one of them. In Tristan Garcia's words, "Our time is perhaps the time of an epidemic of things . . . those of us who love things, but who struggle in the face of their accumulation" (Garcia 2014: 1–2). In other words, things matter, people matter, other lives matter, but it is also possible that one of these things can overwhelm the others. Connections between subjects and objects are essential, but vigilance is also necessary not to tip the balance. Food is the hinge, where another life is the thing that sustains body and mind.

That of course turns out to be a very old Indic concept echoed most audibly in notions of transmigration of souls between animals, plants, and humans; in rasa aesthetics that seamlessly conjoin mood, flavor, environment, and substance; and in ayurveda that conjures body, person, and illness as process rather than as objects. I had to be re-introduced to this alternative ecology of forms by way of post-Heideggerian philosophy, given the inevitable trajectory of a post-colonial subject. I had to re-learn the obvious truths of life in a complicated choreography of misreading, forgetting, and knowing. I re-learned that god, food, and life are essential elements of a Hindu cosmological triangle, and in this triangle food has the "privilege of being a nexus where all possible concerns—cosmological, social, psychological, biological, physical—coalesce" (Moreno 1992: 149). When the Upanishads state that life is food or when the Vedas declare that food is life there is an unmistakable sense of an assemblage attached to food.

Furthermore, cooking, one of the closest things to us, has been driven farthest from analysis, as post-Heideggerian philosophers have understood and the Brahmanas have reminded me. The rediscovery of this riss between pre-theoretical thinking and object-oriented philosophy allows me to do three things. At the grandest level, it allows me to evade the narcissism of the human subject, with all his autonomy and agentic activity that has brought the world to the brink of disaster in the narrow bottleneck of a sustainability crisis that re-poses crucial ethical questions about our relationship to other humans, other species, and the environment. "Food is the field in which we daily explore our 'harming' of the world"—the world at large, the social world of the hungry, and those ill with food, the animal world, and the plant world (Snyder 1995: 70). "Harming" here references *himsa*, the conjoined twin of *ahimsa* (nonviolence), a central Indic concern.

At the intermediate level, this riss between pre-theoretical doing and the world of things shows me a way through the lacunae and riddles that have accumulated in and around my work on immigrants and their food-related work and consumption. My first book, *The Migrant's Table* (2004), was focused on domestic cookery in the remaking of migrant worlds. My next edited book (with Tulasi Srinivas), *Curried Cultures* (2012), interrogated claims of transnational cosmopolitanism and provincialism by way of literal taste. *The Ethnic Restaurateur* takes the analysis to the marketplace of ethnic entrepreneurship and urban culture. My forthcoming project is on immigrant street vendors, where I will lay out the possibilities and problems of producing subjectivity at the intersection of culinary knowledge and the praxis of city-based state regulation.

Most immediately, this engagement with taste and toil allows me to cook with the invocation of theory, where theory is the Sanskrit of the liberal arts academy, central to its rituals of indicating serious intent. Philosophical thinking is a habit developed in a milieu, just as cooking and eating. This particular kind of theorization—practical, provincial thinking—does not allow me to postulate universal processes and posit a god's eye view of the world. It tethers me to the precise place from where I speak today, which is in New York City as an immigrant, in the milieu of food studies scholars. That is, I postulate here, my sense of the city, as revealed by my body in interacting with other bodies and things. In Virginia Woolf's apposite recommendation, this book was born from the body of its author (1929: 93). This returns us to the gains of phenomenology, in spite of the turn to object-oriented ontology, where Merleau-Ponty's (2012) insight, that cognition depends on a *schéma corporel* which locates one's body in the world that encourages an understanding of other bodies, is still relevant. External stimulus can only make sense via an embodied sense of self. Migration is not just about loss of culture or even only about economic opportunity. Migration also has its rewards—mundane, material, spiritual, and epistemological—as I will show in the following chapters of the book.

Notes

1 Michel Foucault said, "For me Heidegger has always been the essential philosopher . . . My entire philosophical development was determined by my reading Heidegger" (Foucault 1985: 8). Jacques Derrida at one point doubted that he could write anything that had not already been thought by Heidegger (cited in Dreyfus 1991: 9). Pierre Bourdieu acknowledged that Heidegger was his first love in philosophy, although he did move on to Blaise Pascal in recuperating the genealogy of his thinking. Yet, he acknowledged that his powerful concept of social fields was "indebted to Heidegger by way of Maurice Merleau-Ponty" (Dreyfus 1991: 9). Merleau-Ponty, in turn, accredited the influence of *Being and Time* on his *Phenomenology of Perception* (2012). Jürgen Habermas, who has distanced himself from Heidegger, nevertheless judged him to be "probably the most profound turning point in German philosophy since Hegel" (1989: 434). Furthermore, "Heidegger's critique of reason has been taken up . . . strongly in France and the United States, for example, by Jacques Derrida, Richard Rorty, and Hubert Dreyfus" (Habermas 1989: 435).

2 Heidegger offers "riss" as a manufactured compound, in his attempt to wrest art, especially drawing, from aesthetics. Riss evokes *Aufriss* (contour or elevation), *Grundrisse* (outline or floorplan), and an opposition that does not let the opponents fall apart but pulls them together in a unitary whole (*Umriss*) (Heidegger 1976). I am appropriating riss here only as the rift that connects, a productive strife. The relation, the riss, is the coming together through antagonism, opposition. I link it to "trials of strength" in Bruno Latour's equally post-Heideggerian project, where the matter hinges on the strife between humans, animals, bacteria, viruses, and things, and humans are not the only *dramatis personae* (1986: 276).

1

Taste, Toil, and Ethnicity

Although immigrants have a long and substantial presence in the United States food system, they appear to have left little trace on American conceptualizations of good taste. This book inserts immigrant bodies and conceptions into American discussions of taste and in doing so jeopardizes the consensus about aesthetics in popular and scholarly domains. An immigrant who enters the American national space, especially a visibly different immigrant, has been turned into an *ethnic* in the last half-century. An ethnic is a proximate but subordinate other, too close to be foreign, too different to be the self. According to the twentieth-century sensory regime of Americanism, an ethnic looks different, sounds different, and prefers different food. Among subcultural and avant garde groups, the term and the people so categorized are sometimes presumed to carry the promise of cultural authenticity. This book narrates that story about subordination and power in the domain of palatal taste that challenges standard theories of aesthetic taste and culture-making in an American city. The central paradox I address is that, although the foreign-born have numerically dominated the feeding occupations, such as greengrocer, baker, butcher, saloon-keeper, tavern-keeper, and restaurateur, especially in the large bi-coastal cities in the United States since the 1850s, we know relatively little about how the transaction in taste appears from their point of view. In contrast, there is a rich literature on the perspective of the native-born consumer, which, in this book, is held at the margin as a mirror to the migrant self.

This blindness about the ethnic provider can be attributed to a number of technical and conceptual reasons. Low prestige of care-work, the unheroic labor of micro entrepreneurship, the inability to articulate in language the taste of the tongue, the limited language skills of scholars working with the American material (especially in the languages of recent migrants), the over-worked migrant without the time to write, and the illiteracy of many immigrants, have compounded our access to that perspective. One example that brings together a number of these reasons should suffice here: although the Chinese have dominated the feeding and cleaning occupations from the middle of the nineteenth century, we do not get a book-length treatment of their perspective in establishing and running the quintessential American ethnic restaurant until the twenty-first century (Lee 2009; Cho 2010). That is an extraordinary deferral. The reason is both the theoretical problem with cooked food in the modern Western imagination, especially within academic scholarship, and the subordination of the cooking subject. Little else can explain such a notable and durable silence.

Food, long considered trivial, now condemned as fashionable in popular culture, has compounded its entry into the academy. Various reasons have been accorded for the absence of food in classrooms, libraries, and museums. Among them is the inordinate attention to mind and thinking in the liberal arts, over the body and other modes of doing things. As modern subjects we are trained to be pleased with our minds and surprisingly blind to our bodies, other than as an object of shallow concerns of vanity. There are a few exceptions. The primitive's body and the diseased body have been allowed entry into the academy for over a century, but only as ontologically inferior things in anthropology and the health sciences. Such a containment of the body is crucial to Enlightenment dualisms.

Yet normative disembodiment is not only limited to the sphere of the West. Strands of Brahmanism—which is one of the points of my departure, as I show in the preface—also make a crucial argument against the abject materiality of the body, especially the socially inferior's body and its lack of liaison with the divine. Perhaps that is because food and the body have long been considered the concerns and cares of the inferior, that is women, servants, slaves, and subject races and castes. Superior men have theorized away the body and its needs, especially for food and for sex (the latter was recovered in the twentieth century West by Sigmund Freud and psychoanalysis), out of the domain of serious deliberation in the academy.

That concordat is disintegrating all around us, in particular in the Western academy, precisely because that is where it ruled the roost, as the importance of the mind and reason are dialed down, and subordinate classes containing women, inferior races, lower castes, and ethnic men have entered the academy and begun to violate its ontological assumptions of superior bodies and high-mindedness. They have reminded us of the necessity of bodies and the love of thinking, a fondness for doing as well as intellection, and the allure of doing and talking about it. New materialisms have refocused our attention on objects, especially the material and affective connections between objects and humans, and the resulting possibility of a paradoxical counterpoint, which is a deep-seated environmentalism. As a result, attention to our relationship to food, as with our relationship to other living and dead bodies, has become unavoidable. Yet we just didn't think our way out of it. It took practice and pragmatism to exit the closed world of the self-assured and superior mind.

Scholarly work such as Marcy Norton's *Sacred Gifts, Profane Pleasures* (2008) has successfully recovered the inadvertent adaptation of Mesoamerican aesthetics in European taste for chocolate and tobacco, transported from the outer reaches of the empire, against the weight of the colonial ideology that good taste only flowed from the direction of the conqueror. In Norton's case, the Spanish taste for chocolate, instead of bolstering established hierarchies of race, class, and roots, spotlighted the internal contradictions of the imperial project and "affected, rather than reflected, discourse" (2008: 691). This book is an analogous inversion of established norms, in which an alternative aesthetics is recovered from the interior of cities, deep at home, rather than from abroad, brought by relatively less powerful people from elsewhere. Surprisingly, in answering her question "When and how do societies assimilate foreign things?" Norton completely misses the role of immigrants and the whole body of literature on it, while acknowledging the historiography of colonialism, consumerism, and food (2008: 661).

These are some of the contexts and conditions that have made possible this project of paying attention to literal taste in talking about aesthetic taste while violating principles of eighteenth-century Western philosophy. They allow us to attend to migrant materialities, which is a result of the cultural democratization wrought by the Civil Rights Movement. That is what connects taste, toil, and ethnicity in this book. The inferior talk back here, and force us to see American cities from the perspective of migrant bodies. The virtue of that is not only a newer, fresher view but also the way it challenges us to transform establishment-style theorizing and sociologizing, by interjecting subordinate practices and theories of the world we live in, forcing us to experience life outside theory qua theory.

The ethnic

Ashis Nandy, the venerable post-colonial theorist, writes bombastically:

> [E]thnic cuisine becomes more and more like a museum or a stage on which culture writes its name . . . for the sake of appeasing our moral conscience and declaring its survival. The Los Angeles Museum of Holocaust displays some artifacts of Jewish culture, thoughtfully collected by the Nazis for the projected museum on an extinct race after the Final Solution. Those were not the days of ethnic cuisine. Otherwise the Nazis would have surely added a wing to their museum where one could include a well-appointed restaurant serving traditional Jewish fare from all over Europe (2003: 251).

Nandy's posture is a provocation, crafted to elicit a retort rather than a considered discussion. Let me first concede some legitimacy to Nandy's ill-tempered diatribe. At one level Nandy's irritability with the collective category of the "ethnic" as a flattening and meaningless pen to hold all non-White, non-Anglophone others is understandable. Nandy was partly reacting to the disrepute that had attached to the term "ethnic" after the break-up of Yugoslavia and mass murder in Rwanda, when it came to be associated with "cleansing." In other post-colonial locations, such as India, the term is polluted with the stench of pogroms in the name of illegitimate group claims against the nation-state (see Calhoun 2007).

In the US the term *ethnicity* has other lineages. It came into play almost simultaneously in the fields of American journalism and social sciences in the late 1950s in what appeared then to be a relatively neutral way of constructing difference (Glazer and Moynihan 1975; Sollors 1997; Guibernau and Rex 1999). "Ethnic food" led this trend in the emerging sub-field of food journalism (as I will show below). Subsequently, theorists of representation—especially Stuart Hall in his 1989 essay "New Ethnicities"—challenged us to re-read the poetics and politics of the term (Hall 1989). By the late 1980s and the early 1990s ethnicity was seen as a benign claim of cultural coherence by any group, previously excluded from the centers of power, now staked below the level of the nation-state. Ethnicity became the dominant mode of framing difference without falling into the problem of race. Among theoretical sophisticates "the ethnic," within scare quotes, is an unutterable referent to color and inferiority, which is mostly covered over in pragmatic silence. In this book I interrogate that precise intersection of dominance and agency to narrate a story of urban culture-making. The time has come to abandon the term for current use, but it remains quite useful in weaving the *history* of the relationship between the presumed normative non-ethnic center and its radiating, multiple, ethnic others, which belongs as much to the realm of fantasy as to fact. The term itself is one of the signs of unequal relationship between the self-proclaimed normative center of the Euro-American imagination, its dominating institutions, and numerous categories of others such as the foreigner, the tourist, the exile, the stranger, the immigrant, etc., in a rich semiotic universe of slippery, relational selfhoods and Otherness.

What Nandy proposes dramatically in the quotation above is also suggested by bell hooks. She posits that the totalizing perspective of "eating the other" is a posture "from the standpoint of white supremacist capitalist patriarchy," where "the hope is that desires for the 'primitive' or fantasies about the Other can be continually exploited, and that such exploitation will occur in a manner that reinscribes and maintains the *status quo*" (hooks 1992: 22; also see Hage 1997). Although most of her essay "Eating the Other" is written in the outraged mode of a critic who cannot find any hope in the commodification of the culture of racial and ethnic others, especially their desires and their bodies, hooks provides two instances of alternative ways of reading such an encounter. She concedes that the "desire for contact with the Other, for connection rooted in the longing for pleasure, can act as a critical intervention challenging and subverting racist domination, inviting and enabling critical resistance," but it remains "an unrealized political possibility" (1992: 22). She cites Stuart and Elizabeth Ewen's critique of consumption in *Channels of Desire* as politically limiting where "communities of resistance are replaced by communities of consumption" (1992: 33). She recommends engaging with the particular form of desire for the Other as the place to begin the interrogation of what exactly is going on. She identifies John Waters's *Hairspray* and Peter Greenaway's *The Cook, the Thief, His Wife and Her Lover* as exemplary instances where desire across the color-line is deployed not merely to conquer and reassert white domination, but to recognize the "particular pleasures and sorrows black folks experience," which refreshingly "does not lead to cultural appropriation but to an appreciation that extends into the realm of the political" (1992: 37). She concludes, "Acknowledging ways the desire for pleasure, and that includes erotic longings, informs our politics, our understanding of difference, we may know better how desire disrupts, subverts, and makes resistance possible. We cannot, however, accept these new images uncritically" (1992: 39). One can live with this assertion a little better than Nandy's exaggerated opening claim, yet there are a number of problems here too.

For one, hooks connects food and sex too closely. They are both forms of literal incorporation, but they are different. It is true that eating together often leads to sleeping together, which is why race and caste purists have always panicked about cross-category commensality, even fleetingly at water fountains or more elaborately at lunch counters and restaurants. Yet, the table is different from the bed. "The table is a social machinery as complicated as it is effective: it makes one talk, one 'lays everything on the table' to confess what one wanted to keep quiet, one gets 'grilled' by a skillful neighbor, one yields to a momentary excitement, to a fit of vanity, to the velvet smoothness of a red wine, and one hears oneself tell all about what one had sworn the day before to hide from everyone" (de Certeau, Giard, and Mayol 1998: 197). Michel de Certeau and Lucy Giard, who are attuned to the specificity of place and space, slow down our move from the table to the bed. Eating together allows one to hold the other at some distance with the table in between, so the relationship can be subject to mutual discussion and negotiation. Eating allows intimacy but not too much of it, which is why we can afford to feed every guest, while it is hardly advisable to sleep with them. That ratio of intimacy and estrangement is an important distinction to be made between the pleasures (and hence the problems) of the table and the bed. hooks' analysis moves too quickly and too easily from food to sex and back again, and I think her argument holds more for eating the other, than eating *with* the other.

The problem is that both Nandy's and hooks' critiques, although targeting the colonizing white view, nevertheless appropriate that imperial viewpoint in surveying colored bodies and ethnic foods. Neither of them asks any of the ethnics (or relevant others under discussion) what they think of all this. That is partly a function of academic discipline. It seems one can say a lot in philosophy and in cultural studies without asking anyone else what they think about the matter under full speculative elaboration. Thus Nandy and hooks appear as perverse inversions of Gustav Flaubert's classic Orientalist appropriation of Kuchuk Hanem, the Egyptian courtesan salvaged by Edward Said, who never spoke of herself, never "represented her emotions, presence, or history." Instead Flaubert "spoke for and represented her" (Said 1979: 6). Thus, in this book I am insistent that the ethnic talk back and tell us what they think.

It would be inaccurate to lay the charge of Orientalism at the door of the philosopher who has written the book on this matter titled *Exotic Appetites* (Heldke 2003). Born of the methodological discipline of philosophy, Heldke cannot ask the migrant purveyor of food what he makes of his experience, without fracturing the bounds of her discipline. She begins with a trenchant critique of her own "easy acquisitiveness" towards ethnic food, which she eventually comes to see as culinary colonialism, which in turn is the window through which she comes to recognize the disturbing attitudes of "contemporary Euroamerican food adventurers" with their "obsessive interest in and appetite for the new, the obscure and the exotic," their grasping of ethnic food to serve their own interests, linked together by "the adventurer's intense desire for authentic experiences of authentic cultures" (2003: 7). But Heldke confines herself to a theoretical critique of the acquisitive attitude because, in her words, "Philosophers' methods are not those of ethnographers, for example, who may at times find themselves scandalized by philosophers' tendency toward abstract generalization, our tendency to see the development of a point as necessitating more theory rather than more examination of concrete circumstance" (2003: xxv). Uma Narayan gently chides Heldke, which also happens to be my position:

> I am not unsympathetic to [the] critique of "culinary imperialism" or to Heldke's critique of "food colonialism." However, I hope to complicate this discussion of "food colonialism" by thinking about ethnic foods from the point of view of immigrants to Western contexts, rather than from that of mainstream Western citizens. While eating "ethnic foods" in restaurants might result only in shallow, commodified, and consumerist interaction with an "Other" culinary culture, it seems preferable at least to the complete lack of acquaintance that permits the different foods

> of "Others" to appear simply as marks of their "strangeness" and "Otherness."
>
> Eating in these restaurants, I also register how "ethnic restaurants" are an important form of economic enterprise for many immigrants to the West, and how Westerners' taste for "ethnic cuisines" contributes to the economic survival of immigrants, the desire for culinary novelty making a positive difference to profit margin (1997: 180).

Narayan touches on the limits of a theoretical critique but, having barely opened the issue, she goes no further. As a philosopher Narayan cannot imagine asking immigrant restaurateurs what they think. Surprisingly, even sociologists such as Johnston and Bauman (2007), in spite of their rich discussion of distinction, cultural capital, and omnivorousness, have refrained from that task which should come naturally to a sociologist. That is precisely what I do, especially in Chapters 2 and 5. In doing so, I draw on the work of Ghassan Hage (1997), refining and specifying it conceptually and methodologically.

Hage develops a three-part argument. He is in line with Heldke's critique in characterizing that obsessive cultural acquisitiveness as cosmo-multiculturalism, which is a competitive discourse that positions "ethnic feeders" with a passive feeding function "in a field where migrant subjects have been erased and where the central subject is a classy and more often than not an Anglo-cosmopolitan eating subject" (1997: 118). It is a form of multiculturalism without migrants, which is linked to tourism and the international circulation of commodities and gastronomic conceptions rather than to the circulation of migrants (1997: 118–19). In Hage's words, cosmo-multiculturalism, or what I will characterize as gastronomic cosmopolitanism, fuses "notions of diversity with notions of classiness, sophistication and international distinction" (1997: 119). Such a cuisine is elaborated by a community of producers, consumers, and interpreters, where a "whole set of internationally sanctioned and largely implicit rules of production and consumption begin to operate as a form of symbolic violence, setting the parameters of acceptable creativity" (1997: 123–4), as we will see in Chapter 4. Gastronomic cosmopolitanism *may* appear to have a positive antiracist message but it continues to be "deeply Anglo-centric in positioning Anglo subjects in the role of appreciators enriched by what are constructed as ethnic objects with no *raison d'être* other than to enrich the Anglo-subject" (1997: 136).

Furthermore, gastronomic cosmopolitanism makes too much of a break with its own past as a stodgy, conservative, closed-minded old self. It is posited that anyone with enough "class" could become an appreciator of Otherness, especially through their food. The working class is constructed in this discourse as "non-multicultural by virtue of its presumed inability to appreciate 'diversity' and ethnic cultures" (1997: 137). Hage quotes a lawyer making the case for cosmo-multiculturalism in the following manner:

> Cabramatta [an ethnic suburb of Sydney, equivalent to the Manhattanite's Queens] is the only place worth eating at. It is the only place *where you are not expected*, where the restaurant owner does not smile to welcome you. He doesn't want you there. He thinks you are a nuisance. When I go to a restaurant like this I know I am going to eat well. I know I will be eating the real thing. I look inside the restaurant and try to locate the owner and as soon as I see that look of disdain on his face I'm in [laughing]. I love it (Hage 1997: 139).

There are a number of things to note here, Hage suggests: first, this whole thing is played out as a game of mastery. "But it is experienced not as mastery over ethnic people as such. There is nothing more anathema to the aesthetic sense of cosmo-multiculturalism than the idea of an explicitly subjugated ethnic otherness" (1997: 139). Yet for gastronomic cosmopolitans, ethnicity is "an object of experience rather than an experiential subject" (1997: 136), even when cosmopolitans insist on authenticity—in fact berate the ethnic immigrant for diluting authenticity for the sake of their neighbor's retrogressive Anglo palate. Here cosmo-multiculturalism is in "direct conflict with the multiculturalism of intercultural interaction" (1997: 144). These cosmopolitans in competitive search of real, authentic ethnic food would not allow the ethnic to negotiate or design their interactions with the larger society.

In his sociological investigations, when Hage talked to the same Vietnamese restaurateur and his son whom the lawyer discusses above, he found that they were actively seeking a non-Vietnamese clientele and deploying sophisticated strategies of subtle exoticism and authenticity, knowing full well "that the absence of signs in English is a good way to attract Anglo customers" (1997: 144). Such knowledge is difficult to incorporate into the cosmo-multicultural fantasy of authenticity. To cosmo-multiculturalism, Hage counterposes the multiculturalism of inhabitance, of real migrants, in complex, sometimes conflictual, relationship, but always in negotiation with white folks and others, and where ethnicity is not detached from ethnic producers. His point is "to valorize a multiculturalism grounded in the reality of migrant home-building and intercultural interaction" (1997: 146). That is precisely what I seek in the migrant restaurateurs' designs on the world they have come to inhabit, and in doing so I hope to sharpen Hage's subtle insights about interrogating those sites where "both the eater and the feeder experience themselves as subjects" (1997: 146). Chapters 2 and 5 bring us most clearly the view from the other side.

That kind of work on inhabitation will also allow us the possibility of getting away from the excessively pinched attitude of theoretical over-cautiousness towards ethnic food that belies the history of its appropriation by the counterculture as a way to critique and re-invigorate the mainstream that Warren Belasco describes in *Appetite for Change* when he notes that "The new Sikh restaurant in downtown Ann Arbor taught us about vegetable tempura, curried squash soup, and tantric meditation" (2006: 218), in the process connecting "us to people and places all over the world," and creating "a visceral, lived daily link between the personal and the political" where the "countercuisine represented a serious and largely unprecedented attempt to reverse the direction of dietary modernization and thereby align personal consumption with perceived global needs" (2006: 217). It might be that such a transformative moment has passed, but banging the door shut to other peoples' food is no way to reimagine the self or the Other and put the relationship between the two on a new footing.

Parama Roy provides an opening for such an interaction in *Alimentary Tracts* (2010). Heavily theorized and deeply entangled in the thicket of literary criticism, it is chronologically selective, hopping, skipping, and jumping from the 1857 Indian Mutiny (against East India Company rule), to Gandhi's austere vegetarianism and spectacular fasting, through the hungers of the low-caste poor, finally to the gastronomic reclamation of curry powder by Madhur Jaffrey. In doing so, Roy walks the fertile borderlands of the ethical and the aesthetic consequences of eating the Other—animal and human. In allowing the Other to enter one's body without the desperate need of purgation, she expertly inverts the critique of hooks (1992), Heldke (2003) and Nandy (2003). She does so by drawing on Jacques Derrida's (1991) suggestion of anthropophagy, not as an abomination but as a "parabolic instantiation of unexpected somatic and ethical engagement with the other" where the "refusal to partake of the other is an important breakdown in or rejection of ethical reciprocity with the other" (Roy 2010: 14).

I think, Nandy's appropriation of the imagined mainstream view in surveying ethnic food enables the post-colonial theorist to avoid identification with the immigrant, as opposed to the affluent traveler or the anguished exile. The point of view of the imagined mainstream persists even in the work of analysts more sympathetic to sociological "facts," such as Johnston and Baumann (2007). In contrast to their work, this book gathers immigrant narratives to refract high theory. And it inverts the lens of the viewing subject—against Nandy, hooks, Heldke, and Johnston and Bauman—to generate a theoretical chiasmus.

Sometimes the shrill clamor of post-colonial theorists erases any alternative signifying possibilities that reside in plain view on sidewalk vendor carts, in ethnic newspapers, menus, and the voices of subjects who are producing various kinds of foods and meaning. Here I want to qualify Spivak's (1988) theorization of the silent subaltern on the very grounds of her quarrel with the Subalternists. Even those reduced to documentary illegibility are not silent. The advantage of ethnographic work, of course, is the recuperation of fragile orality that text-dependent history cannot bear witness to.

The embodied potentiality of food has a theoretical consequence. Those feeding us may have some power over us. Usual paradigmatic vulnerabilities can be inverted. The study of food is capable of generating epistemic implosions, where "a whole set of knowledges that have been disqualified as inadequate to their task or insufficiently elaborated: naïve knowledges, located low down on the hierarchy, beneath the required level of cognition or scientificity" can come alive and burn our fingers (Foucault 1980: 82). Cooking opens up the possibilities of what de Certeau characterizes as an economy of the gift, an aesthetics of tricks, and an ethics of tenacity that upgrades ordinary practices to the status of a theoretical object (de Certeau, Giard, and Mayol, 1998: xxiii).

Post-colonial theorists sometimes speak as if nothing exists between domination and resistance. The vast intermediate landscape of making do, of living, of making ends meet, of insinuating one's intentions between the expectation of others, of poaching, of mimicking, of mocking, of explaining to white folks, of dismissing them, of interpreting the rest of the world to them, of plain fabrication of one's self as the ponderous native informant, the gorgeous pleasures of subversion and subterfuge, may not be available to righteous theorists, but is important to practical others, including migrant restaurateurs peddling food as much as notions of it. Binary conceptions of domination and resistance ignore the peculiar intimacy between the Anglo and the ethnic that has always shaped American cities and public cultures of eating, and theorizing that kind of intimacy without occluding historical and persistent inequalities could be the source of creativity in our work (Suleri 1992). Nandy, Heldke, hooks, and Johnston and Baumann have elucidated on what needs to be stated, which is the long relationship between the imperial imagination and the colonized Other, yet that is not all that needs to be said. Ethnicity is a classification system that produces practical activity, knowledge, and domination. "Ethnic" is both an obfuscating term and a revealing one, as I show in the following pages.

Ethnicity is the perceptual schema by which Americans produce cultural difference. The ethnic is the carrier of difference—marked by feature, language, and culture. It is the production of manageable difference that functions to establish and define the boundaries of who "we" are, who "our" ancestors were, and how "we" mark that difference. The ethnic is never seen as a superordinate class, although s/he is sometimes white (such as in the case of the Irish, Italian, and Jews—and I will show their relevance to my discussion further into this text). The ethnic is the inferior outsider, inside the nation, who can become the locus of our longings, in spite of his inferiority, if touched by some measure of modernity, development, and Americanization. Yet, what makes the American case particularly interesting is that it is unclear that in the encounter between the native and the ethnic, the culture of the former will prevail. There is a failure of nerve, a crisis of cultural confidence that returns the ethnic to the center of American culture in spite of his inhabitation on the margins. In this book the ethnic restaurateur carries that connotation of subordination yet potential strength, the inferiority of the foreign-born yet the possibility of some cultural capital, a person who, due to limits of money, social, or cultural capital, could never play in the domain of high culture yet cannot be excluded from American culture. Those foreign-born restaurateurs who could participate in the social field of the dominant, such as French haute cuisine (and relatively recent instances of Italian, Spanish, and Japanese cuisine), are addressed only through a comparative prism of the disenfranchised, as the focus here is on subtle ways of playing with power in spite of relative subordination.

Yet it is impossible to comprehend the field of ethnic food without interrogating its specific location in American gastronomy as the subordinate and exotic other to the newly valorized chef and restaurateur. Which is why, in Chapter 4, I investigate one of the premier sites of production of a social body learning to play above its class-weight at the Culinary Institute of America. It is a place where the professional is produced in a field dangerously close to those tainted with ethnicity. I address instances of previously subordinate cohorts—Italians, Chinese, Indians, and Filipinos, among others—who have tried to enter the domain of the superordinate chef. Those are instances that illuminate the exacting terms of play at the top of the culinary field.

Since occupations and birthplace were first identified in the Census of the United States of America, beginning in 1850, data has shown a strong correlation between food service occupations and new immigrant groups (used interchangeably with *foreign-born* here). Although occupations cannot be directly compared across Censuses (because the classifications have changed; for instance, cooks, servers, and chefs have been added to the mix of occupations over the twentieth century, changing the ratios between them), we can see that the foreign-born numerically dominate certain occupations, such as domestic servants, hotel and restaurant employees, hotel-keepers, saloon-keepers and bartenders, traders and dealers in groceries, bakers, and butchers. In contrast, members of the so-called white-collar occupations, such as the clergy, lawyers, school teachers, and government officials, have mostly been native-born (see Figure 1.1). For example, in New York City on the eve of the Civil War, about 60 percent of hotel and restaurant employees and 71 percent of hotel-keepers were foreign-born, mostly of Irish and German heritage. (This is in a context where the foreign-born constituted about a third of the labor force) (Ruggles, Alexander, Genadek, Goeken, Schroeder, and Sobek 2004). Scotch-Irish bakers were increasingly replaced by German immigrants, who were dominant by the time of the Civil War. By then, New York City was home to more than two hundred thousand Germans who lived in "little Germany" along the Bowery, and they were the most numerous among the butchers, bakers, and grocers. Germans also constituted about 15 percent of the domestics shaping the kitchen and palates of their Anglo employers (Smith 2014: 44).

About half a century later, according to the 1900 Census (see Figure 1.2), 63 percent of hotel and restaurant employees were foreign-born (Irish and German predominate) and 65 percent of hotel-keepers were foreign-born (mostly German). Restaurant-keepers, a newly significant occupation by 1900, were 67 percent foreign-born at a time when the foreign-born were about 50 percent of the population (Ruggles *et al.* 2004). At this time the vast majority of the city's pushcart vendors were Jewish, and they were moving up the social ladder to employment in groceries, kosher butchers, bakeries, coffee shops, delicatessens, and wine shops. At the same time New York's Chinatown had more than one hundred restaurants, and a decade later a little over a hundred Greek-owned restaurants were counted on Seventh Avenue (Smith 2014: 61).

Even by the 1950 Census (see Figure 1.3), after immigration had subsided due to restrictions (since 1924), 64 percent of restaurant cooks were foreign-born (Italians now at the top, followed by Greeks, Chinese, and Germans). According to the historian Andrew Smith, Italian-American grocers would introduce various kinds of seafood, ice-cream, "olive oil, Parmesan cheese, anchovies, pastas, and coffees" to Americans (2014: 56). Italians ran more than ten thousand grocery stores, almost a thousand butcher shops, and more than a thousand restaurants in the city by the mid-twentieth century.

According to the 2000 Census (see Figure 1.4) that trend continued, with 75 percent of restaurant cooks (and 64 percent of restaurant workers) in New York City foreign-born, but the dominant countries and regions of origin were now Mexico, Central America, the Caribbean Basin, South America, China, and the former USSR (Ruggles *et al.* 2004; Shierholz 2014). By 2010, more than twenty thousand New York City bars and restaurants employed over two hundred and four thousand workers, many foreign-born, accounting for over $12 billion in revenue per annum (NYC Health n.d.). Most of the approximately nine thousand street food vendors in New York City today are foreign-born, with Bengali as the most common native tongue, followed by Cantonese and Mandarin, Fulani, Arabic, Spanish, Urdu, Wolof, Swahili, etc. (Street Vendor Project 2006).[1] By 2010 nearly one half of all small business owners living in New York City were immigrants, including 69 percent of restaurant owners,

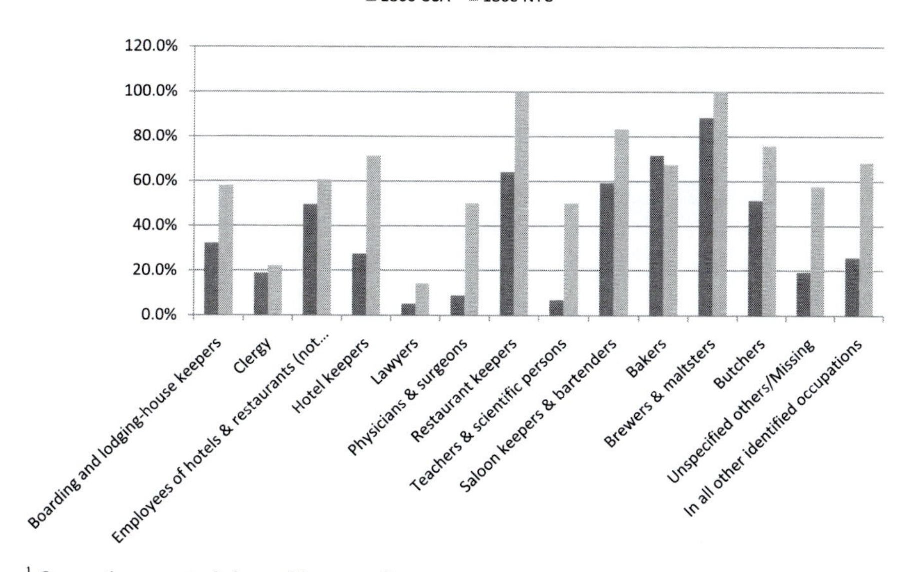

[1] Occupations counted changed between Census.
[2] The 1850 Census, the first one accounting for occupations and birthplace, had inadequate numbers across a number of categories for percentages, which is why 1860 figures are the earliest cited here.
[3] Cooks were counted for the first time in 1910 and chefs in 1980.

FIGURE 1.1 *The foreign-born as a percentage in selected occupations, USA and New York City, 1860.*

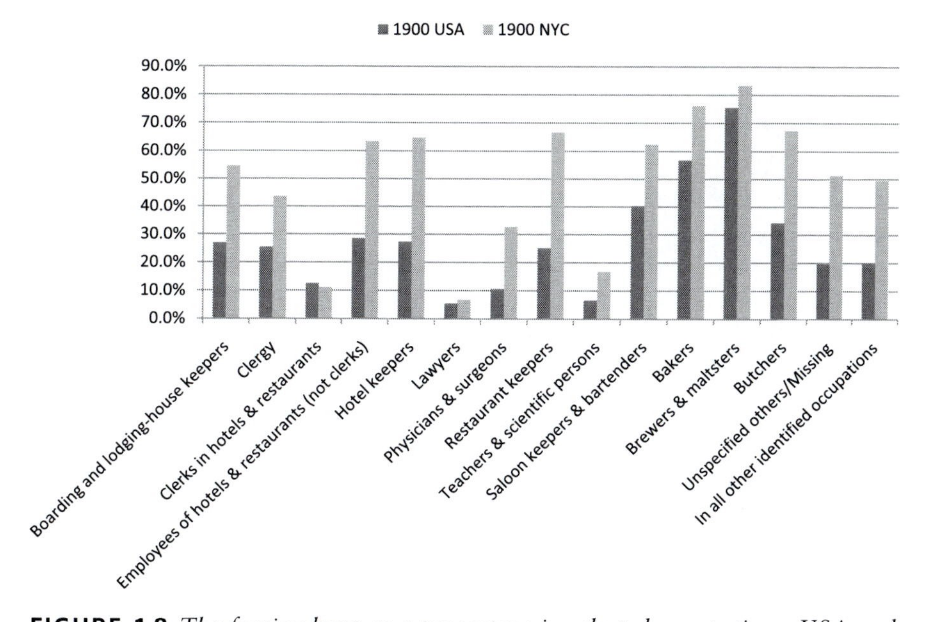

FIGURE 1.2 *The foreign-born as a percentage in selected occupations, USA and New York City, 1900.*

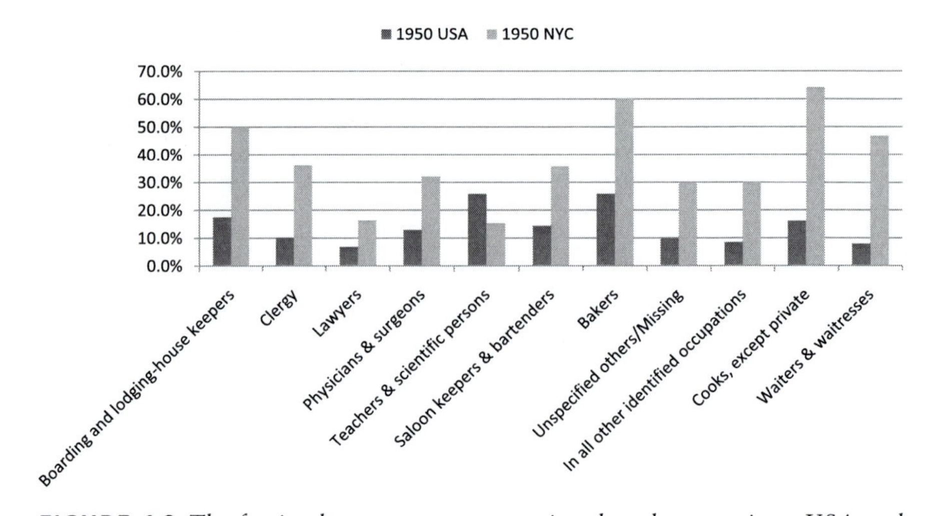

FIGURE 1.3 *The foreign-born as a percentage in selected occupations, USA and New York City, 1950.*

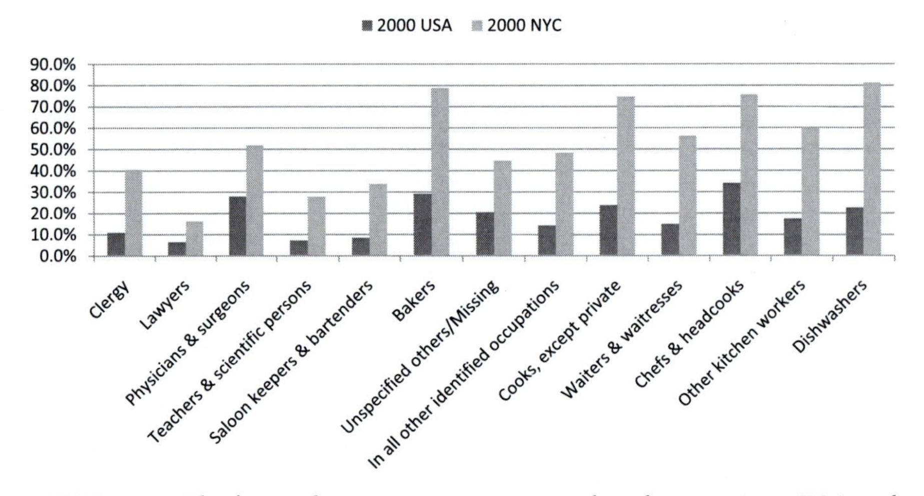

FIGURE 1.4 *The foreign-born as a percentage in selected occupations, USA and New York City, 2000.*

90 percent of dry cleaners, 84 percent of small grocery store owners and 70 percent of beauty salon owners (Foner 2013: 21; Kallick 2013: 80). Given this kind of data it would be perverse to be interested in immigrant lives yet uninterested in food, as a matter either of the political economy of micro-entrepreneurship or the cultural politics of transactions in taste. Yet that was the norm until recently among most scholars.

Although the journalistic material is replete with stories of immigrant restaurateurs there is surprisingly little scholarly work of greater duration that engages theoretically with taste in the metropolis from the point of view of the immigrant entrepreneur (notable exceptions are Möhring 2007; Möhring, Harris, Könczöl, and Motadel 2014; Hassoun 2010; Buettner 2012). Among scholars, historians have been better at recording the doings of immigrant shopkeepers and grocers because, often literate, they have kept records that historians could mine. Labor and immigration historians are particularly good at picking up the scent of food in poor peoples' records (Levenstein 1988, 1993; Gabaccia 1998; Ziegelman 2010; Smith 2014). Good food may matter more to poor people than it does to the rich.

In sociology there is a robust literature on ethnic entrepreneurship. There are a number of common parts to the theory. Low capital requirements make it relatively easier for foreign-born entrepreneurs to enter the highly competitive business of feeding others that most native-born people no longer find desirable. Niche cultural knowledge about esoteric food gives them a competitive edge over better-capitalized mainstream entrepreneurs. Kin or fictive kin networks of loyalty that allow the lending of money on a rotating basis without collateral enable ethnic entrepreneurs to raise the necessary cash for a small eatery without the assets a bank loan would require. Self-exploitation—long hours of work and unpaid labor of kin and fictive kin—permits these enterprises to compete with better-capitalized businesses, and turns sweat and loyalty into capital. Large corporations often cannot respond quickly to fickle changes in fashion, but small enterprises can adapt with speed and thrive for a while, hence there is much greater room for small enterprises selling food and other things that are attuned to quick transformations of taste. Finally, and most importantly for our purposes, both migration and entrepreneurship exhibit serial patterns—that is, people who know each other, have typically migrated from the same regions, work in and own similar enterprises built with money and expertise borrowed from co-ethnics. They effectively develop an informal, intra-ethnic consulting and banking system. Paucity of assets to collateralize bank loans and unfamiliarity with the language and norms of a consumer society deepen this dependence on co-ethnic money, information, and cultural expertise. Co-ethnicity is a powerful labor recruitment and management system that also allows quiescence and exploitation. It is a precise proof of the embeddedness of the economic in the social, as shown most compellingly and recently by Erin Curtis (2013) in the case of Cambodian doughnut shop owners in Los Angeles (also see Heisler 2008; Zhou 2004; Foner, Rumbaut, and Gold 2000; Granovetter 1995; Portes 1995; Rogers and Vertovec 1995; Sassen 1995; Bailey and Waldinger 1991; Westwood and Bhachu 1988; Light and Bonacich 1988; Waldinger 1986, 1990, 1992; Bailey 1985, 1987; Landa 1981; Light 1972).

This, of course, is a broad prototype of an explanation, and a structural one, that needs to be fleshed out with the real activity of real, live, everyday people. The structural model cannot explain, for instance, why and how the first Bangladeshi entered the Indian restaurant business in New York City. That demands biographies and micro-histories. In *Bengali Harlem* (2013) Vivek Bald reveals those potentialities in his finely drawn portraiture of about two dozen itinerant Bengali peddlers of chikan (a textile) circulating from Hoogly through London, Durban, New York, to New Orleans in fin de siècle nineteenth century, sliding into the interstices between the dying throes of the British Empire and the birth of American emporium.[2] As these men left some of their compatriots behind in the United States to keep the tethering posts of their networks in place, they in turn, out of pure necessity and unrestrained desire, built some of the earliest South Asian boarding houses, coffee shops, eateries, and restaurants in their places of habitation, occupying the "thin edge between Indophilia and xenophobia" (Bald 2013: 46).

Much of the ethnicity and entrepreneurship literature attends to economics and politics, as if immigrants are creatures only of political economy who never think about taste, beauty, and how such things might intersect with their practical-moral universe. An apt recent illustration is Roger Waldinger's *The Cross-Border Connection: Immigrants, Emigrants and Their Homelands* (2015), which is an attempt to reframe Oscar Handlin's view of the suffering, oppressed immigrant in *The Uprooted* (1951). Handlin was part of the generation of scholars who refocused the locus of American history from the frontier to the immigrant experience, which he considered harsh and oppressive. Handlin famously wrote in the opening lines of his book, "Once I thought to write a history of the immigrants in America. Then I discovered that the immigrants *were* American history" (1951: 3). Waldinger's thesis isn't equal to Handlin's in terms of drama, but he makes an important point nevertheless. Instead of suffering and loss, Waldinger turns to migrant agency. As a result, his focus is on migrant access to resources here (high-wage labor market) and back home (property, kith and kin); the persistence of transnational connections (instead of uprooting); and the extension of other societies and cultures into territories here. In the process, Waldinger sometimes goes so far in the other direction that he ends up with jarring claims, such as: "the poor exploited the rich, using access to the resources of a wealthier country to make life better back home" (2015: 2). These are unsettling, although rare, rhetorical excesses, given the tenor of the rest of the book. Most importantly, while Handlin devoted a whole chapter to "The Daily Bread" and such mundane materialities of immigrant life, Waldinger's migrants do not eat, drink, sleep, dance, or sing. The index does not list food, shelter, or culture. There are three passing references to food in the whole book.[3] The immigrants do remit money home, talk on the phone, and face the challenges of big ideas such as nation, border, and community, but they do not come across as living subjects. They appear interested only in the nation-state, the labor-market, laws and policy. At least, that is Waldinger's interest and although he makes some very interesting points about remittances, telephony, laws, and transnationalism (with pointed arguments against nationalists and globalists), his migrants are purely political-economic ideas, without bodies and hence innocent of the challenges of nursing those bodies with materials and memories that matter affectively. Waldinger's migrant is a peculiar inversion of the soulful, suffering, uprooted subject of Handlin.

The propensity to ignore immigrant bodies in the disciplinary discussion of taste may be a product of the tendency to see discussions of taste as marginal to the real lives of marginal peoples. In this conception, poor, hard-working people can teach us about poverty and suffering, hierarchy and symbolic violence, but never about taste. That might be one of the unfortunate consequences of the overwhelming dominance of Pierre Bourdieu's framework of analysis, as I will show later. As a consequence, taste loses its contested and dynamic character, and, I would argue, even its fundamentally sociological nature.

My interest in the contested nature of taste explains the focus on the entrepreneur, celebrated here not necessarily as the archetype of the mythic American urban hero, but as an important actor in the aesthetic transaction. My work attends to the otherwise preoccupied ethnic restaurateur because he is the hinge between taste and toil—two streams of theoretical accounts that are put in productive conversation here. Because this is about transactions of taste in the city, I mostly bracket the perspectives of labor that have been documented recently by ROC-NY (2005), Miabi Chatterji (2013, 2010), and Saru Jayaraman (2013). They point out how exploitative the relationship often is between South Asian ethnic entrepreneurs and low-skilled restaurant workers who are sometimes co-ethnics, manipulated by rhetoric of kinship and care to fend off the regulatory reach of the state in terms of labor, safety, immigration, and health laws. Analogously, Mae Ngai (2010) shows, in her study of one upwardly mobile Chinese-American family in *The Lucky Ones*, how the Tapes "broke into the American middle class by helping manage the continued marginalization of other Chinese" (2010: 223). Simone Cinotto points to the same "unnatural convergence of low salaries and low conflict," which was a product of paternalistic control of co-ethnic Piedmontese workers among the pioneer Italian wine producers of California at the turn of the twentieth century (2012: 134).

For a recent instance of hyper-exploitation one need only reference the story of the Fuzhounese (from Fuzhou in Fujian Province) restaurant worker Zhuo Yilin, whose wife and four children were stabbed to death by a mentally-ill cousin, Chen Mindong, another Chinese take-out cook, who shared their Sunset Park apartment in Queens, New York (Yee and Singer 2013: 1). Belonging to a networked diaspora of about half a million Fuzhounese, with low paying jobs and long hours in Chinese take-out, Chen complained to the police on his arrest that "everyone seems to be doing better than him." After his family had borrowed tens of thousands of dollars to pay smuggling rings to get him into New York City, he is in jail today; his cousin distraught over the consequences of his goodwill; his nephew, niece, and sister-in-law dead by his over-worked hands. Sometimes such risky wagers work out, as in the case of "Rain" in a *New Yorker* story: the $70,000 he paid to the smuggler was made up in about five years, after which he was earning $2,000 a month, in comparison to a typical Fujianese salary of $4,700 a year (Hilgers 2014).

It was cook, sleep, wake to cook again, for twelve hours a day, Chen complained. He was one of a vast invisible group. After their shifts ended at midnight they watched TV and video-chatted with their families, six to a room or in internet cafés. The hope was that if they kept working hard they would own a restaurant or a house, maybe even get a green card. Chen Yixiang, Chen Mindong's father, paid about a hundred thousand dollars to his son's smugglers, and still owes them half of this, while his son is in jail awaiting trial for murder. Much of this universe is one of brutally unrelenting work with other people's food. Thus I hope to remain unsentimental about the ethnic entrepreneur, because he should not be reduced to a paper cut-out for the propaganda machine of the American Dream.

Often workers in South Asian immigrant-owned enterprises are undocumented Latino immigrants, who are not only racialized and demeaned by everyday instances of homogenization by the use of names such as "Amigo" and "Jose," used to address all Latino men on the payroll without individual distinctions (a fate not shared by co-ethnics), but exploited beyond the limits of the law (M. Chatterji 2013: 147–48). In one instance, one Latino worker, Santiago, retorted, "It's the same shit everywhere. If he's not calling us amigo, he is calling us worse. They got nicknames for us at every restaurant—they only learn Spanish so they can swear at us!" (M. Chatterji 2013: 148). It is important to record that relationship and name it, but that is not my focus here. In this work I spotlight the urban sociology of value production, arguing that it is productive to pay attention to immigrant restaurateurs who rarely figure in such discussions and urging scholars to do so by getting closer to the dish and the doing.

Bourdieu and bodily practice

In American sociology—one of the disciplines where urban ethnic communities have figured prominently—taste has been studied most extensively over the last decade in the sub-field of "cultures of consumption," which builds on

Pierre Bourdieu's *Distinction* (1984).[4] The latest iteration of such disciplinary attention in North America is Josée Johnston and Shyon Baumann's *Foodies: Democracy and Distinction in the Gourmet Foodscape* (2010). Their work is representative of a major trend in academic theorizing, which is a focus on consumption. The same has to be said of the various identity-producing studies of immigrants and Asian-Americans (Dalessio 2012, Xu 2007). I will argue that a number of these works, especially *Foodies*, while useful in mapping modes of consumer identification and their pursuit of distinction, is limited if we are after a fuller understanding of taste in the metropolis and the work of provisioning, value-production, and taste-making that is put into the exchange by immigrants.

Johnston and Baumann argue that in spite of broadening palates, the gastronomic discussion that has caught fire in bi-coastal American cities (specifically in representative newspapers and food magazines such as *Gourmet*) is burdened with the quest for class distinctions. This, they contend, is happening despite the decline of old-fashioned snobbery and the dethroning of French and Continental cuisines.[5] Their book confirms Bennett, Savage, Silva, Warde, Gayo-Cal, and Wright's (2009) detailed empirical work on the United Kingdom in arguing that taste hierarchies exist, culture irrevocably marks class, and omnivorousness is a rarefied (but not rare) phenomenon wherein the rich and the better educated devour even working class subcultures, while the working classes (especially men) do not consume highbrow genres such as avant-garde art, classical music, art cinema, or exotic restaurant cuisine. They corroborate Warde and Marten's food-related findings based on a study of three British cities (2000) that eating out "continues to operate as a field of distinction, marking boundaries of status through the display of taste . . . The professional and managerial classes are thronging to ethnic cuisine restaurants, while poor, working class, older, provincial people are not. Familiarity with ethnic cuisine is a mark of refinement" (2000: 226).[6]

I would argue that current concerns in cultural sociology are shaped by strong theories of closure and containment, allowing little room for openings and disruption. Repurposing Pascale Casanova's questions in the domain of literature, I would also argue that sociological theories of taste posit a direct political connection between literal taste and social hierarchy, reducing the gustatory merely to the political, and passing in silence the actual aesthetic and stylistic characteristics that make food edible and the center of peoples' investment in good taste (see Casanova 2005a, 2005b). This is opposite to the error committed by connoisseurs and pursuers of pure taste who cannot see any connection between the real political world riven by race, class, and gender, and the world of good taste. It is possible to re-establish the link between literal taste and politics while maintaining the irreducible autonomy of good food. This work navigates between those short-circuits of pure politics and pure literal taste. Furthermore, while Johnston and Baumann (2007, 2010) see fit to exclude immigrant food producers from their analysis because they cannot hear them in the gastronomic discourse they study, Warde and Martens argue that they want to focus on consumption and its meaning for the consumer (2000: 5). There is an implication in some of this work that immigrant concerns relate exclusively to the labor process and the law (as we saw previously in Waldinger 2015), which is to create a peculiarly constricted notion of immigrant selves as only laboring, and to be blind to the role of immigrants in the culture of consumption and the aesthetics of work, as I will show below, through their naming of restaurants, designing menus, and reproducing foods, flavors, and ambience in the metropolis (and I am not alone here: see Buettner 2012; Highmore 2009; Hassoun 2010; Zukin 1995; Yee 2012; Ngai 2010).[7] Three decades ago, when consumption studies began to proliferate, it may have been useful to study consumption exclusively because it had been ignored for so long under the weight of various forms of Marxist and non-Marxist productivism, but I think we have swung too far in the other direction and the stark divide between production and consumption is no longer productive, especially in the articulation of taste in the American city. Warde and Martens's (2000) and Johnston and Baumann's (2007, 2010) focus on consumption, and their consequent elision of producers and their transactions with consumers and critics, is in the final analysis linked to disciplinary narrowing and specializing. This is an important imperative that produces work of detail and density—but it also engenders blind spots, sometimes at the very site where interrogation would have been fruitful. This is where depth could be better illuminated with some breadth and lateral knowledge. This work builds on the insights of each of their approaches, but also seeks to compensate for their errors of omission that, as I will show, have substantial theoretical consequence.

Sharon Zukin has shown that "culture is more and more the business of cities" and "[t]he growth of cultural consumption (of art, food, fashion, music, tourism) and the industries that cater to it, fuels the city's symbolic economy, its visible ability to produce both symbols and space" (1995: 2). She underlines a telling transformation in the symbolic economy where "Large numbers of new immigrants and ethnic minorities have put pressure on public institutions, from schools to political parties, to deal with their individual demands . . . These pressures, broadly speaking, are both ethnic and aesthetic. By creating policies and ideologies of 'multiculturalism,' they have forced public institutions to change" (1995: 2). Not only have public institutions and dominant discourses come under pressure, as Zukin notes, but the whole gastronomic field has had to make room for strangers, as I will show below. One obvious illustration of this is the way in which restaurants, either owned by cosmopolitan, well-capitalized immigrants such as Eric Ripert (a celebrity chef) or by less-credentialed protagonists such as Mohammad Rasool (the pseudonym of one of the protagonists in this book whom you will meet soon), have over the last forty years come to dominate the process of urban culinary value production. Almost every restaurant consecrated by the print media—*The New York Times*, Zagat Surveys, or Michelin—since the gastronomic revolution in the United States (circa 1971) are stand-alone restaurants (or very small chains) that distinguish themselves from big-money-yet-low-cultural-capital establishments such as McDonald's and KFC. Numerically small enterprises dominate in the New York City restaurant market. The New York City Department of Health and Mental Hygiene (NYCDOHMH), which is the licensing agency, lists 25,383 Food Service Establishment licenses at the end of 2014. If we exclude organizations with national brands and more than three units we still retain 17,915 small enterprises from that list (Chisolm and Bubb 2015: 3–4).

In much of the book I engage exclusively with the immigrant restaurateur because s/he is the long-ignored hinge in the transaction in taste. Furthermore, the entrepreneur is an important analytical point at which to enter the discussion about the uses of a displaced body in the transaction in literal taste. With a few exceptions that I will point out, most of the restaurants I analyze in this book are products of capital investments ranging from $20,000 to $200,000 because I am particularly interested in the popular and subordinate dimension of the transaction in taste.[8] In terms of worth and income, most of my respondents are in the lower half of the US population. So capital and profit work here at the Braudelian level of competitive markets, where no one is rich, and if someone is lucky they make a living a notch above the median household income (Braudel 1992). Yet, these are players of some consequence—granted, not dominance—in the emerging gastronomic world of star chefs, print-media critics, commentators, and celebrity bloggers.

This project is about a different scale of entanglement between entrepreneurial capital and cultural symbols in the spatial transformation of a city than the one referenced by Zukin in the story of the Sony takeover of the AT&T building, the transformation of Rockefeller Center, and the up-scaling of Bryant Park, all of which owe more to the collaborative monumentalism of corporations, the patrician class, and municipal governments in mutual pursuit of majestic museums, parks, and architectural complexes (1995: 7). Instead, my work draws attention to instances of entrepreneurship at the molecular level—the street—and the daily encounters in shops between immigrants and natives that produce much of the everyday sensorial cultures of cities such as New York, notwithstanding the modernist ambitions of its planners for ordered rectilinearity. Immigrants have repeatedly poured into this city and made it work in ways that defy high-modernist ambitions about how it should work. By living, working, and playing in the city they have changed its shape.

The exclusion of immigrant restaurateurs, combined with the restricted focus on foodie "discourse," may have allowed Johnston and Baumann (2010) to bind their project narrowly and hence render it doable, but in evacuating the very center of urban culinary production I think they have failed to capture its most dynamic dimensions and sociology has once again missed the opportunity to engage with popular disputations around good taste. I seek to correct that by approaching the transactions in taste from the other end. I pay attention to particular stories of immigrant restaurateurs and make them run up against the silences in the established gastronomic and sociological narratives.

In the case of Johnston and Bauman (2010) we also have the problem of constituting "discourse" too narrowly as representations. My extended definition of discourse without quotation marks includes representations *and* practices. Both discourse and practice became important in American sociological theorizing, as Swindler points out, to circumvent the limits of Talcott Parson's distinctions between ideas in actors' heads and their everyday doings (Swidler 2001). Practice theory moved "the level of sociological attention 'down' from conscious ideas and values to the physical and the habitual. But this move is complemented by a move 'up,' from ideas located in individual consciousness to the impersonal arena of 'discourse'" (Swidler 2001: 75). Discourse socializes ideas in individual heads, thereby making them more potent. This double movement—discourse and practice—refocuses our theoretical attention on contingent, contested activity. Discourses produce certain contingent subject positions (ethnics, immigrants, Anglos, natives, etc.) and objects (ethnic food, Indian food, American cuisine, haute cuisine, etc.). Attention to practices in specific places and their connection to discourses allow a better grasp of the world I am trying to describe.

I also pay particular attention to the gap between representations and practices that Michel de Certeau has forced us to consider in *The Practice of Everyday Life* (1998). Representations do not exhaust the possibilities of what we do, as implied after the textual and visual turns in the human sciences. Representations are more stylized, limited, and fixed than what we can do in practical life. Practices are much more open to subtle possibilities and subterfuge than representations. I will illustrate the matter in some detail below.

Discourses about ethnic food and immigrant stories and biographies are related ways of organizing varieties of social experiences with more or less authorization, yet there is no way to completely sever one from the other. Power over storylines is always partial and contested. Exclusive attention to representational "discourse" winds the circuitry of meaning too tightly and drives authors inexorably towards textuality, away from the materiality of cities where culinary cultures, foodie aspirations, and immigrant words and livelihoods intersect on co-produced street corners that smell different from the dry pages of magazines, books, and web sites. The story is different if we are open to the sensual stimuli of big-city streets peopled by natives and immigrants, built with their sweat and toil, quarrels and collaborations. These olfactory, aural, and textural microcosms of immigrants and natives, living, fighting, dreaming, and interacting in this city of dreadful delight, could be brought to the center of our research on urban food cultures. Much depends on everyday practical relations in the shops, in cabs, in the curry-houses and subways, and scholars could pay attention to that density of social interactions so as not to let our lived world—of person, body, place, and thing—dissolve into "discourse." The challenge is to bring that kind of everyday practice into the analysis without eliding the power of discursive formations. Furthermore, the story here, though propelled by people who come from elsewhere, is grounded in frictional social encounters on specific street corners that should restrain us from over-emphasizing flows and scapes that have come to dictate our recent conceptualizations.

David Howes, a leading protagonist in the sensorial revolution, explains that sensory studies have come after the linguistic turn of the 1960s, inspired by Saussure and Wittgenstein, which gave us culture as language or text, and knowledge as discourse. For a moment in the 1980s, visual culture dominated analysis, and the 1990s witnessed the turn to body and materiality. The sensorial revolution builds on the insights of each of these approaches, but also seeks to correct for their excesses (Howes 2005: 322–3). In a subsequent essay Howes notes that

> The genealogy of this revolution would not be complete, however, without noting various openings towards the senses in the work of certain leading figures of twentieth-century thought, both social and philosophical. These precursors of the full-bodied, multi-sensory approach to the study of the human condition (which can be called "sensory studies" for short) include the historians Lucien Febvre and Norbert Elias, the philosophers Maurice Merleau-Ponty and Luce Irigaray, the anthropologist Claude Lévi Strauss, and the sociologist Georg Simmel (2005: 332).

In this construction, the "senses become the sentinels or theoreticians of society" and this sensualization of theory resists the traditional identification of theorizing with "gazing upon" (in Greek, *theorein*) (Howes 2005: 326). Howes not only provides us with handy mileposts for our theoretical journey here, but also underlines the use of the multi-sensorial register of our bodies—especially, smell, sound, touch, and taste, in addition to the usual distal record of the eyes and the mind—to produce a sensual theory of a body at work in a new locale, in the process transforming the basic infrastructure of a city in a lived rather than a planned way. It is in this lived everyday transformation of habits and thinking about them that a way can be found out of Bourdieu's closed circle of habitus and automatic practice that ties subjects inexorably to social spaces of class and culture. The habitus is the body's dispositional structure that represents the objectification of social structure—as posture, gesture, class, race, gender, ethnicity—at the level of the bodily hexis of the agent. While a lot of everyday practice may be automatic, we should not dismiss the weight of deliberate thinking, especially made available to a displaced immigrant body due to its failure of automatic unconscious replication of everyday gestures, postures, and affinities (see Leschziner and Green 2013).

Shirley Yee shows how conflict may not have precluded intimate interethnic interactions in her compelling study of interracial encounters in a New York neighborhood in *An Immigrant Neighborhood* (2012). Chinese restaurateurs and laundry shops needed white business, just as Irish, Italian, and Jewish suppliers depended on Chinese restaurateurs. Barred by state law from serving as morticians, Chinese and African-Americans used white undertakers. Chinese men sometimes married Irish women as the sheer weight of demographics intersected with desire and geographic proximity. Attending to the mundane problems of inhabitation opens the possibilities of connecting with the history of engagement with ethnic food by the counterculture in critiquing and re-invigorating the mainstream. Here I use the protocols of sociology to invite the ethnic restaurateur to speak. As we shall see, when invited, the ethnic entrepreneur has a lot to say about the city, the consumer, taste, and making a living within the constraints of those constructions.

The ethnic entrepreneur in the heart of the Western metropolis conceives and offers the flavor of her experience by designing a small, semi-public space and a menu, by hiring and managing the skilled hands that can reproduce her recipes. Such choreography is undertaken in the shadow of white Anglophone demand, which nonetheless never overwhelms it. I want to recover that elbow room made by small entrepreneurs of everyday taste. The evidence of immigrant designs on the city is there, but often "inaudibly and always smothered in a stupor of objects" (Merleau-Ponty 1969: 66). In his incomplete work *Passengenwerk*, Walter Benjamin writes, "The revealing presentations of the big city are the works of those who have traversed the city absently, as it were, lost in thought or worry" (1982: 69). Much of the city is made and re-made by people too busy to spend time contemplating what they do and have done. Yet, even those reduced to documentary illegibility are not silent. The advantage of ethnographic work and interviews is, of course, the recovery of fragile orality that history cannot bear witness to. This is also an argument for the kind of interdisciplinarity that food studies provides.

What I am recommending here is the recovery of literal taste to argue about aesthetics in general. In a recent issue of the journal *The Philosophers'*

Magazine (2013) Raymond Boisvert notes that in the eighteenth century, "The new philosophical imagination envisioned humans as a set of containers: bodies for minds and minds for ideas. One unsurprising corollary: the segregation of cooking and eating from philosophy." (Boisvert 2013). Western philosophers have long denied aesthetic legitimacy to taste—in particular, that is, taste on the tongue—while theorizing about taste in general (Korsmeyer 1999; Dickie 1996). This book seeks to recover literal taste and corporeal sensory experience as a means of richer engagement with contested urban cultures.

In their cultural history of Italian cuisine, Alberto Capatti and Massimo Montanari note how pizza and pasta have become the most recognizable signs of Italy the further one goes from Italy (2003: xx). In closing, they cite Prezzolini's question in 1954, "What is the glory of Dante compared to spaghetti?" Instead of insisting on the distinctions between palatal taste and taste in literature, they underline the point of contact between mundane practice and high art, where,

> Spaghetti and pizza belong to a legacy that has spread throughout the world, just as books have . . . Along with the exchange of food products, dishes, and flavours, there is also an exchange of documents and recipes. This lively traffic . . . is vital for good taste. In fact, without realizing it, when we eat spaghetti we also ingest something of Dante (Capatti and Montanari 2003: xx).

On that ringing note Capatti and Montanari flatten the aesthetic hierarchy set in place in Early Modern Europe. Aesthetics was born as a discursive field against literal taste in the eighteenth century, when it was argued that literal taste is unconscious, subjective, and too intimate to allow rational elaboration (Korsmeyer 1999; Dickie 1996).

While reclaiming literal taste and care-work, this study engages with points of contact and sites of contestation between the infant field of food studies (mostly born outside the academy in the realm of journalism) and its godparents in cultural and social sciences. Here, food studies may have the momentary advantage of being "journalistic" (which is usually a poisoned chalice in the academy). My current institutional location allows me to stitch immigrant corporeality both to the materiality of food and to the sociality of the body, and attend to its sensorial range, in the process making elbow room for food studies in the narrow confines of already constituted disciplines, replicating within the university my respondents' labor in the city.

It is often the social friction of a body in motion that makes the naturalized body visible; thus the immigrant is the focus of this work not only because s/he has been absent from the discussion of taste but also because s/he reveals more clearly what cannot be seen in grounded native practices. This is the opposite of the classical anthropological operation of a transgressive ethnographer going out of her community and into the world of others to study the native. An immigrant is an inverted anthropologist who deals practically with the problems of a body out of place. Much has been written about the problems of the anthropological project; in contrast, very little has been theorized about the epistemological consequences of the intrusion of immigrant bodies into metropolitan spaces (in clear distinction from empirical descriptions of what immigrants do here) and what that might do to our concepts and methods of inquiry. Here, it is the boundary-crossing immigrant revealing to the native the truth about his city, at a moment when exotic tastes demanded by a roving cosmopolitan appetite must be fed in a furious gesture of appeasement. Immigrant hands and imaginations, along with capital, both financial and cultural, must be put to work.

My trajectory is akin (but inverse) to Loïc Wacquant's terminus at the black boxer's body in an attempt to understand his milieu of young black men on the South Side of Chicago in *Body & Soul* (2004). He wanted an entrée into the black, masculine world that was closed to him as a white, transplanted, French student of Bourdieu. At the end, it was through his somatic reputation as a boxer that he became "brother Louis." As an immigrant, my body's place in a new world was revealed in the process of following the bodies of other immigrants, which has driven me, like Wacquant, "to thematize the necessity of a sociology not only *of* the body, in the sense of object, but also *from* the body, that is, deploying the body as tool of inquiry and vector of knowledge" (2004: viii).

My attempt here mirrors one of the leading goals of theoretical social sciences, which is to imbricate phenomena within a structure. As Levi-Strauss put it long ago, ethnography is a means of producing knowledge in which "[t]he observer apprehends himself as his own instrument of observation" (1976: 35). Furthermore, the contribution of Merleau-Ponty's phenomenology was precisely that our perceptions and conceptions of the world are shaped by our notions of our own body. Sociology over the last generation has sought to mediate between these points by way of the work of some of the most cited sociologists—Bourdieu's work on habitus, and Anthony Giddens's on structuration. My project pays further homage to the work of Michel de Certeau and Luce Giard, who urged us to insert the author's body into a body of doctrine, and to cultivate ways of knowing that allow for the intrusion of the everyday into theory and history. Everyday food practice "is the place of a silent piling of an entire stratification of orders and counterorders," where Giard seeks to compensate Bourdieu's reticence on doing cooking, and other feminine activities which "are a place of silence or disinterest that his analysis does not trouble to take into account" (de Certeau *et al.* 1998: 183).

It is now three decades since Bryan S. Turner published *The Body & Society* (1984), which was one among a number of early sociological texts to pay sustained theoretical attention to the body.[9] Turner's synthesis sought to account for the path-breaking theorizations of Michel Foucault and practices of the social movements of feminism and civil rights that centered on this tactile, tangible thing—the color, texture, gender of the body. Now, the field is crowded, theoretically (Jaggar and Bordo 1989, Featherstone, Hepworth, and Turner 1991, Giddens 1991, Butler 1993, Falk 1994, Grosz 1994, etc.), yet it is apparent that the sociology of immigration on the one hand, and theories of taste, embodiment, and practice on the other hand, are developing in separate realms. Much of the sociology of the body continues to be devoted to theoretical argumentation focused on gender, sexuality, and disease, belying the sense that all social action, including immigration, is always embodied. Studies of immigration demand a dose of corporeality, and theories of embodiment would benefit from a diverse body of empirical research. That is what I do in this book, while showing how the analyst's sensorial range can be a more versatile tool of inquiry than we have allowed so far in modern epistemes. That is true even when at the end we have to reduce things back again to sign and sound according to the rules of a written academic text.[10]

Sequence of chapters

The next chapter, "Dreams of Pakistani Grill and Vada Pao in Manhattan: immigrant restaurateurs in a global city," plunges us into the bowels of the city, animating two street corners, where two separate immigrants have tried to build restaurants. Based on extended interviews, it will show how the specificity of capital, bodily habits, imagination, and urban location determined the fate of those restaurateurs. Yet that is too close a perspective to get adequately at the structure. For that, I step out into the discourse produced by American tastemakers in the following chapter.

Chapter 3, "Hierarchy of taste and ethnic difference: American gustatory imagination in a globalizing world," is based on reports in newspapers such as *The New York Times*, *Los Angeles Times*, and *Chicago Tribune* throughout their print run, on more recent restaurant evaluations in surveys such as Zagat and Michelin, and on reports of the National Restaurant Association. Here I show how different kinds of restaurants have been historically evaluated over the last one hundred and fifty years, in terms of both popularity and prestige. American taste-makers—that is, journalists and restaurant critics—have framed their appropriation of culinary cultures in two divergent ways: first, as high-status foreign foods, initially limited to Continental and French cuisines, eventually consecrating Italian and Japanese cookery at the end of the twentieth century; second, as the low-status product of the labor and implicit knowledge of the immigrant poor classified as ethnic fare. The appropriation of the first sort is understood primarily in aesthetic terms of taste and masculine notions of skill, while the latter is understood as a matter of necessity, primarily in terms of undifferentiated toil. Here I show how Italian cuisine exited the ethnic category and entered haute cuisine, and I do that by enumerating various surveys and analyzing menus of some of the leading American restaurants through different phases of their expansion and transformation in the long twentieth century (ca. 1880–1999).

Chapter 4, "Extending expertise: men in white at the Culinary Institute of America," is based on an ethnographic insertion into the premier cooking school in the United States, where I taught for ten years between 1996 and 2005. I make the argument that the reconfiguration of American haute cuisine had to be fed by newer modes of training not only in terms of culinary skills and techniques but also by the literal and metaphoric re-classification of white working class bodies into multicultural middle class ones. In the process I elucidate the tensions inherent in the bodily transformation of the American chef, where identities such as the chef are born in strife with others such as ethnic cook (and the housewife).

Chapter 5, "Ethnicity and expertise: immigrant cooks with haute aspirations," is the last empirically substantive chapter, which brings us back to the level of the cook by highlighting the tension between the categories of chef and ethnic through the experience of immigrant restaurateur-chefs and the ways in which that is reflected in restaurant criticism and the rhetoric of cookbooks. The material for this chapter is derived from extensive interviews and cookbooks written by ethnic and non-ethnic chefs. Expertise comes imbricated in gendered and racialized bodies.

In the concluding Chapter 6, I return to some of the themes adumbrated here.

Notes

1. According to Sean Basinski of The Street Vendor Project, major vendor languages of Lower Manhattan in 2006 were Bengali (21%), English (20%), Mandarin or Cantonese (15%), Farsi (10%), Fulani (8%), Arabic (7%), Spanish (6%), French (2%), Tibetan (2%), Urdu (2%), Wolof (2%), and other (5%). All data from Center for Urban Pedagogy and The Street Vendor Project (2006).
2. According to Claude Markovits (2008) these peddlers may add up to a quarter-million merchants and financiers operating outside the subcontinent, mostly in the Indian Ocean world, between 1830 and 1930. Caroline Adams (1987) provides us with an analogous handful of Bengali pioneers in UK.

3 Combining macro- and micro-level analysis, Nancy Foner's edited volume (2013) allows richer attention to material and affective worlds of music, worship, and food in sections such as "Eating, Drinking and Acculturation" (Orleck 2013: 108–12) and "Korean Enclaves in New York City" (Min 2013: 155–9), etc.

4 Other recent directions of research have focused on organization theory (Rao, Monin, and Durand 2003, 2005), small-group interaction, workplace dynamics and aesthetics of work (Fine 1992, 1995, 1996), field theory (Ferguson 1998, 2004), and nutrition-related science-and-technological studies (Schleifer 2010).

5 They base their theoretical contention of omnivorousness on van Eijck (2001); Peterson (1997); Peterson and Kern (1996); Peterson and Simkus (1992); Zavisca (2005); DiMaggio and Mukhtar (2004); Fisher and Preece (2003); Garcia Álvarez and Lopez Sintas (2004); and Vander Stichele and Laermans (2006).

6 They also show that "Frequent eating out on commercial premises is associated positively with having high household income, being highly educated, being younger and being single, and negatively with being a housewife" (Warde and Martens 2000: 226).

7 Even a fleeting perusal of any American newspaper over the last 100 years will show that journalistic literature has been much better at reflecting the transactions between immigrants and natives in the making of urban American culinary cultures.

8 In a comparable study done by Zukin and her students (1995) she underlined a particular limitation for immigrant entrepreneurs: "Another constraint on immigrant entrepreneurs is the cost of opening a full-service restaurant in Manhattan. Investment in a lease, equipment, advertising, and décor can rise as high as $250,000 to $1 million, which prevents many immigrant entrepreneurs from moving beyond the immigrant sector into the mainstream of the industry" (1995: 182). At the upper reaches of the restaurant world, properties such as Junoon and Vermillion rack up to tens of millions of dollars in investments.

9 Norbert Elias's work, leading to (the late translation of) *The Civilizing Process* (1982), pre-figured much of the sociological interest on the body, but was mostly ignored by Anglophone sociologists. Although first published in 1939, it was not fully engaged with until the publication of Stephen Mennell's *All Manners of Food* (1985).

10 Written words so define what we do in the university that there is a temptation to turn every aspect of the world into a text, and write the body out of it. Hence, it is not at all a surprise that anthropology, in which written texts play a minor role as a source of evidence, has most fully engaged with the body compared to almost any other cultural discipline. See Mauss (1935), Connerton (1989), Lock (1993), Serematakis (1994), Sutton (2001), Herzfeld (2004), and Lock and Farquhar (2007).

2

Dreams of Pakistani Grill and Vada Pao in Manhattan: Immigrant Restaurateurs in a Global City

Setting the table

Bread & Butter sits at the dense intersection of a cross-street and an avenue at the lower end of Manhattan. It is barely visible from across the wide avenue, caught in a whirl of honking buses spewing fumes. On the sidewalk a ginkgo sapling struggles to reach the sunlight under the shadow of a three-story walk-up. A crush of pedestrians weave their way to and from the subway station, stepping among untreated epileptics dozing off mid-pavement, and mistreated schizophrenics reduced to panhandling. Robust Nigerian peddlers and slender Bangladeshis sell fruits and vegetables, knock-off handbags, pirated DVDs, cheap jewelry and knick-knacks. Much of this is a good thing for Muhammad Rasool. It brings the customers stumbling across the threshold of Bread & Butter. He is at home speaking forcefully into his cellphone on the sidewalk that bleeds into his storefront restaurant.[1]

The long, narrow space smells of cumin and garam masala, with the sweet, hot hint of clove and cinnamon. The steam table is on the left, behind a glass sneeze-guard, with its row of twenty cooked items ready to be ladled onto Styrofoam plates. The wall on the right is covered by mirrors. Squeezed between the mirrored wall and the steam table are eight two-tops (small tables) with sixteen chairs, and a narrow path that leads to the back of the restaurant. Through numerous interrupted discussions, Rasool is asked how he went about getting the place, how much money he paid, and how he would describe the characteristics of his customers and his workers.[2]

> Muhammad Rasool (MR): I sold some family property in Pakistan to pay down the $20,000. I put in $10,000, maybe $15,000, to renovate the place. My rent is $8,000 a month. I sell on average $6 per customer. I have about 100 customers a day. Twenty for breakfast, sixty for lunch, twenty for dinner. I work here six days a week from morning to night.

Bread & Butter belongs to the lower end of the universe of Indian restaurants in Manhattan. Although I do not have access to check average prices at all restaurants, we can find a surrogate in the average price of an entrée, which stands at $11.16 for all Indian restaurants with menus in Manhattan. There are twelve Indian restaurants in Manhattan with entrées under $6.00, which is Bread & Butter's threshold. The most expensive Indian restaurants in Manhattan, such as Tabla (now closed), Junoon, and Ada, have entrées at a little over $20.00 (as an average of all their entrées), although some entrées in such establishments go above $30.

> Interviewer: How many workers do you have?
>
> MR: One Mexican. One Pakistani.
>
> Interviewer: How did you get into the restaurant business in the first place?
>
> MR: You see after I came to this country I did odd jobs. Worked in a gas station for a couple of months. I had been driving a Yellow Cab for six to seven months. That is when I ate at a restaurant on 42nd Street. It was very crowded and the people were rude. That is where I got the idea that I should have a restaurant. I drove taxi for nine more months, saved some money. I drove taxi at night to pay my workers.

That Rasool's decisions appear as isolated and individualized is an artifact of the interview process. Over the length of our full interaction it was clear that all his decisions are deeply embedded in social relations with co-ethnics. The location and contact information about the current restaurant was provided by a country cousin. The money needed was raised with another by selling some property in Pakistan with the help of other relatives. The manager, for some time was the son of a friend. The legal paperwork for the restaurant was completed by a Lahori compatriot. The cook came from a competitor. The other cook contacted him after seeing his advertisement in a local diasporic newspaper. Almost every day, Rasool meets dozens of co-ethnics as friends, family, and acquaintances who provide him with business ideas, information about better supplies, recommendations for cheaper produce, a good deal for a property, or suggestions about the hot new thing on the menu that might sell well. At the beginning of the business relationship he had a tough time with his partner about matters of money and management and had to involve a number of reputable elders in the community in Queens and at the Mosque to settle the matter extra-judicially. Some money changed hands, and reputations were discounted and others built up. In the evenings, when he heads back to Queens, he often stops by at a friend's business and, over a couple of cups of tea, looks over Pakistani and diasporic newspapers, chats, and picks up entrepreneurial advice, news from back home, and advice about children's careers. By the time he gets home, dinner has been prepared by his wife. Sometimes the college-age children are home and they eat together. On most days it is him and his wife. They would typically watch TV, catch a Bollywood movie, call family late into the night before retiring. Back to work in Manhattan in the morning.

Asked to explain the shape and design of his storefront, Rasool notes,

> It is narrow. This building is 150 years old. I changed everything. From before it is 100 percent changed. The carpenter was a friend, I told him: "Break it down, break it down, until you get to the wall." You know how much more space I got?! Four feet this way and two feet that way!

Here is Rasool literally making elbow room in this already built city. Yet he made a few mistakes in re-designing his place:

> Interviewer: You don't have any pictures up?
>
> MR: Yes, I don't have pictures because I have no room for pictures. The biggest mistake I made was to put the mirror on the wall. Instead of the mirror I should have put pictures. Now where can I put pictures?
>
> I: Why did you put the mirror?
>
> MR: Biggest mistake I made during the construction [laughs and shakes his head].
>
> I: Does it cost too much to take it down?
>
> MR: It doesn't . . . But you see the spirit to do becomes less, and less. A young guy by tomorrow he will change it. I used to do that before . . . but not anymore. That is why I want to retire [laughs].
>
> I: Do you want your children to enter this business?
>
> MR: No. They are like you going to school. I don't want them here washing dishes . . . No I don't want them here.
>
> I: If you were to put a picture there, what would it be?

MR: There is one scenery I see in my embassy, the Pakistan Consulate, it was a picture of Mohenjodaro, I would put that one if I could get that one, it is 10,000 years old . . . general scenery, which attracts everybody.

I: How would you characterize your restaurant?

MR: Fast-food restaurant. Indian, Pakistani spicy food. I also carry less spicy Spanish-American food.

I: Spanish-American?

MR: Yes, because you see we have rice and we have beans, and chicken of course everyone eats. It is the same food without spices. Spanish food.

We find Rasool reorienting himself to his specific Latino public at that street corner, as fewer and fewer South Asian taxi drivers stop by his place (although almost 80 percent of New York City's approximately 40,000 drivers, of approximately 13,000 licensed Yellow Cabs, are of Bangladeshi, Pakistani, or Indian origin). He miscalculated his audience because that intersection is too crowded for cabbies to stop for lunch or dinner. Every street corner in the city has its character. This one is too busy to allow cabbies to stop long enough (unlike, say, the curry houses of Lexington Avenue)—precisely the thing that gets Rasool all the foot traffic. And this corner is different too from the other street-corner in the West Village that can support a different kind of place from Rasool's, as I will discuss below. One day the conversation turned to cooking.

I: Do you cook at home?

MR: No.

I: Where did you learn how to cook?

MR: It is easy. I know it.

I: Did you train for it?

MR: No.

I: You just know it?

MR: Yes . . . It does not take a genius.

I: Who cooks at home?

MR: My wife.

I: Did your wife give you the recipes?

MR: No.

I: Do you consult cookbooks?

MR: No.

I: Did you watch your wife cook?

MR: No, but she gave me confidence. She didn't tell me how to cook, but she gave me confidence. If you don't know how to cook then your partners take advantage of you. Once I called my wife on the phone and asked her how to make *aloo gobi* and she told me how to do it. Then I did it. I ask her, how do I cook this, how do I cook that? She tells me. I do it. It does not take a genius you know.[3]

I: What do you mean?

MR: You see this Mexican guy who works for me? He learned just by watching me. Now he is my best cook.

I: How come?

MR: It is business. It is only business. It is not real. People come in, they take a look at it and think it must take all these people to make complicated things. But it is simple. It is business. It is just business.

There are a number of things to note here. First, the failure of the interview as a tool to elicit tacit knowledge about cooking, which forced me to redesign the study to deploy more ethnographic techniques to get at *doing*. Second, the phrase "It is business. It is just business," is a complex, cryptic opening into differing values in differing domains. It implies a short-term horizon. It implies a domain of necessity which is held in opposition to cultural essence. It allows for certain kinds of manipulations and transformations. In Paul Stoller's work, that segregation of domain between culture and business is precisely what allowed the Nigerian vendor El Hadj Harouna Souley to explain away contradictions between a moral worldview and some of the dirty everyday activity with the words: "Money has no smell" (Stoller 2002). The analogue in Rasool's words, "It is business," allows him some ethical and aesthetic leeway.

Rasool's construction of culture against commerce has a long lineage in South Asia. Utsa Ray has shown (2009, 2010) how middle-class Bengali men and women (*bhadrasamaj*) transformed the urban Bengali discourse on taste in cities such as Kolkata (Calcutta) in the late nineteenth and early twentieth centuries to produce a new desiring subject who valued domestic cookery more than street foods, and in doing so inscribed middle-class home cooking as the only legitimate standard of authentic Bengali cooking, one that can never be matched either by migrant male Odiya cooks, hired in increasing numbers by the same class, or by street vendors. Middle-class Bengali men and women endlessly complain that there is no good Bengali food outside the home, unlike French or Italian or Punjabi food, they say. Here the complaint is a disguised compliment, about the subtlety of the palate developed far from the madding crowd of the poor and non-Bengali (Odiya, Bihari, Marwari, Nepali, etc.) streets.

There are signs of a civilizing process of Bengali desires by the end of the nineteenth century where "*katu* (*jhal* in colloquial Bengali) [hot/spicy] and *amla* [sour] had stable extreme positions in the spectrum of Bengali taste hierarchy." (Mukhopadhyay 2004: 43). Nationalist heroes such as Bankimchandra Chattopadhyay and Vivekananda repeatedly condemn tamarind and chili consumption, associating them with uneducated rural women and the uncouth bazaar. Although the marginalization of chili and tamarind in the construction of Bengali haute cuisine awaits its historian, classic Bengali recipe books from the end of the nineteenth century onwards contain them both in the section on chutneys and pickles, excising their "excessive" use in good Bengali cuisine (Mukhopadhyay 2004). Yet it is perhaps their very repression in the dominant hierarchy of taste that produced their efflorescence as a subaltern counter-discourse of street-foods, a minoritarian tradition that escapes the dominating form of taste. Furthermore, street foods are paradoxically considered an element of the male domain and yet irresistible to young women, who for precisely that reason must avoid the lure of *dustu-khide* (unruly appetite) to shore up the claims of decency. Middle-class discourse about the great virtues of Bengali cuisine hinges on the gendered and classed character of its construction, as a product of the affective labor of the housewife and her servants. A recent study of Indian street culture notes that "the street has for long been the object of anxieties about social miscegenation and mixtures of commerce, residence and community" (Gambetta and Bandyopadhyay 2012: 2). That story is always about culture against commerce.

In Vu Pham's detailed study of a Vietnamese-American crustacean restaurant in San Francisco (Pham 2006), a slightly different wording, "After all, it is a business," is used to find room for one's dubious activities and intentions. In this case it is used to self-certify a mix of Vietnamese French colonial nostalgia that panders to white neocolonial fantasies. Crafting fairy-tales of refugee self-invention and upward mobility, and the privileging of personal familial triumph over critiques of colonialism. Pham sees "after all, it is a business" as the mode of dubious aesthetic massaging of a western wound. In Rasool's case it allows him to act insincerely. He ignores such delicate neocolonial convolutions, but his dreams are no different from those of some Anglophone Indian elites playing in the New York food market with lots of capital and MBAs. One of these concepts is *inday*, named by Basu Ratnam, Phil Suarez, and Jean-Georges Vongerichten. They are hoping to spread the gospel of fast, casual Indian food (without being too Indian) in the mid-market niche. There are other somewhat grandiose attempts to reconstruct colonial Indian pastiche as a Kipling-esque company, serving cutlets, *burra* kebabs, tea sandwiches, *chota* pegs, and gin and tonics, with million-dollar investors and dreams of Gymkhana Clubs and Mogli Eats. These business plans may still see the light of day. Here, points of public contention are digested into aesthetically reconciled marketing memorabilia, where, as Marilyn Halter (2000) and Arlene Davila (2001) show, marketing and ethnicity are completely at home. That is one end on a continuum of compromised behaviors.

Rasool's insistence that what we have here is mere commerce, not culture, is antithetical to the marketing of his culture. This is echoed in diasporic newspapers' sparse coverage of commercial cookery in the features, although the classifieds are plastered with advertisements for restaurants and cooks. The two major expatriate Indian weekly newspapers—*India Abroad* and *India Tribune* (which I have analyzed from 2001 to 2014)—have carried about two dozen stories each year (in fifty-two weekly issues) on the culture of cooking, which typically conclude with a page of recipes written by women for women. The focus of the food articles is to collate a pan-Indian cuisine in the diaspora, introducing the readers to dishes from "elsewhere" in India—a theme Arjun Appadurai noted in his seminal article on cookbooks in the Indian national space (1988), which appears to have been extended to the diaspora today. Both newspapers have a cautious, middle-brow approach to food contained within discourses of domesticity, and reflect the tastes of anglophone, achieving, middle-class Indian men in the US.

That goes hand-in-hand with a celebrity-oriented culture of chefs who have gained recognition in the mainstream media—such as *The New York Times* or on Food Network—be it Floyd Cardoz when he won the Top Chef Master competition, Padma Laxmi as the sultry and sensuous host of Top Chef, or the opening of Hemant Mathur's *Tulsi* (Pais 2011a, 2011b). This conservative, celebrity-oriented, nation-advertising approach sits well with Rasool's valorization of his wife's home cooking (and his resistance to its commodification), the presumed realm of culture. Here we get the faint trace of the divide of modern post-colonial nationalism into culture inside the home and commerce outside it, in public (Chatterjee 1993; see Walsh 2004, Burton 2003).

Most importantly, Rasool's reticence underlines the explanatory power of Appadurai's argument about what happens when commodities cross the relatively constricting cultural containers that he characterizes as regimes of value (1986: 15). In *The Social Life of Things* (1986), Appadurai draws on Georg Simmel's work on money and economic value and Werner Sombart's theory of luxury consumption as the motor of Early Modern European Capitalism to "demystify the demand side of economic life" (Appadurai 1986: 58). First, Appadurai sidelines the marginalist presumption that demand flows directly from needs and desires rooted in human nature. In contrast, Appadurai shows that a desiring subject who generates demand has to be culturally produced. Most importantly for our purposes here, the value of things, especially things that cross boundaries between communities, has to be sorted out in complex and sometimes mutually incomprehensible ways, as subtle and as symbolic as the doings of the cargo cults of Oceania. And, things that are not allowed to be commodified, such as land and relics, may acquire commodity form in new contexts. Sites that allow commodification, such as the bazaar, may do so by demarcating it clearly from the household, but such divisions may falter under new regimes of value. Finally, things may be allowed the commodity form in certain phases of their biography, such as gifts before they become so but that, once gifted, are ideally diverted from their path as a commodity.

So is a plate of chicken vindaloo produced in Rasool's restaurant a commodity accessed by whoever pays for it or a gift of another culture that cannot be fully commodified? It depends on the nature of the transaction and the intentionality of the actors involved. The more subtle and sophisticated the customer, the more s/he resists the complete commodification of the relationship, in spite of the cash nexus. The seller of the cultural artifact located at the bottom of the social hierarchy, such as Rasool, wants to commodify it quickly, if fleetingly, and is inclined to segregate it from home cooking. In contrast, ethnic celebrity chefs (and other high culture intermediaries) are invested in the exchange as a long-lasting cultural transaction. That is why the quest for authenticity becomes so acute. The search for authenticity is an anxiety produced by access. Before it was available to many, the mere knowledge of its existence, if not the taste, was a distinguishing sign. Now that it is available to so many, we need experts to judge whether the thing is any good. That biography of a commodified fragment of a culture in another context, such as a dish you can buy, is now overlaid on the Romantic regime of value that accentuates Western tastes for things of the past and from other places. Buffeted by such demands, Rasool appears to carry in his metaphysics at least two registers of value. One of money, price, and "only business," "not real," important and useful to the calculus of making a living, but different from the high moral purpose and aesthetic pursuit of "culture." Yet culture is the very thing that some of his customers come to him in their hunger for an authentic replica of another culture; this is the second register of value. In the transaction between Rasool and some of his customers who seek a quick ethnic fix there develops a gap in the commensurability of regimes of value. Both sides are getting something valuable out of the exchange but not the same thing.

Beyond the back-and-forth of figuring each other out that goes on between the entrepreneur and the customer, there is also something more here in the case of Rasool. It has something to do with the limits of language (that I could not press on without Punjabi—the interviews were conducted in Hindi and English), about doing, and about the social embarrassment of cooking and middle-class Lahorean masculinity. Rasool does not embody the skills of cooking that his wife can lay claim to. But what he does incorporate is the taste of the real thing, and he can mobilize the memory of that taste to feed his imagined South Asian cabbie customer and the real Hispanic one. Yet, beyond my own linguistic limits, and Rasool's inability to cook with skill, what is intriguing is how people like Mohammad Rasool have not figured in the scholarly discussion on taste.

What's in a name?

Taste is here directly linked to building something. The process of designing a restaurant can begin with the mere act of naming it. The first visible Indian restaurant in New York City, named Ceylon India Inn, was established in 1913 on Eighth Avenue and Forty-ninth Street, where it became a center of Indian nationalist activity. But the owner, K. Y. Kira, sought to re-orient its focus from inside the community to outside it—as was becoming common in view of the demand for ethnic food among a new Anglo-American middle class (see Chapter 3)—by moving its location and discouraging Indian seamen and students from lingering too long.

By the 1920s, we see the discussion of South Asian food shift to the takeover of the Royal British Navy by "little brown men"—often called lascars—who ate rice and curry on board ship. In an article in *The New York Times*, John Carter explained that "the shift of economic forces during and since the [First World War] has left little of her British character, save the officers, who are English" (Carter 1925: SM9). He complains about the lascars, "Their religion demands that they shall eat no meat unless it has been slaughtered in accordance with the prescribed ritual. The diet of Indian Moslems consists of mutton, curry and rice: rice, curry and mutton ad infinitum. This mutton must be fresh-killed, by a Moslem, although it does not matter who cooks it. Accordingly, vessels with Moslem crews must carry a flock of live sheep aboard" (Carter 1925). There were other perverse problems with these Orientals, Carter continues, specifically their propensity to contract strange ailments from curses and promptly die from them, to the great inconvenience of the captain. Although they were paid lower wages, to Carter it wasn't clear that employing Orientals made it cheaper to run a shipping line, because a crew of "fifty British will handle a vessel for which seventy lascars would be hardly enough. Moreover, Orientals, for all their philosophies of Nirvana and of indifference to death, nearly always grow panic-stricken in an emergency, with corresponding risk to vessel and cargo" (Carter 1925: SM9). It is these lascars who, on jumping ship, would give us the first chain of cheap curry houses in the Western metropolis.

There was also a Caribbean connection to South Asian food by way of the Harlem Renaissance. Richard Huey, who sang the hit "Bloomer Girl," opened Aunt Dinah's Kitchen in 1935, serving southern fried chicken, Mexican chili, sweet potato pie, and East Indian curry (van Gelder 1944). Harlem may have also been home to east-coast America's first Indian restaurants directed towards its own community, which unfortunately did not leave any trace in print (Bald 2013: 174). By the 1930s, there is also evidence of an Indian member of the Harlem Restaurant Owners' Association, and by the late 1940s, advertisement for Indian restaurants such as India's Garden Inn proliferate in the pages of the African-American *New York Amsterdam News.* The 1939 WPA Guide to New York City (Federal Writers Project 1939/1995) listed four "East Indian Restaurants." There is no documentary evidence of other Indian restaurants until the late 1940s, but according to Bald's oral informants there may have been a handful of unnamed ones in small basements and side-streets of Harlem. By the mid-1940s, others had also noticed a number of Bengali hot dog vendors operating in East Harlem, down Madison, Lexington, and Third Avenues (Bald 2013: 173–4). Arguably, the place that served more Indian meals than any other in Manhattan by the mid-twentieth century may have been at the four-story building at 100 West Thirty-eighth Street, home of the segregated British Merchant Sailors' Club for Indian Seamen, which had a mess hall that seated eighty people and in its first year served 198,200 meals (Bald 2013: 182).

It appears from the sudden frequency of discussion about curry in the course of the Second World War that media coverage of the Indian National Movement led by Mahatma Gandhi, the requirements of a low-protein wartime diet (with its flavor challenges for the Anglo palate), and exposure to the taste of Allied Indian troops, conspired to put curry on the American plate, at least of gastronomes and journalists such as Jane Holt of *The New York Times*. Holt often worked in conjunction with The Civilian Defense Volunteer Office (with an interest in civilian nutrition, especially vitamin deficiency) and trade organizations such as The Spice Traders' Association. Where Jane Holt left off, Jane Nickerson continued, in her "News of Food" column, announcing the "first direct shipment of curry powder since the war" to arrive from Madras on September 7, 1946 (Nickerson 1946). Nickerson then also informs us that the East India Curry Shop was "a restaurant that probably serves the most 'authentic' curries in town" (1946). Access, by then, was already producing anxieties about authenticity.

The four Indian restaurants listed in the Manhattan Telephone Directory by 1949—the earliest reference to a cluster of Indian restaurants—were named India Bengal Garden, India Prince, India Rajah, and India Restaurant. The Bengal Garden was opened in 1948 by a previous line cook, Habib Ullah, his Puerto Rican wife Victoria, who welcomed guests at the front of the house, and two investors, Ibrahim Choudry and a Mr Ali, "who had saved up $20,000 selling hot dogs from a pushcart on 110th Street" (Bald 2013: 178).

At the dawn of post-colonial nationalism such insistent use of "India" in the name must have made sense both to South Asian entrepreneurs and to their American customers. Perhaps that is why the categorization of India Rajah under the class "Hindu," in a 1939 *New York Times* classified ad, did not have staying power. *Hindoo* was a United States Census category used from 1910 to 1940 to classify Indians who were Hindu, Muslim, Sikh, or Parsee (Gibson and Jung 2005). It was also an increasingly popular term used to classify South Asians and distinguish them from Native Americans. There was a certain exoticism to that classification. Tobacco growers often branded their products under names such as Hindoo, Mecca, Mogul, and Bengal (Bald 2013: 17). Tin Pan Alley songwriters produced tunes such as "My Hindoo Man" and "Down in Bom-Bombay," which were sung in middle-class American homes. In 1904, Coney Island's Luna Park created a veritable Delhi Darbar, with imported camels, elephants, and hundreds of Indian performers, borrowing from the iconography of the Raj and King Edward VII of England's accession to the imperial throne. Affluent men in American cities "outfitted their smoking rooms with plush Oriental rugs, hookahs, tiger skins, elephant tusks, daggers, scimitars and images of 'eroticized Eastern women'—goods that simultaneously conveyed the conquest of far-off lands and conjured the fantasy world of the eastern harem" (Bald 2013: 18).

The classification of India Rajah as Hindu declines in the print record after 1940. The owner wasn't Hindu, the chef de cuisine was "Ali Jan of Benares" (Ashley 1939: 100), and "India" may have been a better referent, both for the customer and the entrepreneur. But it took a while for the public and the experts to develop the necessary distinctions between Indian, Hindu, Parsee, Turkish, and Arab, as evidenced by the following confusion in an early restaurant guide for New York City, titled *Dining in New York*, by Rian James (1930). The Rajah, classified by James as a "Turkish (Parsee)" restaurant in the 1930 edition, located west of Broadway on Forty-eighth Street, is described thus: "a dingy little red sign swings high over the stoop of an erstwhile aristocratic brownstone front. Upstairs you will find The Rajah, about as big as a medium-sized clothes-press, and not nearly as sanitary; but you're in Turkey now—and if you were terribly fussy, you wouldn't have gone to Turkey in the first place. Besides, the food is worth the trip" (1930: 65–6). One of the clues that this is probably Indian food is James's description of it:

> The table d'hote starts with Tamarind—a lemon-colored drink made from vegetables—as an appetizer. A watery, albeit true-to-type, native soup follows. Then, the real business of the Turkish dinner sets in. Choose lamb, chicken, or beef curry—oh, such a fiery curry sauce! A heaping plate of rice

> with an ample portion of cabbage is placed beside your curry. The trick is to pour your curried meat into the little well of the rice, mix thoroughly, and then enjoy . . . You'll enjoy your dinner, speculating about the other queer-looking diners, and learn, astonishingly enough, that all sheiks don't wear goatees, ride white horses and brandish swords (James 1930: 66–7).

In ranging widely, James conflates the Arab world with Turkey and India in a classic case of early twentieth-century Orientalism. Some of the comestibles—such as the drink called Tamarind—appear in contradictory guise in different sources. Even two decades later, Robert W. Dana, author of *Where to Eat in New York* (1948), writes about it as "pomegranate nectar," which "is a sweet beverage boiled from the tamarind roots that grow on Indian riverbanks" (1948: 100). Despite confusing two different fruits with very different taste profiles—tamarind and pomegranate—and displacing the fruit with the root of the tamarind, adding the local color of "growing on Indian riverbanks" is a desperate attempt at verisimilitude. Lawton Mackall identifies it more plausibly as "pomegranate cocktail (spiced juice, no alcohol)" (1948: 206).

Yet that parenthetical "Parsee" in the classification of The Rajah was too specific to be ignored. When I first ran into the reference, I wondered what a Parsee (a Zoroastrian exile from Persia to India) was doing in Manhattan with a Turkish restaurant that had an Indian name (The Rajah), and that advertised itself as "Hindu" (in the advertisement section of the 1939 *New York Times*). Later, I gathered from other sources that The Rajah was once owned by Rustom Wadia, a Parsee from Bombay, who came to the US in 1923 to study engineering at Union College in Schenectady, New York (India Abroad 1992). He ate his first American meal in an Indian restaurant in Manhattan around the transportation hub in midtown, eventually becoming its co-owner in 1926, taking it over fully in 1944. Wadia's enterprise was clustered with a number of other successful mid-town ventures such as Longchamps on Madison Avenue, which specialized in Anglo-curries, Sarat Lahiri's (an itinerant musician) Bengal Tiger Restaurant on West Fifty-eighth Street, and Trudie Telle's (an American missionary) East India Curry Shop on East Sixteenth Street, which had Darmadasa (whom we shall meet again) as a cook.

So the name The Rajah, the provenance of the food, and the sign under which it was served, all had to be slowly sorted out over decades of transactions between immigrant proprietors, their own classificatory systems engaging with real and imagined customers, with those of American newspaper critics, commentators, advertisers, and guidebook writers, before the people and the food could be put in their mutually comprehensible categories. What appear at first glance to be mere errors of classification are also traces of a process of transaction in type.

Interestingly, a number of restaurants that appear for the first time in guidebooks serving foreign cuisines for Americans, such as Indian, Thai, Korean, and Japanese, were originally clustered around Midtown. That is in contrast to Chinese, Italian, and Kosher restaurants, serving large domestic immigrant populations, which were clustered on the Lower East Side in the early years of the twentieth century. Harlem may have been home to East Coast America's first Indian restaurants directed towards its own community, which did not leave much of a trace in print. Midtown restaurants facing outward were better covered in Anglo newspapers, hence more legible in the historical record.

By the end of the 1950s, "India" can still be found in some of the restaurant names, such as Bombay India, Ceylon India Inn, and Pakistan India. The 1956 edition of *Menu: The Restaurant Guide of New York* identified three Indian restaurants serving curries, *samosa*, shish kebab, and *rijsttafel*.[4] But by 1969, sub-national places and non-place names were added to the repertoire, such as Punjab, Karachi, Rajmahal, Koh-i-Noor, and Natraj. Yet, clear national identifiers had to be positioned in small print underneath the names, such as "unique Pakistani, Indian cuisine" under Rajmahal or "Authentic Indian Curries" under Punjab. The 1978 edition of *Mary Waldo's Restaurant Guide to New York City and Vicinity* lists 19 Indian and Pakistani restaurants. By 1979, newer restaurants such as Raga, Mumtaz, Nirvana, Shaheen, and Tandoor no longer needed "India" in their names as the entrepreneur and the audience began to figure each other out, sometimes with the intermediation of critics. Perhaps the category had also become overcrowded. By 1989, Dawat had to both explain itself and pull itself into gastronomic "discourse" by claiming that "*Dawat* Means Invitation to a Feast" and that they served "The 'Haute' Cuisine of India . . . under the culinary supervision of Madhur Jaffrey, who has been called, 'the finest authority on Indian cooking in America' by Craig Claiborne." They managed to say all that in their tiny advertisement in the NYNEX Yellow Pages (1988–89: 1,481). Much of this history of transactions in type was reticulating through the simple question I had asked Muhammad Rasool:

> I: How did you come to name this place Bread & Butter?
>
> MR: You see, I used to call it Taj Mahal but my business was not working. Day after day I dragged my tired body home on that [commuter] train. One day I fell asleep. The train jolted to a halt. I woke up and looked around . . . which is when it came to me. No one, not one person in this compartment knows what Taj Mahal is, but each one of them knows about bread and butter, so to make my business run I had to change the name to Bread & Butter!

The logic of naming Indian restaurants in New York appears to be distinct from that of Chinese and French restaurants, revealing their spatial and social location. The first recorded cluster of eleven Chinese restaurants in New York City in 1898, listed by Louis Beck in his *New York's Chinatown*, included Hon Heong Lau, Me Heong Lau, King Heong Lau, Way Heong Lau, Gui Ye Quan, Mon Li Won, and Kim Sun, and were all located on Mott and Pell Street in Lower Manhattan, marking their insider audience and subaltern status (Beck 1898: 49). Until the last quarter of the twentieth century the Indian population in the United States was, in most locations, too small and dispersed to support enclave eateries, such as we find among, say, the 4,000 or so Chinese in New York's Chinatown in the 1890s. Although we do not know for sure from the archival record, according to the oral historian Bald's interviews with descendants of Bengali Harlem residents, most of the Indian restaurants in Harlem that catered to Muslim South Asian seamen, peddlers, and West Indian migrants might have had more specific names, such as Ameer's, Syed Ali's, etc.

Chinese restaurants in New York have gone through a fascinating century-long cycle that began with early confinement within Chinatown; then suddenly, around 1903, they break out of that area in the Lower East Side, following the lead of a Chinatown merchant named "Charley Boston," who also went by the name of Lee Quong June (or Li Quen Chong) (*New York Times* 1900, 1903). He closed his restaurant on Doyer Street and reopened on Third Avenue and Rivington, then pushed up further onto Seventh Avenue, near Thirty-fourth Street. Other "Chop Suey Resorts," in the current terminology, followed quickly, ending up with more than a hundred eateries between Fifty-fifth Street and Fourteenth Street, from Bowery to Eighth Avenue, with names such as Chop Suey Bowl, Chop Suey House, Chop Suey Café, Chop Suey Palace, Chop Suey Food Garden, and Chop Suey Parlor, by the 1920s (Liu 2009). In Los Angeles, in 1900, there were a couple of Chinese restaurants, frequented almost exclusively by the Chinese, which jumped to fifteen by 1910, now covered in the typical write-ups in Anglophone newspapers. In 1905, San Francisco had forty-six Chinese restaurants, growing to seventy-six by 1925 (Chao 1985: 223). This was not just a New York or a West Coast thing. There is evidence of one Chinese restaurant in Chicago in 1900; by 1915 there were 118, with only half a dozen or so in Chinatown (Liu 2009: 12).

The sudden fashion for chop suey in American cities is a reminder that the surprising ubiquity of sushi at the end of the twentieth century, or the current popularity of Ramen noodle shops, have precedents. By the Roaring Twenties, American urban culture had gone chop suey-mad, eventually to be consecrated in a Louis Armstrong jazz number, "Cornet Chop Suey" (1926), and a cool, iconic Edward Hopper painting, *Chop Suey* (1929). Harvey Levenstein links their proliferation to the expansion of lower- to middle-class service jobs for men and women in the city, who were not catered to by the old working-class saloons or the new higher-class restaurants (1993: 185). By 1925, the journalist Bertram Reinitz was pointing out the new role of chop suey in feeding working women, the "telephonists and typists" (Reinitz 1925: XX2), who typically made a lunch-hour exodus to Chinatown from Franklin, Duane, and Worth Streets. Taking stock of the year's major developments at the end of the term, he writes, "Hot tamales have acquired unprecedented popularity as party provender . . . and chop suey has been promoted to a prominent place on the midday menu of the metropolis" (1925: XX2). He noted that from a casual commodity, the chop suey had become a staple, now vying with sandwiches and salads for the attention of young, female palates. This new American palate was so established that by 1942, the US Army mess hall handbook listed chow mein, chop suey, spaghetti, and tamales.

In another contrast in naming traditions, establishments that gave off signals of much higher status, were the elite American restaurants of the first half of the twentieth century, which invariably had French names such as Le Pavillion, La Côte Basque, La Caravelle, Lutèce, La Grenouille, and Le Périgord, leading the New York restaurateur Drew Nieporent to characterize it as the Le/La phase of American fine dining (in Bruni 2005: F4). Mere names of restaurants can provide a rich record of social location and transactions in taste.

From naming to cooking

Walking down the steps from the sidewalk, I found myself in a dark, low-ceilinged room. My eyes landed on the gourd-shaped IKEA lamps over each table. Then they were drawn to a large calligraphic backdrop on the far wall, which was a cross between a fluid Arabic verse from the Quran and the famous terracotta horse figurines from Bankura which pay homage to Vishnu, the Hindu god. Begum Hasina welcomed me as if she already knew me. Dacca is in the East Village in Manhattan on Sixth Street—New York City's own little stretch of Brick Lane—a block it shares with a dozen other Indian restaurants run by branching Bangladeshi expatriates descended from Sylheti lascars who, by jumping ship, have given us a network of curry houses stretching from Amsterdam to New York. Dacca is the brainchild of three Bangladeshis linked by marriage—Hasina, the spirit occupying the place, her husband, and her brother-in-law Dulun.[5] They opened the restaurant because, in their words, they wanted to bring Bengali home cooking to Americans (Burnett 2007). So they have put *khichuri* (a rice and lentil mess that is the very apotheosis of domestic cookery) and *maacher jhaal* (fish in mustard sauce) on their menu. This has drawn some critical attention from reviewers on the web and food critics in the print media. On MenuPages.com, among a dozen ecstatic evaluations, a typical one stated, "Best on the block . . . [Dulun] and his family are warm and welcoming and ensure a great meal" (Menupages.com 2007). Peter Meehan noted in *The New York Times*, "I swore off the restaurants on the block, and anything on Sixth between Cooper Union and the F.D.R Drive. [Dacca] . . . brought me back. [Dacca] is proof that interesting, authentic Indian cooking is not relegated to the outer reaches of the city" (Meehan 2004).

Dacca provides a variation on a theme. With an average entrée at $13.02, Dacca sits among the middle third of all Indian restaurants in Manhattan. Of the 202 Manhattan restaurants that characterize themselves as Indian, there are 177 separate properties with distinct menus, while the rest are alternate properties of chains with the same menu, such as Baluchi's (Menupages.com 2009).[6] More than 90 percent of Indian restaurants in New York City can be characterized as the standard curry house, of which Baluchi's is a good example.

Curry houses typically list appetizers such as *samosas*, soups such as *mulligatawny*, tomato and lentil, and various kinds of kebabs. They include *tandoori* breads, *biriyanis* and *pulao*. Main courses include chicken, lamb, and fish in pre-made base sauces with a last-minute twist such as *vindaloo* (added vinegar), *tikka masala* (added tomato paste and butter), *dopiaza* (added fried onions), and *makhni* (added butter). The vegetarian options are typically *chana masala, aloo gobi, saag paneer, mutter paneer, malai kofta*, and *baigan bharta*; sides include mango chutney, tomato chutney, *raita*, and pickles; and desserts such as *rasmalai, gulab jamun, kheer*, mango ice cream, and *kulfi*. The names of these dishes are beginning to be standardized as a kind of global curry-house Hindustani, but they often carry traces of Bengali locution, such as *khichuri* (contra the Hindustani *khichdi*), *bendi mosala* (contra *vhindi masala*) and *luchi niramish* (contra *puri-bhaji*).[7] The reason that East Bengali accents abound in nominally Hindustani-looking menus is because currently more than one-half of Indian restaurateurs in New York City are Bangladeshis.

In the context of rampant hybridity it is not surprising, then, that Muhammad Rasool from Lahore puts *vindaloo* from Goa on his menu in Manhattan. No one orders the *vindaloo* at Bread & Butter. It is too expensive at $7.95. It may also be a bit too much for the crowd it caters to, but it is right there in smudged ink at number 23 on the menu. "A piquant . . . curry from the famed Beach City of Goa, meat marinated in a unique spicy 'masala' w/cumin seeds & potatoes." The language is formulaic, magical, ritual-like in its ubiquity here and in all low-cost Indian restaurants, and points to something sad and touching, obvious and insistent, as revealed by the momentary confusion of a young man.

Sebastian D'Souza is an American-born Bangladeshi who, along with a group of six intricately linked male family members, manages Sonar Bangla, one of the downtown Indian restaurants, a stone's throw from Ground Zero.

When asked whether some of the dishes there have echoes of home, he surprisingly picks the *vindaloo*. He says, "Yes of course, we have it often at home . . . my mother cooks it. Like most Bengalis we love our *vindaloo*." His father hastens to explain, "We are Catholic Bangladeshis, and *vindaloo* is Portuguese. So we have it often." In a way, that explains everything—shared Catholic world. But in another way it does not explain a thing. There are many other kinds of Catholics, so why must these two groups—Bangladeshi Catholics and Goan Catholics—imagine themselves as proximate, especially when they are thousands of miles from home? Perhaps because they are thousands of miles from home and pushed towards each other by their appearance to outsiders.

Sometimes there are problems of turning into explicit language what is obvious to the practiced body. Take for instance, a savory, lentil-stuffed, fried-dough appetizer called *kachori*. As Figure 2.1 shows, it is intriguing how the *kachori* got on the menu and came to be named through a series of borrowings as apparent from the spellings and the misspellings on the menus. I wonder if the *kachori*, by its very nature, is untranslatable, or are such borrowings a mere sign of laziness? What are the specific problems of translation that motivate the restaurateur to give up? Language sometimes falls much shorter than the broader sensorial range we experience with our bodies—does it smell right, have the right crunch of puff pastry, does it have the brittle heat of dried red chilies? The body ranges more widely and can be deployed more deftly, as a tool of enquiry that exceeds mere sign and sound. That is partly the power of food and also the limits of turning something so multi-sensorial into language.

Kachori (or **Ka-chori**) is listed in the following ways in 16 restaurants in Manhattan, out of a total of 188 menus analyzed:

"too different to put into words, but recommended" at Amin
"too difficult to put into words, but recommended" at Bombay Grill, Baluchi's, India Place, Indigo, Indian Bistro, Sitar
"Kachori Chaat … ask an Indian friend" at Chennai
"assorted fritters" at Curry in a Hurry
"deep fried lentil pastry w/mash potatoes, chic peas, & 3 sauces" at Kinara's, Prix Fixe menu
"two chickpea & green pea balls, hot & sweet" at Madras Mahal, under "appetizer from Gujarat"
"savory, lentils and potatoes filled pastry pocket topped with yogurt and tamarind chutney" at Nirvana
"dumplings filled with fresh lentils, seasoned with Gujarati spices and dry fruits. A specialty of Gujarat" at the relatively upscale Salaam Bombay
"crisp lentil dumpling stuffed with spiced chickpeas, crispies & drizzled with yogurt, mint & tamarind sauce" at Yuva, as an appetizer
named but not described at Curry & Curry and Madina

FIGURE 2.1 *The mystery of* kachori.

Furthermore, the varieties of spellings for *kachori/katchori/kochuri/ka-chori* in today's Indian restaurant menus echo the unsettled appropriation of *curree/curry/currey* in eighteenth-century English cookbooks and *pasta/paste* in twentieth-century American equivalents. Words and dishes settle into certain known things with prescribed dimensions (the prescription and names becoming more stringent with print) slowly among a community of producers, consumers, and critics.

Of course, many of the steps in the process of transmission and translation are no longer remembered or inscribed anywhere that can be traced back. These are forgotten stories: the way that *vindaloo* got on the menu at Bread & Butter (Rasool told me that he does not recall, "Perhaps taken from another menu?"); how *vindaloo* relates to Sebastian D'Souza's mom's cooking in Queens; how Floyd Cardoz's "South Indian Mushroom Soup" with tamarind at the high-status and high-priced Tabla may or may not be a riff on *vindaloo* while simultaneously fleeing from it; why Madhur Jaffrey's menu at Dawat (which she now disavows) puts its duck "*vindaloo*" within quotation marks.

From cooking to eating (and judging)

Jackie, a particularly thoughtful and erudite respondent and customer at Saravana Bhavan, an Indian restaurant in the Murray Hill neighborhood of Manhattan (which is sometimes referenced colloquially as "Curry Hill" because of the two-dozen restaurants, grocery stores, etc. located in that neighborhood), reflects on the mercurial nature of power in the encounter between the customer, the server, and the entrepreneur. Much of the complexity surrounding Indian food, for her, comes from the difference in language: different still from the Romance languages which many Westerners are at least familiar with, even if they cannot understand.

> Indian languages (usually Hindi, I assume) are utterly incomprehensible on a menu to me. When I finally make it to Saravana Bhavan, I recognize items like curry and chutney as they are assimilated into the Western lexicon, however kara dosa and bisibelabath are totally baffling. As kara dosa is in the earlier section of the menu, I assume it is an appetizer.

These blind guesses are made only on the basis that, as a restaurant operating in America, the proprietor would organize the menu according to local custom. Without knowing how meals are eaten in India, she defers to her own upbringing and orders *medhu vada* (lentil doughnuts) and some naan first, then a curry for the main course, and *gulab jamun* and *masala* tea for dessert.

For an insider that combination of *medhu vada* and the naan would be incompatible.

> Unfortunately I am completely lost on whether the chaat is a chunky dip, a side dish, supposed to be mixed into something else, or some other form of dish I don't know about. Food arrives and I reach for my fork but stop. Is the proper way to eat this with one's fingers? Do Indians eat with their fingers or is that a remnant image from British imperialism? Would I be foolish and insulting or respectful if I attempted it? How am I supposed to know how to eat this food?[8]

Laurie, another customer, speaking about the same restaurant, notes, "The Hotel Saravana Bhavan has a Taj Mahal-like feel with white textured walls and bright lights that seem to promote purity and simplicity," but without the blatant religious motifs that are so common in other Manhattan Indian restaurants she has visited. The restaurant's website gives virtual tours of different chains around the world, mostly in the United Arab Emirates and Malaysia. In each one, including the New York property, the servers wear white shirts, the atmosphere seems calm and refined, there are no women on staff, and there is a lot of stainless steel. Customers in the other branches of the chain are seated in large wooden chairs, with a warm pink and red color scheme surrounding them, and lots of upholstery. There is always a sweets counter, and pictures of dishes on the wall. None of these were present on the property at Twenty-sixth Street and Lexington in Manhattan. The Manhattan Saravana Bhavan appears to be attempting to distinguish itself from the dark, ornate, and upholstered "typical" Indian restaurants in the neighborhood, as it is also a little more expensive than the typical Indian restaurant. "I paid $20.00 for two cups of tea, a masala dosa, a side of rice, with a 20 percent tip."

Laurie, also commented on the available silverware and the ubiquity of stainless steel plates and glasses, but concluded that it was "a mix of sensitivity to local service, culture and taste which was nicely fused with the maintenance of tradition, whether that tradition stemmed from the ancient mass temple feedings of the southern Indian town of Udupi, or the more current mélange of European and Indian style dining."

Alisa, another respondent, changed the terms of the discussion. She began by drawing attention to the threads of mint that top an innocent-looking bowl of thin lentil soup:

> I scooped up one of the rectangular prisms of bone marrow. It wriggled and limped in my spoon. It tasted of pure fat. The headiness of the broth alone was delicious for a bite or two, but the overwhelming fattiness imparted by

> the marrow forced me to stop eating. "What is going on," I thought. "Why don't I like anything? This is Tabla. This is Floyd Cardoz. This is supposed to be the future of Indian cuisine. What is wrong with me!?"

Things improved with the lentil patties. She was excited to eat something vegetarian. She downed her first morsels without tasting the crunch of the cashew or appreciating the complexity of the yogurt sauce (spicy and tasting faintly of curry). Visually, it was the most stunning dish of the night—a shallow pond of yogurt sauce cradled four lentil mounds hidden under a mask of verdant mint chutney and burnt-sienna tamarind sauce.

The lentil patty finished entirely too soon; she eyed the platter of goat *tandoori* with suspicion. It looked tame enough, like thin slices of medium-rare filet mignon, splayed on a white plate with nothing but wedges of lime and few herbs as garnish. It did not look anything like the fiery red chicken *tandoori*, with its mass of onions and peppers, that she was used to at inexpensive Indian restaurants.

> Delicately spiced with ginger and garam masala, I speared piece after piece, eating with the voraciousness of beggars. I was so thrilled to be finally enjoying something. I had been feeling all-together too *memsahib*-ish thus far. Then again, perhaps the recognizable plainness of the goat tandoori had moved it out of the realm of the exotic and into the realm of the familiar not so different from the transformation of curry into a British dish in the 19th century.

Alexa, another commentator I interviewed, connected the discussion to a broader transformation in both demographics of cities and division of labor at home:

> As a child I saw the transformation of Iowa City, and my palate, from being comprised of uniquely American cuisine to a city rich with global tastes. First, it was Mexican cuisine—with migrant workers beginning to settle. Then, Asian, with the expansion of the University of Iowa Medical Hospital and the influx of Asian students and families. Most recently, Indian cuisine has come to dominate—every time I return home my mother takes me out for Indian. Hand-in-hand with this globalization was industrialization. Foreign ingredients were being shipped in—"fresh" in the "ethnic" aisle of our supermarket. As the taste for global cuisines increased, the frozen dinner aisle expanded too—boasting frozen enchiladas, dumplings, and curry . . . Ethnic restaurants were, in those days, cheaper and more accessible to my mother. Also, they validated going out—my mother could not make these dishes at home. So we had to go out to eat.

These reflections point to the fact that consumer-oriented studies have given too much power to the customer, critic, and foodie in the process of making meaning. In fact, ironically, consumer-oriented surveys rarely get close enough to the consumer's point of view and anxieties. Value production in the realm of ethnic food is not an Anglo monologue. It has never been so. It is even less so now, after the cultural democratization that gives all subaltern cultures (including those of the foreign-born) a robust sense of legitimacy and in fact even some slight disdain towards normative, mainstream culture. The foreign-born have always participated in the negotiations, not as equal partners, but as substantial ones.

Throughout these transactions there is a desperate search for authenticity by consumers. Authenticity is haptic, haunting, in a crowded and noisy marketplace. It is the craving for touch—its magic and its intimacy—in an increasingly distanced, ocular, and aural world. From art, through craft and designer goods, to commodified food, the quest is to be touched, in this case by an Indian, and in other cases by the artist or the designer via his signature or fingertip on a keyboard. Academics, working in high-cultural institutions, dismiss the uses of authenticity not only because of its potential for ahistoricism but also because of their disdain for touch over sight and sound. In the Western intellectual tradition, indifference towards touch is long and durable, traceable to Plato and Aristotle's agreement about its radical inferiority to sight and sound (Smith 2007: 93). An institution built on writing culture must discourage gesture, touch, and savor, perhaps even speech (Lowe 1982: 13). In contrast, everyday life is filled with touching gestures, such as a hug, a handshake, a kiss, an embrace, many of which can be turned erotic.

An erotics of authenticity is crucial to the ethnic quest. The ethnic, although subordinate, is blessed by touching authenticity, the putative Other of the late twentieth-century urban American modernity. The contemporary search for authenticity has strengthened ethnic hands further in the trial of strength based on their capacity to bring new allies into their effort to wrestle value out of the transaction in taste. Customers, even the most thoughtful ones, are ciphers in a circulation of ideas and judgments about foods that today routinely include not only ethnics but high-culture critics, which wasn't the case until about the 1980s in most American cities. That happened slowly and hesitatingly.

Critics constitute a cuisine

Until 1961, an authoritative native informant was always invoked in discussions of Indian food in *The New York Times*. On March 12, 1939, we see one of the earliest discussions of curry in the context of gastronomy in an article by Charlotte Hughes (1939). It goes into a long and sophisticated discussion of the thing. "Curry is a very ancient dish, antedating Hollandaise sauce and apple pie by centuries." It asserts that "Curry has come to be a lot more popular in New York in the last few years, with curry restaurants springing up here and there and with hotels putting curry dishes on their menus."[9] She goes on to elaborate that "Curry powder is a blend of fifteen or twenty spices" that needs proper blending, as explained by "Darmadasa, of the East India Curry Shop" (Hughes 1939). In 1946, Jane Nickerson, another *New York Times* reporter, depended on the proprietor of the same shop to explain curry, getting an answer colored by the typical exaggeration and bravado that a native informant displays towards what he construes to be a naïve American—"fifteen to twenty spices" (Nickerson 1946). In 1948, an anonymous American reporter depended on C. B. Deva, an "import–export trader," a transplanted native of Lahore, and the proprietor of India Prince, to unpack the mystery of curry (*New York Times* 1948). Later, in 1955, Nickerson found Dharamjit Singh, a "crimson-turbaned Sikh" (Nickerson 1955).

Craig Claiborne, often consecrated as the first American restaurant critic, depended initially on the exotic housewife as his tour guide. In his February 25, 1960 piece on Indian food, Claiborne relied on Manorama Phillips, a middling Indian bureaucrat at the United Nations. "Miss Phillips is a diminutive, dark-haired young woman with a mercurial smile who has lived in the United States for nearly four years," he describes. "When she arrived from India, the pangs of homesickness were severe and she literally dreamed of the dishes of her native land" (Claiborne 1960: 22). Professionally, Miss Phillips worked for the Government of India Trade Center and roomed with an American woman. Her three-room apartment was furnished with Indian accessories. When she entertained, which was frequently, it was either for tea, when she served a spiced tea punch, or for a curry dinner. "Her guests are seated on pillows covered with brilliant fabrics. In keeping with tradition, flatware is never used at the table" (Claiborne 1960: 22). The article is accompanied by a six-by-six-inch photograph of Miss Phillips in her apartment, clad in a sari, and framed by exquisite Indian handcrafted textiles. Here is the brown body as evidence of authenticity. Words needed the aid of pictures, and pictures the help of body, clothing, sari, artifact, to produce meaning. A very Heideggerian point, where life and the environment of things and other bodies are inseparable.

It points to the ratio of configuration between immigrant bodies, urban demand, and cosmopolitan gastronomic dialogue that goes into the construction of a "discourse," barely hammered into place by numerous performers with real and borrowed authority. The story of the curry, the *kachori*, and the *vindaloo* connects "discourse" to practice, and to the problem of transplanting durable dispositions. Yet, the immigrant dreams not only of a better analogue for the *kachori* and the curry; his fantasies are more substantial.

I: If you could change this place . . . to make it your dream place, what would you do?

Muhammad Rasool (MR): I will take this mirror out and put the picture there such as the scenery of Mohenjodaro. I will put a small stand there with three containers of soup. I will sell cheap soup, self-service soup, pita bread, and put a grill there [at the window to the sidewalk]: serve *shawarma*, chicken *shawarma*, lamb *shawarma*.

I will put the clay oven—the *tandoor*—there. I will get a young guy with a cap [toque] on his head. We will just have meats in the *tandoor* and salads. I will call it Pakistani Grill!

If I was permitted in Islam to sell liquor, maybe as an exception, I would open a big restaurant . . . still an Indian Pakistani place but beautiful like an American place.

Rasool would rebuild this corner of the city—pushing the glass-front out, putting the grill on the sidewalk, pursuing his customers with dreams of soup and *shawarma*. He could turn this into a Middle Eastern place, at some distance from South Asia, but successfully playing between the scope of his ecumenical Islamic imagination and the confused compass of his audience's geography.

Rasool arrived with the burden of feeding his body, and came to eventually use it to feed his customers and his household as well. He came with his morals, motivations, and aesthetic standards, all practically developed in his previous social context. He arrived with his tongue, taste, and hands tied to the Lahorian lower-middle-class milieu when he immigrated in 1988 at the age of thirty-seven. He learned to deploy his body, especially his hands and his tongue (both for talk and taste), in the midst of a dispositional crisis under the scrutiny of others. He brought memories of things he had eaten but never cooked, morals entwined with a division of labor at home and at work, and an insistent distinction between commerce and culture. He has crafted his place in this world that is not of his own making, and in the process has supplied what was demanded through his labors, turning his culture into commerce, which he resists and yet profits from. Rasool had to develop a sense of his new city, and yoke his senses to the making of a living in that city.

The ongoing sociological discussion—of taste, ethnic entrepreneurship, changing gastronomic categories, field theory, shared meaning in restaurant work, and professional identity—can only partially account for Rasool.[10] Not in the sense that no sociology can ever fully explain an individual and his trajectory, but in the sense that scholars have failed to look at his menu, ask for his recipes, or seek his judgment in explaining transformations of taste in the city.[11] Rasool and many like him have peopled American cities for centuries. They have cooked, developed recipes in an implicit dialogue between their bodies and their customers' conceptions, and crystallized that dialogue in thousands and thousands of menus (menus where migrants struggle to name, standardize, and translate their dishes). Many more have been erased without a trace and, with a few exceptions, scholars have rarely taken this practical knowledge as a point of departure for an analysis of the world of taste.

When Rasool was asked, "Do you look at online reviews of your restaurant?" he provided a desultory response. It was clear that he was unable or unwilling to play in the gastronomic world of Manhattan, which is very different from the position of another entrepreneur I now want to bring into the picture. She also brings a very different approach to the embodied materiality of cooking and entrepreneurship. She still carries much of the palatal sense of her pre-immigration being and is adept at translating her practices to perform in the gastronomic field of Manhattan. And she seemingly has the dual advantages of more money than Rasool and a lot more cultural capital.

Vada Pao: Mumbai street food in New York City

Vada Pao is indistinguishable from any small West Village eatery. It sits tightly between two other restaurants. The sidewalk is narrow too, but less crowded, with hardly a delinquent in sight. The foot traffic is younger, calmer, whiter, and characterized by touristy wanderings, rather than the grim purpose and raw ambition of immigrants on the move. When we entered Vada Pao in the early afternoon, the sidewalk was devoid of traffic and the place appeared to be slowly stirring from a tropical siesta. The only thing missing was a slowly whirring ceiling fan muddling the heat amidst the creeping bougainvillea.

Chitrita Mukherjee is the entrepreneur behind Vada Pao.[12] She is thirty-four years old, a comfortably Anglophone Indian immigrant, born in Kolkata, but dreaming up a place like Mumbai (Bombay) in New York City. When we asked her, "What would be your ethnic self-identification?" she seamlessly suggested the cosmopolitan phrase "South Asian," rather than the narrower "Indian." In contrast, Rasool's imagination was tied to the nation and the taxi driver's occupation in the big city. Mukherjee's connection was to the world, the region in it, and her professional training as a designer. Her handiwork has garnered substantial critical attention in the world of gastronomic "discourse" as "a sleek sandwich shop that specializes in upmarket spins on Bombay-style street food, with a focus on *pao*—meat and vegetable sammies served like sliders on *ghee*-griddled buns."[13]

Pao Sliders or Kathi Roll:
Choose any filling below:

- **Pao $3** **Kathi Roll $5** **{Add Egg $1}**
  - **Vada**
    Potato, chickpea flour, coconut garlic chutney
  - **Bhaji**
    Mix vegetables, kutchumber salad, lemon juice
  - **Spinach Lentil Tikki**
    Tomato mustard chutney, chickpeas, chilli mayonnaise
  - **Tandoori Achari Paneer**
    Pickle marinade, mint yogurt, roasted peppers, mango chutney
  - **Unda Omlette**
    Eggs, onion, green chillies, chilli garlic ketchup
    - **Chappli Kebab**
      Ginger, chilli garlic ketchup, tomatoes, lettuce
    - **Chicken Tikka**
      Tandoori chicken, mint chutney, roasted onions
    - **Shami Kebab**
      Minced lamb, lentil, kutchumber salad, mint yogurt
    - **Tandoori Pulled Goat Leg**
      Kutchumber salad, cilantro, lemon juice, Mexican sour cream
    - **Parsi Beef Keema**
      Mince beef, coriander cumin masala, tomato

FIGURE 2.2 *A portion of Vada Pao's menu.*

I: What is the concept here?

Chitrita Mukherjee (CM): *Vada pao* has a very strong, authentic, regional identity as Mumbai street food. Plus we wanted to streamline our operations. We went with our interpretation of the *pao* as a slider.

I: What brought you to this enterprise?

CM: I came to the US to do my Master's in architecture and urban design at Columbia University. I was attracted by the Parson School's program in lighting. I got my Master's in Lighting Design.

I: How did you get to food?

CM: I was fascinated by the food scene here [in the US]. We loved all the choices available to us. We thought Indian food had this market gap where you could find very expensive, good Indian food, or two-day old curries. We wanted fresh Indian food, which would be portable, sold at a value, to students and young professionals. To people like us.

I: Let us talk a little more about the concept of Vada Pao. How did you get to this version?

CM: I had my baby shower at my friend's restaurant and I was talking to her that I needed a change. She said she wanted to do something outside of her current venture. We started discussing concepts and hoped to learn from our mistakes and missteps.

I: You are Bengali, why not a Kolkata concept?

CM: I don't think the repertoire of Kolkata street food is large enough to provide us with a range. You have *kathi* roll (which we have), *jhaal muri, puchka.* The Bombay repertoire both works better and is underserved. For instance a Delhi concept would also work with *parathas* and kebabs. But no one does *vada pao*—only two or three places do it in Queens but they don't do it right. Plus a slider works as a good translation of *pao.*

I: Is the Delhi concept crowded?

CM: Yes . . . in a sense that is generic Indian restaurant food now.

I: I was surprised by the name Vada Pao, because it is so local and specific. Weren't you afraid that it might not make any sense to your American audience?

CM: Yes, I worry about it. My fallback position [laughs] is that I can always go back to lighting design if the concept fails.

I: How many customers do you have in a typical weekday and on the weekend? If you were to guess their demographics what would it be?

CM: We have about 100 customers on a typical weekday. And about 150 customers on an average weekend day. My weekday and late-night customers are about 30 percent visibly Indian and 70 percent non-Indian, probably young professionals and students. On weekends I have more Indian families coming from New Jersey and Philadelphia for the stuffed *parathas* and now *vada pao.* My check average is between $8 and $9.

I: What were your thoughts in designing this place?

CM: Lower-end version of high-end cuisine. A lot of our design was influenced by trying to do it in the cheap and yet make a statement. Since the concept is Mumbai street food we wanted to put up a large image of the VT train station [in Mumbai]. Earlier, this wall had a plain finish, now it is a textured finish, a slightly unfinished look, a little like a *dhaba.* For the tables I wanted to get a distressed look as in a *dhaba*—Indian street food eatery—where tables have a lot of graffiti. But instead of graffiti we wanted iconic Mumbaiker images such as of the cricketer Sachin Tendulkar.

I: Are the cooks Indian?

CM: I have two Indians (one Gujarati, one Mumbaiker), one Mexican, and one Nepali in the kitchen. The cook is Indian, Goanese, who has cooked at The Taj in Bombay, then he worked on a ship (that is how he came here), and he has worked in a couple of restaurants here in the US.

I: Did the cook bring his recipes or did you teach him the recipes?

CM: Well, a little of both. He knew how to make chicken *tikka*, *achari* chicken, and *bhaji*. We asked him to follow our recipes, and the spice mix is our own.

I: Did you consider hiring a chef who did not have an Indian background?

CM: We didn't know where to source the chef from. We were asking our friends in the Indian restaurant business and putting ads in Indian newspapers. That is where we were getting our chefs. That is how we got Mohan.

I: You said you cook at home. How did you learn to cook?

CM: I come from a joint family with thirteen to fourteen people. Sunday would be a day when everyone cooked something. It was very competitive. I had an uncle who had studied for a hotel management degree but did not pursue a career in it. Yet, every time we would make a dish he would ask us to break it down, analyze it. That is something I took for granted. I thought if this is going to be my vision then I should put together the menu and the recipes.

I: How would you characterize your relationship to the media?

CM: For the first time we have a PR rep. We were covered very early on by *New York* Magazine. It seems Florence Fabricant came and ate here and wrote about us. I did not even know that she had eaten here until I saw the write-up.

I: Do you read online reviews?

CM: Yes, all the time. We have a Google alert every time someone posts something on Yelp or MenuPages; we get a notification. I read it.

I: Has customer feedback influenced your concept?

CM: No, I wouldn't say that it has. But it has influenced our service. Most of the feedback is that the food is good but the wait is too long or the service is bad. I make use of customer feedback to inform the cooks and servers.

Transactions in taste

Rasool and Mukherjee have designed their restaurants in Manhattan within the constraints of their material, symbolic, and bodily resources (of skill and imagination). One started with a $35,000 investment, a Bachelor's degree (from Pakistan), and the limits of his Punjabi-Pakistani masculine habitus. He didn't know how to cook. Now he doesn't want to cook. That is women's work, servants' labor. His food, his location in the city, his labor force, the limits of his skills and imagination, have set his restaurant adrift from even any generic notion of Indian food. On the other hand, he is more flexible, less invested culturally in his construction of the place, and thus willing to play to the audience that he gets, almost all of which is local foot traffic. Rasool characterizes his customer base as "5 percent Indian and 95 percent local." What he is selling more than anything else are gyros, french fries, chicken curry and rice for lunch and dinner; eggs, toast, and coffee for breakfast. Less than six months after our interview the Urdu sign is gone, replaced by two large announcements for "$5.00 lunch or dinner." Since he does not cook, his menu and recipes are drifting more and more towards the habitus of his "Mexican" cook and their joint understanding of American tastes, specified by his audience of sidewalk vendors and commuters. With less capital and less embodied skill, Rasool's transactions with his customers have to concede a lot more ground than Mukherjee's, but he can fulfill their need for nourishment. She, on the other hand, responds to her customers' demands for better service but not for different food, which she treats as a cultural artefact. She is more successful at translating the *pao* as a slider, which is a product of her greater familiarity with Anglophone-American popular culture.

Rasool does not want his three grown children or his wife to work in his restaurants. He has enough resources to be able to keep them away, unlike, for instance, the Latino vendors of tacos, tamales, and *pupusas* in Red Hook, Brooklyn, studied by Zukin (2010).[14] Additionally, Rasool has the ability to pay $8,000 per month as rent, and his legal status, as well as his Bachelor's degree, which is productive of his competency in spoken English, did make some difference during the process of applying for various permits and paperwork. However, Zukin (2010) shows that despite the absence of these advantages, the more materially impoverished Red Hook vendors have been quite successful in latching onto the gastronomic "discourse" of the city. The Red Hook vendors also don't seem to create a dichotomy between culture and commerce, and in fact frame their commercial venture as a cultural one, and I think that is one of the reasons they are more successful in playing to the gastronomic audience.

The Red Hook vendors have effectively used numerous intermediaries, such as immigrant advocates and foodie bloggers, to successfully legitimize their vending and accumulate substantial cultural capital as an authentic urban space. In contrast, Rasool fails to draw himself into that "discourse." As Stacie Orell, a student of mine, pointed out, part of their success may be attributed to the recent perception of Red Hook as being an up-and-coming trendy neighborhood, whereas Rasool is in a neighborhood that doesn't have that sort of cultural cachet. Maybe the vendors chose their location wisely, but then again, vendors are by definition mobile, whereas a storefront is not. Did the vendors really draw themselves into the "discourse," or did the "discourse" find them by virtue of their locale? I think it is probably a little of both.

Rasool does have some degree of cultural capital, some of it embodied in his tongue as language, and as taste, which he can remember. Furthermore, he is forced to fit his somatic experience of Pakistani food into the category of Indian food, which for reasons either of translation or global hierarchical valuation appears to work better in Manhattan. For instance, as a category in Restaurant Guides published within the telephone directories of the last five decades, "Pakistani" fails to take hold. A high of six Pakistani restaurants in 1969 falls to three the next decade, then two, one, and finally none at all in 2010 (although in reality they proliferate in Jackson Heights, Queens, and Coney Island Avenue, Brooklyn). The relative paucity of national cultural capital available to a Pakistani practically dictates that Rasool has to concede to the demands of his audience. Yet, he resents being lumped within the category of "Indian," given the work of imagining contested national communities in South Asia.

Rasool's cultural advantages are less than those of Mukherjee, who started with almost $100,000, a Master's degree from a premier American university, and the vocabulary of design that allowed her to connect the rough newness of the vernacular to the smooth texture of the cosmopolitan omnivore. Hence, only she can imagine the common street foods of India as containers of capital. Approaching them through a designer's eyes, Mukherjee grasps their pop-cosmopolitan possibilities. But those are not her only advantages. She can cook, partly because, as a South Asian woman of a particular cohort, she must. She could explain to us the art of making good stuffed *parathas* and the analogic taste of a *kathi* roll. Yet she also claims more than she can legitimately command when she minimizes her cook's somatic memory of making chicken *tikka*, *achari* chicken, and *bhaji*.

That is not the whole story either—of gender, generation, and class. In Mukherjee's words, her "hotel management uncle" delivered an unusual familiarity with cooking, which is an extraordinary accomplishment against the Bengali grain of *bhadrolok* (proper, middle-class) masculinity (see Janeja 2010). This is partly where biography exceeds sociology. Cooking skills and the ability to access what she calls a "global Indian" imagination, accentuated by an accidental catering gig for the New York premier of *Slumdog Millionaire* (after which the call of the *vada pao* was more insistent), connects her to networks that are crucial to her self-conception as a successful entrepreneur. As a designer, she coped very well with fitting her bodily habits into a new, albeit tight, space in this large city, hinging her economics to aesthetics, habits to consciousness, and inhabitation in a locale to global gastronomic "discourse."

By *design* I mean not only the physical infrastructure of the restaurant, but also the concept, the name, and the menu, and the ways of reproducing it through investment, recruitment of labor, recipes, and cooking. I use the word *design* because: (1) of its ability to convey an attempt to re-make the world within material and conceptual constraints; (2) of its functionality—you have to deliver a certain kind of food, repeatedly, at a price, at a place; and (3) it relates the body to space, economics to aesthetics, habits to consciousness, and inhabitance in a locale to global gastronomic discourse. The entrepreneur is the bridge here between capital and culture, and I have interrogated that intersection between the aesthetic and the economic, taste and toil, and how the practiced body holds the two together despite the academic separation of such concerns in far-flung disciplines of economics, sociology, cultural studies, philosophy, marketing, and design.

Yet, as a particular economic enterprise, Vada Pao failed to meet Mukherjee's income expectations and she had to close down her business. Rasool's restaurant survives today, years after our interview, while Vada Pao was sold, replaced by another Bollywood concept. Rasool is more successful in re-localizing his practice precisely to that street corner between Papaya Dog and CVS, perhaps because he was never attuned to the global gastronomic "discourse" on Indian food. What I initially presumed to be Mukherjee's advantage—attention to the global hierarchy of taste—may be her precise disadvantage, making her unfit to occupy the street corner she had landed on. Her customers may not have cared for designer Indian food, and the price they were willing to pay for it was much lower than for French or Italian or Japanese cuisine. That needs a broader and a longer historical frame to be explained. At the level of specificity of the individual we do get agency in this chapter but many of the structural features are hidden from view, for which we have to step out of the particular restaurant and the perspective of the restaurateur, and that takes us into the next chapter.

Notes

1 Where I have taken material only from the public domain—such as Baluchi's menus—identifiers have not been eliminated. Where my material is based exclusively on interviews, names and identities have been changed.

2 All the interviews were conducted by Jackie Rohel, Sierra Burnett Clark, or me, sometimes in combination, sometimes individually.

3 This is almost *verbatim* the same conversation that one of my doctoral students, Grace Choi, had with a Bangladeshi restaurant owner in London.

4 Both this source and *Mary Waldo's Restaurant Guide*, discussed below, were accessed during archival research done by a student at the Museum of the City of New York.

5 The names of the restaurant and the restaurateurs have been changed.

6 In my judgment, *MenuPages* provides a more comprehensive listing than *Zagat*, the *Yellow Pages*, or *Yelp*. On 29 November, 2009 there were 202 self-identified Indian restaurants in Manhattan and Brooklyn, 85 in Queens, and a handful in the Bronx and Staten Island, bringing the total to about 300 in NYC. On June 10, 2015 Menu Pages was listing 408 Indian restaurants in New York City, with Manhattan 205, Brooklyn 76, Queens 127 and none in Bronx (Menupages.com 2015).

7 The subtle linguistic displacements here would be unavailable to a body unfamiliar with the ring of an East Bengali accent in West Bengali ears. The researcher's body embedded in details of tacit social practice is a useful tool of inquiry unaccounted for in the typically single-minded pursuit of visuality.

8 All quotations from field notes.

9 Yet, neither "Hindoo" nor "Indian" restaurants are listed in any of the following guidebooks: Appleton (1900); Rand, McNally & Co. (1901); Lewis, Scribner & Co. (1903); Moreno (1903); Merchants' Association of New York (1906); Rand, McNally & Co. (1909); R. L. Polk & Co. (1920–21); Chappell (1925). The supposed ubiquity of Indian restaurants and curry is probably a late–1920s and 1930s phenomenon.

10 Johnston and Baumann 2007; Rao *et al.* 2003, 2005; Warde and Martens 2000; Warde, Martens, and Olsen 1999; Warde 1997, 2009; Ferguson 1998, 2004; Ferguson and Zukin 1995; Fine 1996; Waldinger 1986, 2001; Aldrich and Waldinger 1990; Bailey 1987; Berger and Piore 1980.

11 Fine (1995, 1996), Ferguson (2004) and Rao *et al.* (2005) do pay attention to the details of menus, media, and recipes. But their concerns do not include immigrants and the processes of transplanting bodies. Sharon Zukin (2010), on the other hand, does consider immigrants, but not the processes of cooking, skill, and embodiment.

12 Once again, names have been changed, but matched to ethnicity.

13 Citation suppressed to protect identity.

14 What the vendors paid to regularize their carts wasn't that different from Muhammad Rasool's upfront costs (about $35,000).

3

Hierarchy of Taste and Ethnic Difference:

American Gustatory Imagination in a Globalizing World

American taste-makers—that is, journalists, restaurant critics, and professional chefs—have framed their appropriation of twentieth-century culinary cultures in two divergent ways: first, as high-status foreign foods, initially limited to Continental and French cuisines, eventually consecrating Italian and Japanese cookery at the end of the century. Second, as the low-status product of the labor and implicit knowledge of the immigrant poor classified as ethnic fare. The appropriation of the first sort is understood primarily in aesthetic terms of taste and notions of skill, while the latter is understood as a matter of necessity, primarily in terms of undifferentiated toil.

As we have seen in Chapter 1, there is a long-term pattern of ethnic succession. Food-work done by German and Irish immigrants in the mid-nineteenth century was carried out by Italians and eastern Europeans at the end of the nineteenth century, who in turn were replaced by Latinos and Asians at the end of the twentieth century. Tastes have changed too. French cuisine gave way to New American, Japanese, and Italian cuisine in America's most expensive restaurants, which were accented by Asian and Latin American ingredients at the end of the last century. There is a two-fold ethnic succession here: one in the ethnicity of the labor force; the other in the sphere of food served. The two are shaped by each other in counterintuitive ways. In this chapter I read the long-term work of historians closely and interrogate large sets of data produced by newspapers with durable print-runs, and restaurant guides and surveys in the short run, to outline an argument about hierarchies of taste based on race and ethnicity.[1]

Public edibility

According to Rebecca Spang and Jennifer Davis, restaurants first appeared in Paris in the 1760s as restorative places, and it was only by the late 1790s that the word was "set loose from its moorings in the culture of medicalized sensibility, and 'restaurant' became the fashionable word used for any Paris eatery" (Spang 2000: 173; Davis 2013: 5). For a while the terminology remained fluid between restaurants, inns with tables d'hôte, and cookshops, only to settle again by the nineteenth century on what we would today recognize as a restaurant—a sort of public parlor, with separate tables, individualized table settings, printed and elaborate menus offering a wide range of dishes, silverware, attentive service, music and lighting, lavish furnishings, and opulent interiors, to create a private space of romance in public. "For decades into the nineteenth century, Anglophone authors and publishers continued to italicize the word restaurant and restaurateur, marking them and their referents not only as foreign, but as untranslatably so, evidence that something had happened in France that had occurred nowhere else on the planet" (Spang 2000: 175). People have eaten out in cities for a long time and they continue to do so in innumerable ways, but they have eaten in restaurants only since the French Revolution, and French restaurants have provided the template for commercial fine-dining in the West.

Restaurants emerged slowly in the USA, and only in the first decade of the twentieth century did they outshine saloons in public discussions in American newspapers. Figures 3.1–3.4 show the rise of the restaurant and the congruent decline of the saloon, signaling a shift from a public culture bifurcated between

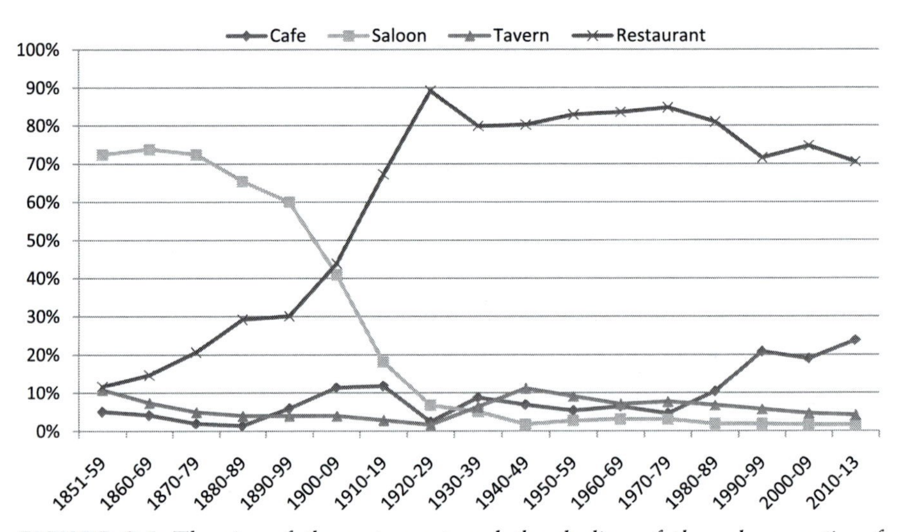

FIGURE 3.1 *The rise of the restaurant and the decline of the saloon: ratio of coverage in* The New York Times *(NYT) (1851–2013).*

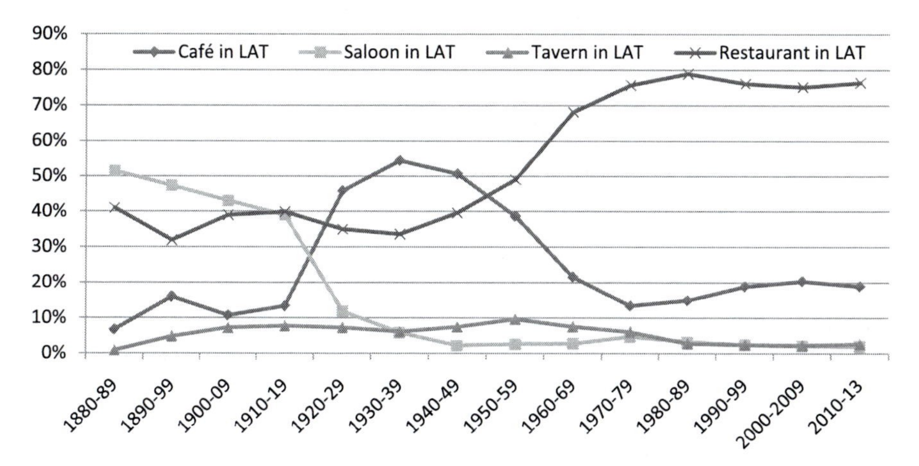

FIGURE 3.2 *The rise of the restaurant and the decline of the saloon: ratio of coverage in the* Los Angeles Times *(LAT) (1880–2013).*

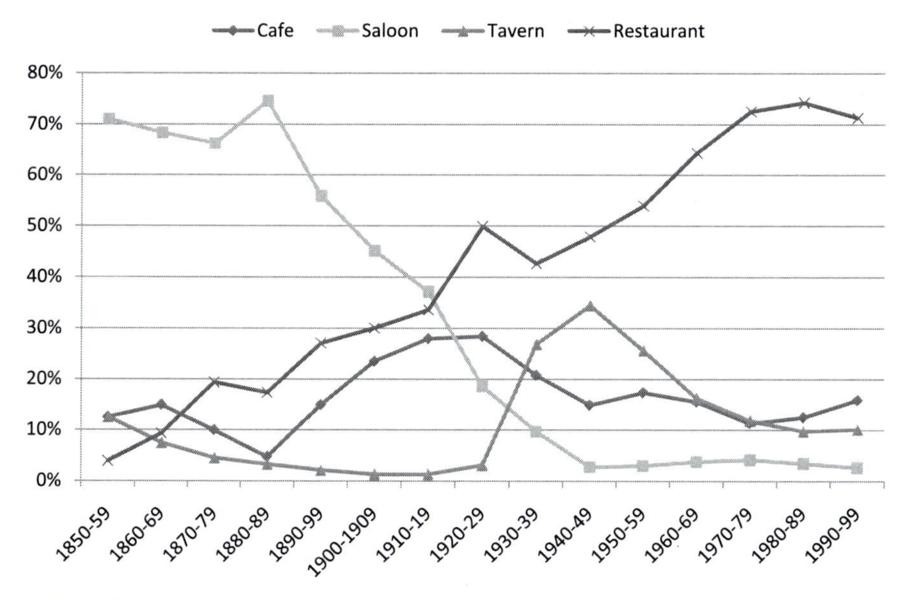

FIGURE 3.3 *The rise of the restaurant and the decline of the saloon: ratio of coverage in the* Chicago Tribune *(1850–1999).*

the patrician and the working classes in the nineteenth century, marked by the saloon and the tavern, to middle-class hegemony in the twentieth century, shaped by the increasing number of restaurants. The American restaurant would become a hegemonic space by way of middle-class disparagement of the tavern, the saloon, and the aristocratic parlor, the very institutions that restaurants were historically derived from.

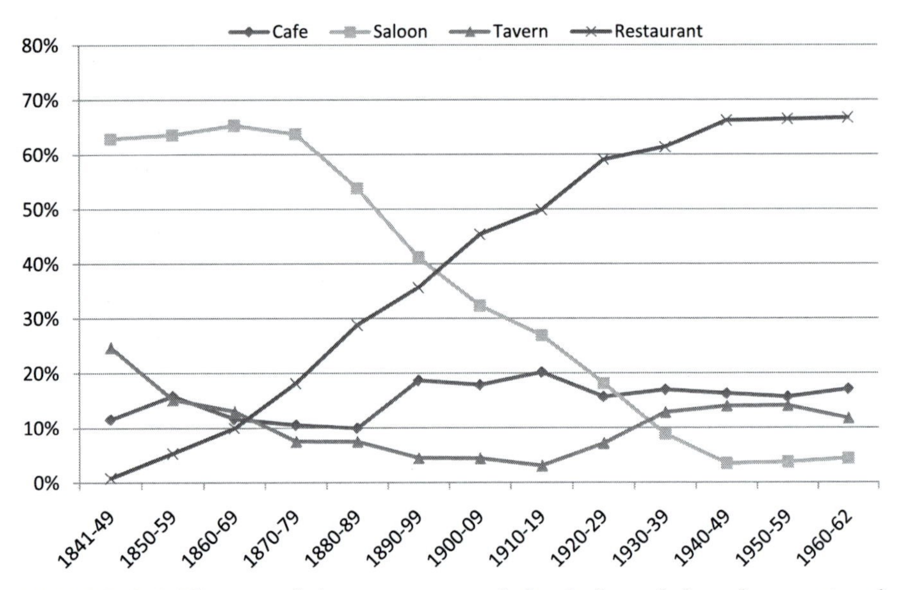

FIGURE 3.4 *The rise of the restaurant and the decline of the saloon: ratio of coverage in the* New York Tribune/Herald *(1841–1962).*

According to Sharon Salinger (2002), there were a range of class-segregated taverns in the eighteenth century, especially between the middling sort and the poorer ones, when these establishments were legally bound to provide food and shelter for man and horse. Laws in most settlements in the eighteenth century restricted tavern access to slaves, servants, sailors contracted to ships, and women. And taverns were often distinguished by class according to the licenses they acquired, for wine and brandy (upper class) or beer and cider (working class), and by their location at the waterfront (laboring class) or at city centers (gentlemen). At the cusp of the American Revolution, cities such as Philadelphia, Boston, New York, and Charleston had one tavern per 55 to 133 residents. Per capita concentration was the highest in New York, at one tavern per 55 people.

When in 1773 New York City had 396 licensed taverns, they were the most important public places, as evidenced by their use as the setting for meetings and public demonstrations around the new Sugar Act of 1764 (Smith 2014: 15). Taverns were robust sites of public discussion among free white men, and the owners often became some of the best informed on local and national events by aggregating talk among their various customers. Taverns were also where militias converged and newspapers were available. The importance of taverns declined after the Civil War, slowly rising again for a few decades, then declining consistently in public visibility through the second half of the twentieth century, and almost vanishing by the twenty-first century along with the saloon.

Along with taverns, as in Europe, coffee houses were central to doing business in the early colonial period, and sites such as the King's Arms (probably the first, and for a while only, coffee house in New York City), Exchange Coffee House, the Merchant's Coffee House on Wall Street, and the Tontine Coffee House at the corner of Wall and Water Streets played an important role in questions of governance and public disputation among free and established white men. Coffee houses became less important as the patrician class withdrew from public engagement with deepening franchise, and saloons became more visible. Coffee houses both became more ubiquitous and were transformed into leisurely cafés. Rather than a place of deal making, they became less political and more consumption oriented. Cafés themselves declined in importance from the pre-Civil War era, to hit a low in the 1880s, rising temporarily in public discussions in the 1890s and 1900s, declining slowly after the Second World War, to rise again in importance from the 1980s onwards and hit a high in the 2010s, signaling the rebirth of café society, leisure, and informalization.

The saloon was the dominant working class public space through the nineteenth century, into the first decade of the twentieth century, when restaurants replaced it consistently across the major urban print-media markets. The saloon and the restaurant so dominate the nineteenth and the twentieth centuries respectively that they hide the more subtle movements of taverns and coffee houses.

Restaurants became visible in the first half of the nineteenth century (in 1830) and became a durable semi-public institution by the middle of that century. Delmonico's, the most durable of the lot, began in 1827 as a modest confectionary run by two eponymous Swiss brothers. They expanded their operation to a restaurant in the Parisian model by 1830 and hired a French chef. By the 1840s, Delmonico's had become a destination for downtown elites, with a printed menu in French and English, pages of entrées and wines, and lavish appointments. Grand hotels' dining rooms such as Astor House began to play in the same domain of haute cuisine by the mid-century. In the 1850s, dinner at Delmonico's would set the customer back by at least two dollars, which was two days of a manual laborer's wages (Lobel 2014: 121). That was in contrast to the sixpenny working-class eatery and the twelve-cent chop house for the commuting middle classes. At the bottom of the pile of eateries was probably the oyster cellar, which provided some rare opportunity for African-American entrepreneurs such as Thomas Downing, who ran arguably the most famous such establishment from 1825 to the 1860s and died a rich man, reportedly with a fortune of over $100,000. This was the time when ice-cream parlors also began to expand to attract ladies excluded from many eateries. One of them, Taylor's Epicurean Palace, set the mid-nineteenth century standard for a sumptuous feminine parlor, with a darkened and subdued atmosphere, built at a cost of a million dollars with daily receipts of $900 (Lobel 2014: 129).

For the 160-odd years (1851–2014) for which we have the print-run of major American newspapers such as *The New York Times* and the *Los Angeles Times* (Figure 3.5), we can see a persistent mention of public eating and drinking places such as cafés, saloons, taverns, and restaurants in 3–8 percent of documents (articles, advertisements, reviews). There is a slow upward trend over the whole print-run that spikes up to 6 percent in the 1920s, and then again since the 1980s into the 2010s, marking the two heights of American discussions of eateries. Once restaurants become dominant sites of public discussion in the Anglophone print media in the United States, we also see the increasing discursive valence of articles and reviews (about food

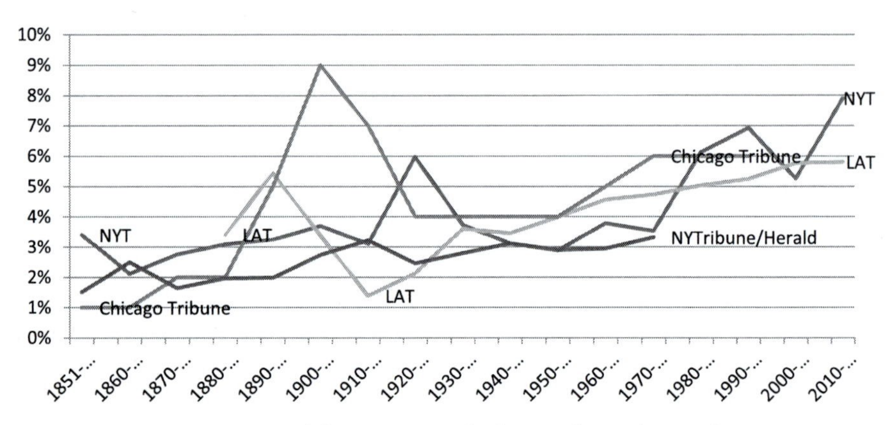

FIGURE 3.5 *Percentage of documents with the words "café", "saloon", "tavern", and "restaurant" combined in the* New York Tribune/Herald, NYT, Chicago Tribune, *and* LAT *(ca. 1851–2013).*

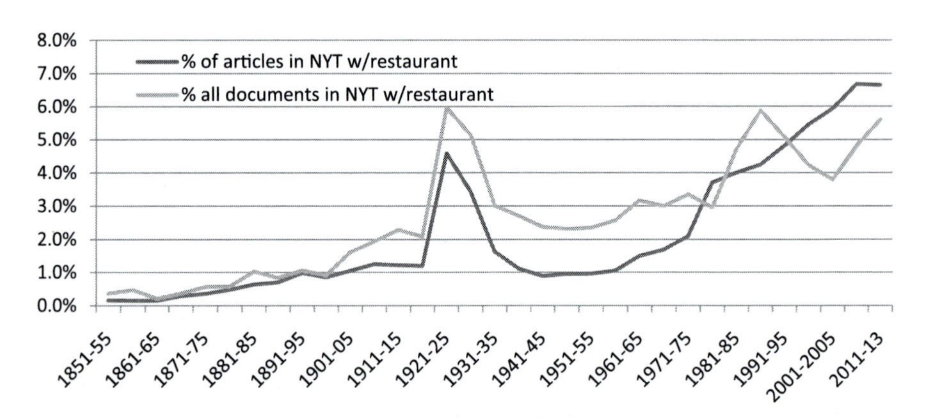

FIGURE 3.6 *Twin peaks of public discussion of restaurants in the US.*

and drinks), especially since the mid-1990s, when they outstrip classifieds. In the first decades of the twenty-first century the cultural and critical discussion begins to outweigh the commercial media.

Retrospective ethnics

In his path-breaking book *Revolution at the Table*, labor historian turned food scholar Harvey Levenstein reaches the conclusion that early Americans never liberated themselves from the British culinary heritage, though they tended to eat more corn, pork, and molasses, imbibe more whiskey and cider, and drink less tea and ale (Levenstein 2003). This pattern of culinary Anglo-conservatism "continued to be the case after 1783, even though the proportion of immigrants of non-British origin rose" (Levenstein 2003: 4). It was the Germans who most strongly influenced American cooking by the mid-nineteenth century.

Many of the immigrant families, visible in the earliest US Census records, with their daily imperative of working, shopping, cleaning, and cooking, figure prominently in Jane Ziegelman's popular book *97 Orchard. An Edible History of Five Immigrant Families in One New York Tenement* (2010).[2] Structured as vignettes of succeeding families at one address (97 Orchard Street in New York City), Ziegelman tells the compelling stories of the German Glockners and Irish Moores of the 1860s, eastern European Jewish Gumpertzs a few decades later, and the Rogarshevskys and the Baldizzis of the early twentieth century. This is a story about how immigrants have transformed American palates and food businesses.

Food is at the center of her analysis, but so is labor: how tenement housewives were like "freight elevators, hauling groceries, coal, firewood, and children up and down endless flights of stairs" (Ziegelman 2010: 7). Her stories maintain a crucial balance between taste and toil (without which discernment merely measures the consumption of other people's hard work). The story of food, cooking, and housework is interwoven with a history of gendered shopping in public markets such as the Essex Street Market and the Fulton Market.

Butcher-turned-historian Thomas De Voe's extensive work on the city's already declining public markets (Browne 1869; De Voe 1862) registered a two-fold shift by the mid-nineteenth century. In 1843, the Common Council of the City of New York had repealed the law that required meats to be sold only in public markets by licensed butchers. De Voe came from a long line of native butchers who made a comfortable living because of the higher entry costs into the trade due to the licensing and access to established social networks necessary to gain admittance to a market stall. Deregulation destroyed that protection and immigrant butchers—Irish and German—poured in, which became a necessity as the city spread from its northern limits on Chamber Street (in 1790) to Fifty-fifth Street on the eve of the Civil War, leaving behind the dozen markets clustered on the edges of Lower Manhattan. The shift was from city-supported, public market monopolies, to a more laissez-faire system of private shops (a Census counted over 2,200 by the 1850s) that could keep up with the spreading and class-segregating population by neighborhoods (Lobel 2014; Horowitz 2005, 2008; De Voe 1862).

The population had doubled every decade in the first half of the nineteenth century—due to Irish and German immigration—and the spaces of a walking city of commerce and residence gave way to functional and class stratification. Native-born Protestant butchers reacted by aligning with similarly threatened shoemakers, tailors, and printers in forming the American Republican Party, which won 23 percent of the vote in 1842 but failed to reverse the tide of a shifting immigrant-based small-entrepreneurial market in the feeding, clothing, and shoe-making trades (Lobel 2014: 58). By 1834, German immigrants had already opened the first brewery. In particular, Bavarian brewers such as George Gillig, Joseph Doegler, Frederick and Maximilian Schaefer, and Franz Ruppert would become crucial in the shift in the taste of American beer, and by 1872 there were seventy lager breweries in New York (Smith 2014: 107).

Levenstein finds evidence, by the 1880s, of a bifurcated working class. The well-off skilled and semi-skilled comprised one side, consisting mainly of white native-born Americans and immigrants of Anglo-Saxon, Celtic, and northern European ancestry who ate more meat, eggs, potatoes, and more fruits and vegetables, much of it canned, than their United Kingdom counterparts (2003: 100–1). On the other hand, there were "new immigrants," mostly of central, eastern, and southern European ancestry, all with lower skills in the labor market, which were reinforced by ethnic disdain.

The latter were the target of new professionals—settlement house workers, home economists, nutritionists, and public health advocates—each seeking "to teach the immigrants how to Americanize their diets in an economical fashion" (Levenstein 2003: 103). Levenstein notes that this evangelical enthusiasm did *not* derive from smug self-satisfaction about their own food culture but from their scientific expertise. "Nutritional science reinforced what their palates and stomachs already told them: that any cuisine as coarse, overspiced, 'garlicky,' and indelicate-looking as the food of central, eastern, and southern Europe must be unhealthy as well" (Levenstein 2003: 103–4).

Ziegelman records the conflicts and confluence of the taste of reformers and immigrants as inscribed on the Bill of Fare for the Immigrant Dining Room at Ellis Island. She also notes how in the mid-nineteenth century, "the Irish were big in the fish and oyster business, Germans worked as dairymen, grocers, and butchers," and how immigrant food purveyors fed their own communities and the rest of the city (Ziegelman 2010: 27). From the first decades of the nineteenth century, immigrants were peddlers of fruits, vegetables, and fish, bakers of bread, slaughterers of livestock, waiters, cooks, and brewers of beer—shifting with the shifting populace from high alcohol English ales, to the crisp, bottom-brewed, refreshing German lagers that would come to characterize American brews. German immigrants established groceries, delicatessens, beer halls, bakeries, and butcher shops, which served as both community spaces and sites of transmission of the taste for comestibles among outsider cohorts, "where the native-born could sample their first bratwurst, or pretzel or glass of lager" (Ziegelman 2010: 55).

American scholarship on food has paid the most attention to the 20 million or so "new immigrants" between 1880 and 1924. That is partly driven by the density of documentary collections powered by Progressive Era enthusiasm to reform the food habits of immigrants. In *We Are What We Eat*, Donna Gabaccia develops the argument that Americans have always been creoles with hybrid tastes. By the end of the colonial era, "region more than ethnicity defined American identities" (Gabaccia 1998: 35).

The gradual formation of the national food market, along with railroads and roadways, and the mass media revolution (print, radio, and TV), in alliance with new refrigeration technologies, produced a national diet. But the immigrant labor that made the national market possible at the end of the nineteenth and in the early twentieth centuries also produced enclave eating, as racism, xenophobia, and cheap housing contained new immigrants in demarcated urban neighborhoods. That is also where the ethnic entrepreneur operated, supplying the produce of the old land which was often new to the rest of Americans, such as Napa cabbage and radishes introduced by Japanese farmers in California, and broccoli, wine grapes, figs, and olive oil by Italians. Sometimes, small eateries and restaurants evolved from grocery stores, a delicatessen, or a family boarding house (Gabaccia 1998: 81). Andrew Smith, the prolific historian of New York City food, shows how a number of immigrants—such as the German-born sugar refiner William Havemeyer, the Austrian-born candy maker Leo Hirschfield, Carl and Peter Luger of steakhouse fame, and Richard Hellman, the mayonnaise baron—entered and dominated the earliest food businesses in baking, butchering, sugar refining, candy making, groceries, canning, and pickling (Smith 2014: 17–69).

Corporate nationalization on one hand, and ghettoization of the poor urban immigrant population on the other, produced two scripts on American cuisine. One eroded ethnic and regional accents to claim mass-produced foods as national icons where hot dogs, Cracker Jacks, fried chicken, and Fritos lost their ethnic signifiers. Then there were ethnic enclaves such as Chinatown and Little Italy catering to insiders.

Hasia R. Diner's comparative work on immigrant cuisines, *Hungering for America*, asks: how did America transform the taste of immigrants? She crafts her project around two subsidiary queries: what is the fundamental difference between pre-immigration and post-immigration foodways of the Italians, the Irish, and eastern European Jews in the United States; and why did the Italians and eastern European Jews develop an American identity around the specificity of their foods while the Irish did not? (Diner 2001).

The most important difference between pre- and post-immigration foodways, she notes, is abundance. Rosolino Mormino, a resident of Napoleonville, Louisiana, wrote his brother in Italy with telling eloquence: "In America bread is soft, but life is hard" (Diner 2001: 48). A dietary study of Italians, done by the US Department of Agriculture and Hull House in the 1890s around Chicago, reported that olive oil become essential to Italian identity, as did meat. "In Italy few from the lower classes ate [meat] more often than three times a year. In America meat appeared regularly on their menus" (Diner 2001: 56). Dishes that continued to keep their Italian names, such as *minestra* (vegetable soup), got richer and more complicated. "Pizza in Roseta Valforte [in Italy] was a flat, thin disc of bread with salt and oil. In Roseto, Pennsylvania, tomatoes, onions, and anchovies gradually covered the dough" (Diner 2001: 53). Migration effectively elevated the cuisine of the poor Italian to that of their elites.

Class elevation also occurred with eastern European Jewish food after immigration. "The formerly poor started to eat *blintzes*, *kreplach*, *kasha-varnitchkes*, *strudel*, noodles, *knishes*, and, most importantly, meat every day. Their once meager cabbage or beet *borschts* now glistened with fat" (Diner 2001: 180). Marcus Ravage, a Rumanian Jewish migrant in New York in 1900, noted with astonishment, "In New York, every night was Friday night and every day was Saturday [sabbath], as far as food went" (Ravage 1917: 75–6). Furthermore, a national cuisine was born in the diaspora which eventually de-emphasized regional styles. Angelo Pellegrini wrote that immigrants came to America "ignorant of cuisines beyond their own regions. In the Little Italy of the American metropolis the southern Italian ultimately learned about *osso buco* and *veal scaloppini*, and his neighbor . . . from the north met up with pizza and eggplant Parmesan" (Pellegrini 1971). Furthermore, as Niccola de Quattrociocchi, a native of Palermo, wrote in the 1920s, "One evening [while strolling in New York], we went to an Italian restaurant where I was introduced to two very fine, traditional American specialties called 'spaghetti with meatballs,' and 'cotoletta parmigiana' . . . I found both extremely satisfying and I think someone in Italy should invent them for the Italians over there" (de Quattrociocchi 1950: 30). Other new elements crept into their repertoire, such as the drinking of beer with their food rather than wine (Diner 2001: 60).

Diner argues that "The Italian story may best represent the experiences of most immigrants" (2001: 26). In *The Migrant's Table*, I show that the more recent Bengali-American story at the turn of the twentieth and the twenty-first centuries is different precisely because the respondents in my study were more affluent both in their native contexts and in the New World (Ray 2004). The hagiography of American abundance among Irish and eastern European Jews, or even the muted critique of American foods and tastes by Italian-Americans, stand in sharp contrast to the attitude of the Bengali-American interlocutors in my study. Only two of my respondents, out of 126, mentioned abundance, while others were highly critical of American foods. That is mostly because of their class background, the way they have crafted an identity that left behind the hunger of their poorer compatriots, and because they take full advantage of the cultural terrain, absorbing the current normative critique of American foods. Bengalis have culturally benefited from their re-insertion in a world where the excesses and limits of the agro-industrial system and its consequences on the body—in terms of both taste and health—have become common sense.

Ethnic food and the long shadow of gustatory difference

Between 1851 and 2013, the words "ethnic" and "restaurant" are found together on more than eight thousand instances in *The New York Times* (*NYT*). The first article using both those terms separately, was published on October 8, 1959, titled "Use of Native Spices Adds Interest to Unusual Cuisine of Balinese," and was written by the *NYT*'s first serious restaurant critic, Craig Claiborne. On the other hand, the phrase "ethnic restaurant" can be identified on 273 instances, with Claiborne leading that category again, on July 15, 1964, with an article titled "Variety of French Food Sampled on West Coast."[3]

There were 631 hits for "ethnic food," with the lead article by James J. Nagle, titled "Tastes Widening for Kosher Food" on November 6, 1960.[4] Thus the phrases "ethnic food" and "ethnic restaurant" became visible in the *NYT* from the 1960s onwards, and each one of those articles was about the food of a group that was not considered to be a part of the normative mainstream—to wit, "one hundred percent Americans" (Edwards 1982)—by the author. The use of the term "ethnic restaurant" peaked in the 1970s, slowly declining into the 2000s, for which *The New York Times* index identifies only eleven records in 2010, and none at all in 2013. It appears that the era of "ethnicity" as a catch-all category between race and nation may be ending among high-status journalists, which is precisely the time to take a look back at its half-century-long career in defining the American relationship to gustatory difference.

There are no references to either of the phrases—"ethnic food" or "ethnic restaurant"—in the American Periodicals Series, which is a comprehensive collection of periodicals published in the United States from 1741 to 1850.

"Ethnic" appears on its own in that collection, in a March 1805 issue of the *General Assembly's Missionary Magazine*, only to distinguish non-Christians from Christians. That is congruent with the idea of "ethnicity," which is derived from the Greek noun *ethnos*, meaning nation or people, and is used to refer both to people in general and "other" people in particular (Sollors 1997: x–xi).

On October 8, 1959, Craig Claiborne writes, "Because New York is a city of sophistication and with tremendously different ethnic groups, the public here has extraordinary opportunities to dine on the 'exotic' fare of a hundred regions," marking the new dispensation towards gustatory difference. "One of the most fascinating of the many Far Eastern restaurants here is *A Bit of Bali* . . . Since the management obviously has respect for authenticity, dining there can be a rewarding adventure," he concludes, anxious that the thing barely grasped would elude his reach (Claiborne 1959). That is a concern still contemporary to our own times—the search for difference and the fear that contact will contaminate the exotic.

Of course, there had been exotic food long before the 1960s, but Americans did not call it ethnic. On August 6, 1871, the *NYT* noted, "the fact is patent that restaurants and boarding-houses are fast multiplying, and threaten at no distant day to usurp the place of the family dinner table as well as the family mansion" (*New York Times* 1871). Anxieties about the "domestic" in its multiple resonances—of family, home, hearth, and nation—are typical in much of the commentary on "restaurants" at this time, which are mostly referred to as "German, French, and Italian Dining-Saloons" into the late 1920s. Restaurants clearly belonged to the *demimonde* and would only replace saloons as new sites of middle-class sociability as the century progressed.

Yet, there is a hint of urban excitement often balanced by ethnic disgust. One can see the excitement in an 1852 piece on Philadelphia subtitled an "Era of Saloonism," which ends with the following:

> Scores of waiters, like dumb mutes, stand ready to receive your orders, and to convey them to that concealed and invisible sanctuary whence issues so many multitudinous preparations, whose fantastic names tickle the ear, and whose superlative qualities please and exhilarate the palate . . . You are persuaded that, lost in the mazes of the city, you have entered, by accident, into some secret avenue, which has conducted you into an elysian state of existence—some Mahomedian paradise, adorned with marble and gold; perfumed with frankincense and myrrh; and lighted by the brilliant eyes of beautiful houris (Victor 1852: 2)

Perhaps the earliest instance of even-handed and systematic coverage of New York City eateries—cheap and exalted—was conducted by the *New York Daily Tribune* in 1845, when it counted 123 "eating houses or refectories" (excluding oyster bars), listing the name of the owner and their location. These establishments provided employment to nearly a thousand Germans and Irish immigrants, the author noted, where, for fifteen to sixteen hours of work a day, waiters were paid ten to twelve dollars a month, plus room and board, while cooks were paid between eight and ten, and dish-washers made four to five dollars (*New York Daily Tribune* 1845: 5).

This mid-nineteenth-century equanimity, even some urban excitement for the exotic, recedes by the 1880s, precisely when immigration takes off, until we get someone like Helen Bullitt Lowry in the 1920s, who had to rehabilitate and normalize the "old world" of Greeks, Jews, and Italians through their foods in New York. According to Gabaccia this is when American food was both nationalized due to technological developments in transportation and refrigeration, and ghettoized in the ethnic enclave (1998). Until the 1920s, ethnic food was often subject to open disgust even in reputable newspapers which carried titles such as "Found in Garbage-Boxes Stuff that is Utilized for Food by Some People" (*NYT* 1883) and shrill announcements such as "An Octopus Eaten by Chinamen" (*NYT* 1880). We also see a less insidious ethnocentrism about monotonous and insipid "Teutonic cookery," where all the meats taste the same and is slathered over by the same viscous sauce (*NYT* 1898). Distaste and disdain clearly mark the outer boundary of a civilized taste community. Only the democratizing process of the mid-twentieth century Civil Rights Movement would make such attitudes appear crude and impolite, in due course.

In contrast to ethnic places, society restaurants such as Delmonico's are welcomed with open arms. On April 7, 1862, the *NYT* warmly embraced the new up-town location of Delmonico's with the following words:

> When the best families were clustered around the Bowling-green, and gentlemen dandies who promenaded on the Battery were expected to wear white kid gloves, the name DELMONICO first became known to the lovers of good living in the City . . . The establishment (which was formerly the mansion of Mr. MOSES II. GRINNELL) has been fitted up with faultless taste, and is without any exception, the handsomest place of this kind in the City (capitalization in original; *NYT* 1862: 5).

Every new location of Delmonico's was received with rapture, and contained by some vague patrician referent such as "formerly the mansion of Mr. Moses." And every society ball held in one of these venerated restaurants was announced with much fanfare in the dailies. On January 19, 1873, the *NYT* published a long and relatively even-handed piece titled "German Restaurants." According to the un-named author, they are distinguished by their cheapness and abundance—a consistent ethnic marker. They are said to serve "the odd things that foreigners love," along with the roasts, pumpkin pies, and dumplings that Americans prefer. For the Frenchman there is "lentil soup, in which masses of Bologna sausage are floating, while the Irishman is vigorously to [*sic*] work on something like fish-balls smothered in red cabbage," all of which is served with an "enormous supply of coarse German bread." One customer orders a "weiner snitzel—a tremendous name, which, however, when brought, is only veal cutlet with the bone removed." Another "says he feels delicate, and will have calf's tongue with raisins. This delectable dish, when it makes its appearance, is not very inviting in appearance." For all this, the author notes, the "price marked on the carte is fifteen cents. Further investigation into the mysteries of German cuisine shows beef a la mode served with macaroni a very peculiar but highly satisfactory way of eating it," all served by waiters who are "clearly German" (*NYT* 1873: 5).

That mix of inviting exoticism and disdain continued into the first decades of the twentieth century when Helen Morgan, in an article, referencing the emerging omnivorousness, titled "Our Wide Taste in Food," could write: "Strange dishes have been taken from one home to another, until, as a consequence, an American family of 1935 might reasonably concoct a meal like this: fruit cocktail, sauerkraut, spaghetti, mutton or lamb or meat balls, corn on the cob, garlic salad and apple pie." She assures us that "Undoubtedly any one subject to [such] nightmares would not survive, yet such a hodge-podge is not impossible" (Morgan 1935: SM17). From our vantage point, marked by even greater mixing, the menu hardly looks a hodge-podge. But the ethnic as exotic, and maybe as someone with slightly disgusting eating habits, continues as a minor theme even after cultural democratization. We can smell traces of it as late as 1999, when Richard Weir writes "Not for the Faint of Palate. Guinea Pig, Cow's Spleen, All Part of City's Diet."

Popularity and prestige

When we classify the talk on restaurants in the American print media as related to ethnicity over the last 150 years (which is about the outer limit of the print-run of major American newspapers), we find that the data on restaurants is too thin until about 1880 to make any generalizations. Figure 3.7 shows that French, German, and Chinese restaurants dominated the conversation in the decades after the Civil War. Discussions about French restaurants increased in the last decades of the nineteenth century with their increasing popularity among the elite, and interest in Chinese restaurants subsided modestly, while the category "German restaurant" fell off precipitously through the First and the Second World Wars. It is since the 1940s that interest in Italian restaurants has increased, and it continues to climb. The persistence of Chinese restaurants in public

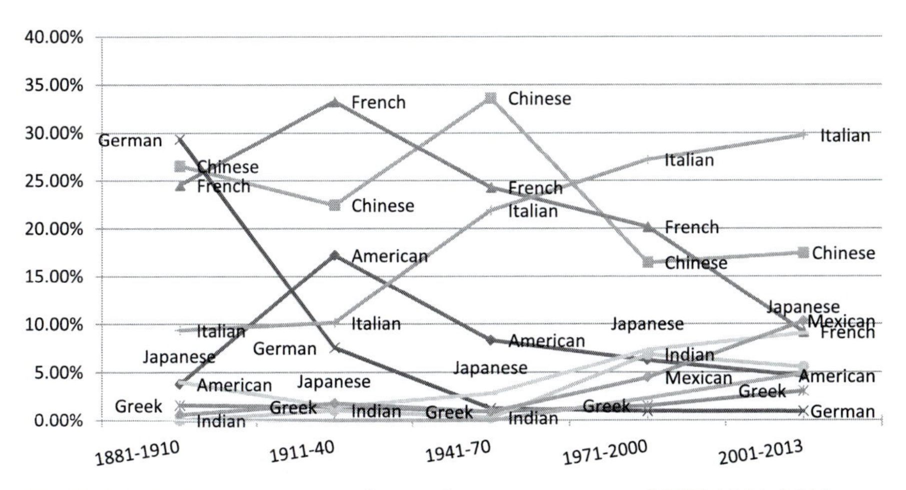

FIGURE 3.7 *Comparative popularity of cuisines over time:* NYT *1881–2013.*

consciousness is remarkable, although their relative decline is understandable given greater competition from numerous other exotic cuisines since the 1970s. Italian restaurants climbed in terms of volume in American discourse only after Italian immigration fell off. In comparison, French restaurants came from a high point in the first decades of the twentieth century to fall in comparative popularity in public discourse to below 10 percent in 2013, where they sit today with Japanese and Mexican. The French trajectory is unrelated to immigration, as its foreign status trumped its ethnic limits long ago. Nevertheless, the high-status French category has been losing out to Japanese and New American cuisines, which are recently resurgent haute cuisine categories.

Over the last 150 years, the discussion about German and Continental restaurants has declined, the first precipitously and the second consistently. The German case is an intriguing instance of invisibility due to ubiquity. Germanic cuisine was everywhere and could not be distinguished from the standard American diet of meat, potatoes, dairy, and lager beer—and anti-German sentiments through the two World Wars squashed any residual possibilities of a nominally distinct culinary identity. Categories of cuisine that increase in visibility after the 1960s are quite remarkable, because in general the ratio for almost all cuisine declines because of the increasing number of named cuisines, related to omnivorous tastes.

I wanted to measure the difference between the coverage of ethnic restaurants in the *NYT* and other national newspapers. An analysis of the *NYT*, *LAT*, and *Chicago Tribune* throughout their print-runs show a marked similarity of coverage, where French, Italian, and Chinese restaurants are the most discussed, followed by Japanese, American, and Mexican. Most articles about restaurants in major American newspapers are about Italian restaurants, showing two peaks in the coverage: one in the 1881–1890 period, mostly focused on cheap eateries; and then once again after 1981. The popularity of Italian cuisine is given a fillip by accumulating prestige, as it begins to lose its ethnic status and acquire haute markers in major markets. In a report titled *Ethnic Cuisine II* (2000) the National Restaurant Association noted that, according to their study based on a survey of 1,230 customers, while younger customers sought out Thai, Indian, Vietnamese, and Japanese, older customers often opted for Italian, among others, which is "so well known and prevalent that" it is "no longer considered ethnic." This is a development that I will discuss in some detail later. The most visible difference between the major media markets is that, predictably, the *Los Angeles Times* covers Mexican cuisine more extensively than do the *Chicago Tribune* or *The New York Times* (where it is covered minimally).

In addition to newspapers, I have most closely analyzed data from Zagat, MenuPages and Michelin surveys, which shows the rising popularity of some cuisines such as Italian, declining popularity of others such as Continental, and the surprisingly stalemated location of Chinese cuisine, along with the dramatic increase in the prestige of Japanese, New American, Spanish, and Greek. Before I elucidate what various surveys show about the popularity and prestige of various cuisines, which is the hierarchy I am interested in delineating, let me say a few things about the strengths and limitations of the surveys themselves.

Michelin is the most recent guide to the New York City market (entering it in 2005) and sometimes considered the most high-brow, to a fault, especially when snobbery has been on decline, as most sociologists of culture claim (increasingly replaced by omnivorousness, according to Peterson and Kern 1996; Johnston and Bauman, 2010). Nevertheless, Michelin guides are highly respected among chefs, and argued over, because of their long history of game-changing reviews of French cuisine in France, the high temple of Western culinarity. They also tend to be the most expansive, the evaluation conducted by anonymous inspectors (some French and some American), and the most idiosyncratic. Their claim is that they are "meticulously researched, objective recommendations to approximately 950 delicious restaurants in the Big Apple, a city where cuisine reigns supreme" (Michelin 2014). Michelin is insistent that it is not a directory, thus only the best make the cut, and that their evaluators are anonymous "local" inspectors (this was added after widespread discussion surrounding early editions as too French, and ham-handed about local modes of judgment).

Zagat, on the other hand, is a middle-brow product, born of an impulse of the eponymous lawyer couple and their friends. It is sedate, not very populist or avant garde, but considered comfortably middle class, in the sense of reflecting the tastes of thousands of its reviewers, mostly professionals, who eat at their own expense and provide details in a self-volunteered survey. Zagat-rated restaurants are neither exhaustive nor randomized. The Zagat Guidebooks were begun in 1979, limited to New York City, and formalized in 1980, but no public version is available at the Library of Congress from before 1986 (which is the earliest one I cite in a number of Figures and Tables below). The selection gets filtered through two layers of opinion-makers. First, tens of thousands of self-selecting surveyors volunteer to rate a restaurant. Next, it reflects the preferences of the editors themselves, who cull the reviews and assign overall scores by no publicly discussed system. Yet, in spite of these weaknesses, Zagat reviews do reveal some trends as opinion makers. Accordingly, the 2014 Zagat NYC is the product of surveys undertaken by "38,000 avid diners like you" (Zagat 2013), who evaluated 2,050 restaurants (most of which are listed by Zagat staff on the survey instrument and some of which are volunteered by reviewers). Zagat does not reveal its method of collation and classification. It appears mostly to be staff judgment based on survey inputs, with the previous year's survey as the baseline, taking into account the preceding year's collated chatter in print and digital media.

One of the more populist digital listings, accounting for the largest number of restaurants, is Menupages. I provide an illustrative example in Table 3.1 below. In January 2014, Menupages listed 2,020 Chinese restaurants in New York City, compared to 62 by Zagat 2014 (print), and 61 by Michelin (print). In all, Menupages lists 16,234 restaurants in NYC, out of an estimated total of about 25,383 eating and drinking establishments (based on municipal tax, health, and labor law statistics), compared to a Zagat total of 2,084, and a Michelin total of 939.

At the end of 2013, Menupages further strengthened its populist credentials by initiating the first comprehensive list of eateries in the more working-class borough (compared to Manhattan) of Queens, which is a residential neighborhood of some of the greatest ethnic diversity in the United States and has for decades been a destination for gourmets in search of authentic Asian and Latin American cuisines.

Now to the substantive claims based on the surveys discussed above. Zagat data can be used fruitfully to show the popularity of certain kinds of ethnically marked cuisines among the Anglophone, middle-brow public, especially in contrast to the more popular Menupages (or Yelp), and the more high-brow Michelin. Zagat surveys confirm the evidence from newspapers that Italian restaurants have been popular and have consistently made up more than 25 percent of rated restaurants between 1986 (earliest publicly available data) and 2014. In contrast, French restaurants have declined in terms of percentage of all restaurants rated, to just under 10 percent from a high of 24 percent in 1986. Continental cuisine has declined precipitously in popularity among the middle-brow, to just under 1 percent of listed restaurants

TABLE 3.1 Michelin, Zagat, Menupages coverage of NYC restaurants in 2014

Ethnic/national Categories	Michelin 2014 (print)	Zagat 2014 (print)	Menupages (accessed Jan 2, 2014)
American	93	260	1,006
Chinese	61	56	2,020
Contemporary	104	n.a.	n.a.
Continental	0	9	0
Filipino	0	0	23
French	42	174	347
Greek	19	30	143
Indian	21	40	383
Italian	146	371	1,945
Japanese	82	99	941
Korean	22	13	219
Mexican	42	44	960
Nuevo Latino	0	16	89
Soul	7	4	0
Spanish	22	26	125
Southern	7	21	159
Thai	16	36	387
Vietnamese	8	20	136
Others	720	860	n.a.
Numbers listed	939	2,084	16,234
Number of categories	61	98	48

from a high of 10 percent in 1986. Chinese restaurants have also declined in relative popularity, but less precipitously, from a high of 8 percent of all Zagat-rated New York City restaurants in 1986, to a low of four percent by 2010, rising to 5 percent in 2014. On the other hand, American and Japanese restaurants have improved their position to about 20 percent in the case of the former and 8 percent in the case of the latter.

How does the NYC case compare with the data from other American cities? Table 3.2 shows that among the most visible, counted, and recommended cuisines there is substantial similarity between NYC, Chicago, Los Angeles, and San Francisco, with some interesting variations. What has been classified as American or New American cuisine is substantially less ubiquitous in NYC (19 percent) than in Chicago (32 percent), Los Angeles (33 percent), or San Francisco (36 percent). New York City diners are more omnivorous at the higher end of the market than the others. Yet, both NYC and San Francisco are much more Francophile (at 13 percent each) than Los Angeles or Chicago

TABLE 3.2 Comparative popularity of ethno-nationally-marked Zagat-rated restaurants in four selected US cities in 2010

Ethnicity/nationality	NYC	Chicago	LA	SF
	%	%	%	%
American	19	**32**	**33**	**36**
Chinese	4	4	4	4
Continental	1	1	1	0
French	**13**	9	8	**13**
Greek	2	2	1	0
Indian	3	3	2	2
Italian	**28**	19	20	15
Japanese	7	8	11	6
Korean	1	1	1	1
Mediterranean	5	3	4	8
Mexican/Tex-Mex	3	6	6	4
Pizza	6	6	3	4
Soul/South	2	2	1	2
Spanish	2	2	1	2
Thai	3	2	2	2
Vietnamese	1	1	1	2
TOTAL MARKED[1]	100%	100%	100%	100%

[1] Due to rounding, not all columns add up to 100.

(9 percent each). Italian continues to be the most popular haute cuisine in NYC (28 percent), while it is about half as popular in San Francisco (15 percent, partly because the category "California Cuisine" includes a variety of Mediterranean options), and a little more than half as popular in Chicago (19 percent) or Los Angeles (20 percent). San Franciscans prefer a broader range of Mediterranean cuisines than residents of other cities. Predictably, Mexican and Tex-Mex cuisines do much better in Chicago and Los Angeles than in NYC and San Francisco. Yet, it is difficult to ascertain from the Zagat data whether these are local preferences or outsider-tourist choices because although Zagat claims its surveyors are local, it is primarily used by tourists.

If we follow the trend lines (Figure 3.8), it appears that an American restaurant cuisine has been born, at least discursively, in the last two decades of the twentieth century, and a foreign cuisine—Japanese—is beginning to complement another foreign cuisine—French—in the estimation of American taste-makers. Here we reach a question of classification and its consequences. I call Japanese and French cuisine "foreign," rather than "ethnic," foods for a simple reason: demographics. In the 2012 American Community Survey (ACS), less than 1 percent of the NYC population claimed a French ancestry (67,761, to be precise, out of a total of a little over 8 million residents), yet 10 percent of Zagat-rated restaurants with clear ethno-national markers are French. Similarly, only 25,672 people living in NYC claimed Japanese ancestry yet 5 percent of Zagat-rated New York City restaurants are Japanese. At the other end of the social hierarchy of taste we see, for instance, that 5 percent of rated restaurants are Mexican/Tex-Mex restaurants (classified as such in the guides) for a Mexican population that adds up to 308,952 (which is distinct from

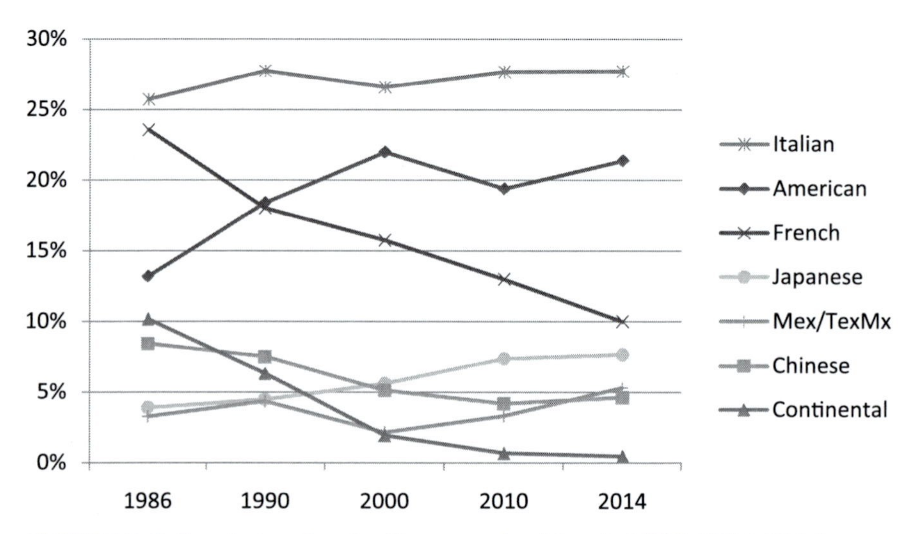

FIGURE 3.8 *Popularity of major Zagat-rated cuisines in NYC (1986–2014).*

2 million other Latinos in New York City, whose cuisine mostly does not register in the Zagat guides).

Check averages in Zagat-rated New York City restaurants listed in Table 3.3 also show a clear hierarchy of taste if price is considered a surrogate for status. Japanese restaurants have leapfrogged from number six in terms of price in 1986 to the second rank in 2010. In 2011 (not shown in the table below to avoid clutter), Japanese restaurants were the most expensive restaurants in NYC. Another upwardly mobile cuisine is Greek, moving up from twelfth in 1986 to fifth in 2010. There is also the steady promotion of American and Spanish cuisines. Older ethnic categories such as Southern, Mexican, Chinese, and even Thai have all suffered in their prestige ranking, due partly to cheap ubiquity and partly to the call of the new Asian categories such as Japanese, Indian, and Vietnamese. The Italian case is perhaps the only exception, where we have seen both the proliferation of cheap ubiquity and the high price/prestige category, and I will address that issue below.

Note that the top two cuisines in 2010 (see Table 3.3) are, for the lack of a better word, foreign foods. The top six cuisines, with the exception of Japanese, are ones which have come to be identified with white folks (also with high per capita income).[5] Among them, only Italian has significant demographic weight in terms of the ancestry data of New Yorkers.

In Table 3.3 there is a pattern in terms of the distribution of the "Very Expensive" to the "Inexpensive" restaurants—Columns F, G, H, and I—as it relates to ethnicity. The higher ranking cuisines—French and Japanese—are the only ones that reach double digits in terms of percentage distribution of Very Expensive restaurants (Column I). American and Italian follow closely, with almost half the restaurants in the Expensive category (Column H). The middle group around Greek restaurants clusters mostly in the "Moderately expensive" category (Column G). Most of the restaurants in the Chinese, Tex-Mex, and Soul categories cluster in the "Inexpensive" category (Column F). The one difference between Chinese, on one hand, and Tex-Mex and Soul, on the other hand, is that there are a substantial number of "Expensive" Chinese restaurants, while there are no Soul or Tex-Mex restaurants in that category. Furthermore, Mexican, at number eight, does much better than Tex-Mex, at number 15, affirming the prestige of foreign foods in the American imagination.

Proximity to poor ethnics undermines the prestige of a cuisine (as measured by price, although cheap ethnic food often acquires value as authentic). Yet, that is not the only way the variable between the self and the other gets weighted. American cuisine is also doing very well among the taste-makers, at least since the 1970s, so there has been an upward adjustment in American cultural self-conception largely in national terms. American gastronomic nationalism has finally been born after a long gestation period of much self-doubt, marking the *belle époque* of American cultural self-confidence.

TABLE 3.3 Hierarchy of taste: check averages of NYC Zagat-rated restaurants in 2010

Ethnicity/ nationality claimed	Number of people in NYC claiming an ancestry in 2012 ACS	Rank in terms of decreasing check average	Average price of meal in 2010 dollars	Total number of restaurants in printed Zagat 2010	Inexpensive Restaurant as % of all restaurants within that group (up to $25)	Moderately Expensive Restaurant as % of all restaurants within that group ($26–40)	Expensive Restaurant as % of all restaurants within that group ($41–65)	Very Expensive Restaurant as % of all restaurants within that group (over $66)
A	B	C	D	E	F	G	H	I
French	67,761	1	47.81	202	4	**37**	**47**	**12**
Japanese	25,672	2	46.72	101	9	**44**	**35**	**12**
American	n.a.	3	42.83	270	13	**34**	**44**	**9**
Italian	606,826	4	42.27	389	7	**41**	**49**	3
Greek	74,821	5	38.71	32	9	**56**	**31**	3
Spanish	8,233	6	37.73	30	3	**77**	**20**	0
Indian	205,098	7	33.85	43	**26**	**60**	14	0
Mexican	308,952	8	32.88	39	**31**	**49**	21	0
Korean	96,335	9	31.43	17	**29**	**53**	18	0
Vietnamese	15,206	10	29.08	26	**39**	**46**	15	0
Thai	4,169	11	28.63	45	**40**	**51**	9	0

Chinese	497,788	12	28.47	63	**49**	**32**	17	2
Southern	n.a.	13	28.44	24	**50**	**38**	12	0
Soul	2,059,279	14	24.50	11	**64**	**26**	0	0
Tex-Mex		15	22.00	4	**50**	**50**	0	0
Total/ Average	**8,336,697**		**28.14**	2,003	n.a.	n.a.	n.a.	n.a.

[1] About one-third of Continental restaurants are also listed under other cuisines, mostly French.
[2] 7 out of 11 Soul Food restaurants are also listed under the category Southern.
[3] "Spanish" population in column 1 is distinct from Latino.
[4] African-American population is cited in the ancestry column for Soul due to the association.
[5] Totals and averages are for the whole city and include other ethnicities/nationalities not listed in the table.

My hypothesis is that American taste-makers have a threefold classification system by which they venerate a few foreign cuisines in turn (Continental, French, and Japanese) or "slum it" with the real ethnics (Soul Food, Tex-Mex, Dominican, etc.). Falling somewhere between the two poles are Chinese, Indian, Korean, Thai, and Vietnamese food—all Asian, by the way, which hints at a larger dynamic of cultural capital at work in the global political economy of signs which is, I think, unrelated to food per se. Ethnic foods never reach the heights of foreign foods. But some ethnic foods do better than others, which is related to the per capita income of the group (as shown in the previous footnote). My related hypothesis is that the popularity of a particular ethnic cuisine among the middling sorts is unrelated to the total number of people of a particular heritage: in fact the two may be inversely related. Italian cuisine brings an interesting complexity to that pattern. American cuisine, on the other hand, evokes an association between culture and nation on which the French have long had a monopoly. That national identification goes hand in hand with a complex love of and loathing for ethnic interlocutors. Proximity, especially within a class hierarchy, can be a cultural liability much greater than foreignness. The intimate Other is always disdained, while the distant Other can be safely eulogized. These two polarities of identification—nation and ethnicity—mark a complex adumbration between the self and the Other in the American aesthetic imagination that I will develop in the concluding chapter.

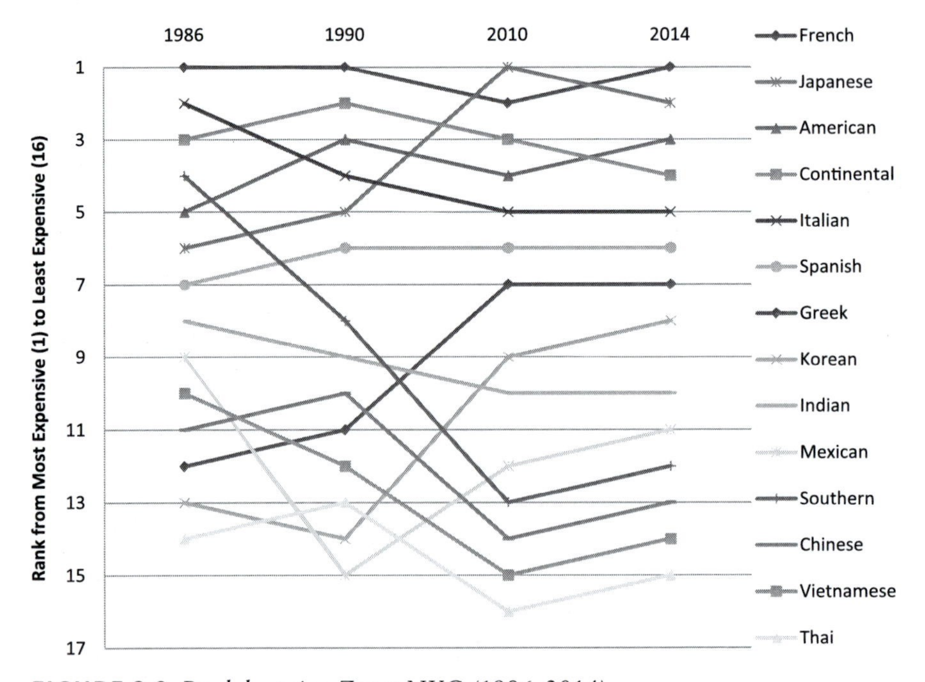

FIGURE 3.9 *Rank by price, Zagat NYC (1986–2014).*

Middle-class appropriation of ethnic restaurants?

Andrew Haley deploys a wide range of evidence to argue that, by the 1920s, "the tables had turned, and increasingly the middle class, not the upper class, determined what would be served in America's restaurants" (2011: 236). He opens with the lyrics to a delightful popular song, "A Bowl of Chop Suey and You-ey," played by the orchestra at the high-class Hotel McAlpin, and a report in *The Steward*, a culinary industry journal. The teashop at McAlpin, the report noted, had "dainty little American born Chinese girls" serving a Chinese luncheon. According to Haley, this is a sign of the emerging "cosmopolitan" taste of the rising middle class, displacing the haute cuisine, haughty maîtres d'hôtel, and French language menus of the plutocrats in the early twentieth century.

The nascent middle class of clerks, managers, and professionals (such as lawyers and doctors), the byproducts of the industrial and the managerial revolutions between 1880 and 1920, were transforming "the tang and feel of the American experience," in C. Wright Mills's formulation (1951). Comfortably salaried and with more leisure time, this middle class changed the expectations of the good life, which increasingly included urban, public, heterosocial entertainment. Barriers of ethnicity and tightly gendered spaces (such as saloons and elite restaurants for men and accompanied women, and teahouses for women) were breached, as the salaried professional expected to spend a night on the town with his wife, sometimes eating in reputable but inexpensive German, Italian, Chinese, and Mexican restaurants. That did not lead to equality, but it drew ethnic restaurateurs and white, middle-class women into the ambit of professional, middle-class hegemony.

In the Gramscian sense, *hegemony* here implies more than mere domination. It promised the alignment of the interest of the middle-class consumer with the economic ambition of the ethnic entrepreneur, and an expanding sphere of leisure activities for middle-class women, as both employees and housewives. By the second decade of the twentieth century, at least eight percent of Americans dined in restaurants regularly, and that number would keep increasing (Haley 2001: 6). The American industrial revolution was producing a class of managers, supervisors, and intermediaries both in the labor process and in the consumer product chain that had to be fed and entertained.

With the separation of spheres and a cult of domesticity taking hold, a new form of companionate marriage had already been articulated, on one hand, and the segregation of cities along class lines and the resultant "slumming" had shown the possibilities of internal urban cross-class tourism, on the other hand. The re-gendering and re-classifications of spaces such as home, work, and entertainment, and the reorganization of time into leisure, work, and recuperation, had also fed reform crusades including temperance, women's rights, nutrition, and slum clearance. Conflict and collaboration with ethnic and Anglo restaurateurs was inevitable in the making of a hegemonic bloc. Haley illustrates the struggle between the rich and the middling folks in the remaking of the businessman's lunchroom, which became more important because of longer commutes, apartment living, and the middle-class servant problem. Lunchrooms typically offered table and counter service. By the late 1870s the lunchrooms were considered respectable and moderately priced, with cost ranging from $0.25 to $1.25.

In a typical New York lunchroom, businessmen were offered "beef a la mode, lamb pot-pie, knuckle of ham with spinach, hashed turkey with poached eggs, chicken and oyster patties, roast pork and apple sauce, roast turkey and cranberry sauce, roast venison, wild duck, roast Spring chicken" (*New York Times* 1881). Then there were table d'hôte restaurants that served multicourse dinners, often with table wines, at a fixed price. Many served Italian, German, and French bistro-style food. There were inexpensive beefsteak restaurants or chophouses that served beefsteak for $0.15, potatoes and vegetables for $0.05, pies, tea and coffee for another $0.05, to "well-dressed people, evidently with plenty of money in their pockets" (Haley 2011: 79). Department store restaurants and coffee and cake saloons were added to the offerings available to the middle classes.

The highly competitive and precarious nature of the restaurant business played to the power of the middle-class patron. This is where Haley challenges Bourdieu's model of class habitus as an exclusively conservative force, as he makes room for new aesthetic attitudes and options in the war of positions between the ascendant middle class and declining elites (2011: 90). This is also where placid "continental cuisine" is restored its proper sociological place, saving it from posthumous approbation as mere aesthetic error.

Haley shows how members of the emerging middle class, "eager to find alternatives to inaccessible aristocratic establishments, colonized and transformed foreign eateries into restaurants that catered to middle-class tastes" (2011: 94). We come across the surprising claim (in light of all the current boosterism) of an 1872 *New York Times* editorial arguing that the United States could become a great culinary power only if Americans learned to celebrate what could be found in various foreign and cosmopolitan restaurants in the city.

German immigrant restaurateurs, with enough capital, were leading the crusade to make their restaurants acceptable to middle-class families (often with German heritage) against the stereotypes of greasy, filthy, garlicky, spicy foods. In New York, Philadelphia, Buffalo, Detroit, and Milwaukee, native-born middle classes joined a growing German middle-class in patronizing a wide range of northern and middle European restaurants (Haley 2011: 99).

Ethnic entrepreneurs often developed hybrid menus, in response to demand or to generate it, as evidenced by a Chinese restaurateur's rejoinder to a police captain's question in 1903, as to why he did not just stick to Chinese dishes rather than range into ham and eggs, mutton chops, and French fried potatoes. He said that he understood that a man might wish to treat his wife or an out-of-town friend to a dish of chop suey after a theater, but would not eat the stuff himself. "Consequently, he lets his wife have her chop suey, while he orders from the American side of the bill" (*New York Times* 1903). At about this time, the *New York Sun* (1901) observed that a large part of the clientele of Italian restaurants was already American. Newspaper reporters again played an important role in opening up the possibilities of a middling restaurant which "may be French, Italian, Hungarian or even German, and the price may be 30 cents or $1.25 a head" (*New York Times* 1885).

Slowly, the middle-class's ability to display cultural capital came to depend on the capacity to make judgments about cuisines other than French, an omnivorousness that would come fully into play by the end of another century of development and cultural democratization, as shown by Johnston and Baumann in *Foodies* (2010). As a reporter from Milwaukee noted, writing about German immigrant food in 1901, "the fear vanishes and something akin to joy fills your soul, for you have experienced a distinctly new gustatory sensation" (*Milwaukee Sentinel*, July 1901; cited in Haley 2012: 66).

Ethnic restaurateurs eager to capitalize on the expansion of the dining repertoire of the middle-class followed their clientele out of ethnic enclaves. In 1901 the *New York Daily Tribune* noted the spread of Chinese restaurants out of Chinatown up along Third and Sixth Avenues. By the 1910s, city blocks in the Twenties and Thirties in Manhattan were home to the city's Italian restaurants and modest French bistros. In 1910, 100 teachers, solid agents of middle-class socialization, passing through New York on their way to a convention in Boston, stopped and ate at a restaurant in Chinatown, and then a Hungarian one in the evening (Bishop 1911: 387). By the 1920s, inexpensive middle-class restaurants occupied the brownstones between Forty-third and Forty-seventh Streets near Times Square (*New York Times* 1920). The ethnic restaurateur recognized the growing power of the middle-class diner and his wife in the transformation of taste in the metropolis.

For Haley, these are clear signs that the tables were turning on aristocratic taste, modeled after European aristocracy's manners and mores, which seemed increasingly narrow and outmoded. Yet, "Dining at a Chinese restaurant did not undermine support for the Chinese Exclusion Act; eating spaghetti did not bring an end to nativism . . . Cosmopolitan dining had a limited influence on attitude towards immigrants because it was so self-centered" (Haley 2011: 116). According to Cindy Lobel, this "cosmopolitan cuisine" served the imperial, social-Darwinist presumptions of the middle-classes, analogous to the role of minstrelsy and world's fairs in their display of exotic peoples (Lobel 2014: 9). Thus, the cast of "cosmopolitanism" that Haley and Lobel attribute to their subjects is narrow and expedient, often construed as a form of American nationalism against European cultural attitudes and racial superiority, which forces me to keep it within quotation marks. I think Johnston and Baumann's "omnivorousness" (2010) is a more apt term here than "cosmopolitanism."

As much as looking up the class hierarchy with disdain, the middle-class surely would have looked down on working-class entertainments that were emerging at the turn of the nineteenth and twentieth centuries, as shown by Kathy Peiss (1986) and Lewis Erenberg (1984). Working with dance halls, amusement parks, and movie theaters, Peiss shows how working-class women transformed urban American popular cultures at the turn of the nineteenth and twentieth centuries. She also showed how these new forms of leisure reconfigured the spatial and temporal organization of home, work, and play. The ethnic restaurant is an extension of the same logic of reconfiguration of leisure in the twentieth-century American city. And it is a specific place of middle-class hegemony that successfully excludes the working-class (now increasingly defined as palatally closed-minded). But the middle-class would come to appropriate ethnic cuisine with a particular kind of disdain for ethnics.

The invisible ethnic restaurateur

In spite of the centrality of ethnic entrepreneurs—German, Jewish, Italian, and Chinese—in the cultural reconfiguration of dominant American tastes, we have seen very few scholarly monographs on these entrepreneurs. Work is just beginning to emerge on the North American Chinese restaurateur. The 2010 Census identified 3.8 million Chinese in the USA, and scholars have counted more than 40,000 Chinese restaurants, "more than the number of McDonalds, Burger Kings and KFCs combined," as Jennifer 8 Lee writes (2009: 9). Nevertheless, the academic output on McDonalds and McDonaldization has been much heavier (Ritzer 1996; Watson 1997). That may be because counter-cultural academics have come to see McDonald's as a harbinger of cultural homogenization under the sign of American imperialism (although James Watson's collection is an argument against it), and the shape of the neoliberal future of de-skilled work, corporate control of commodity and labor markets, rationalization, withdrawal of the welfare state, and the decline of taste. Unfortunately, so much single-minded attention to powerful American corporations makes the less powerful even less so. Hence it is salutary that we are finally catching up with our analysis of the Chinese restaurant in North

America, the home turf of many of the threatening global fast food brands (Coe 2009; Lee 2009; Cho 2010).

The technique behind Jennifer Lee's *The Fortune Cookie Chronicles* (2009) is to interview restaurateurs and workers who were suddenly connected on March 30, 2005, when hundreds of people across the United States won the Powerball lottery. It appears that customers had bought lottery tickets with the same numbers inscribed in their fortune cookies that had been distributed in Chinese restaurants in forty-two American states. That allowed Lee, fluent in Mandarin Chinese and Cantonese, to get further than the usual questions asked by most Americans until then, such as why Americans eat Chinese food, or why Chinese food is popular among American Jews (Tuchman and Levine 1993). Her research in the digitized archives of historical newspapers, and particularly illuminating interviews with immigrant Chinese restaurateurs and workers, provide a view that could not be matched even by the more conceptually astute and material-culture driven analysis of Lily Cho in *Eating Chinese* (2010), which, as it turns out, has more theoretical axes to grind (that I will address later).

Lee deftly sidesteps the issue of authenticating expatriate Chinese food by calling food such as General Tso's chicken and chop suey "Chinese, born in America" (like herself), or "American which just looks Chinese" (like herself again; Lee 2009: 16). In Louisiana she tastes Szechuan alligator, which was probably unavailable anywhere in China, but was still recognizably Chinese. Challenged by cream cheese wantons in the Midwest, Philly cheesesteak roll in Philadelphia, and chow mein sandwiches in New England, she comes to the brave conclusion that "Chinese food, perhaps, does not have to originate in China" (2009: 22–3). She then pursues fascinating tales of presumably the first Chinese food delivery system developed on the Upper West Side of Manhattan in 1976; nails down the Japanese inventor of the fortune cookie; and considers the explosion of Chinese restaurants in New York City from six in 1885 to more than 100 chop suey places in 1905, all confined between Fourteenth and Forty-fifth Streets and Third and Eighth Avenues (Lee 2009: 34, 45, 57).

Most persuasively, she follows the fate of the 286 illegal Chinese immigrants abroad the ship *Golden Venture*, which ran aground in Queens, New York on the night of June 6, 1993. Of the 286 passengers on that ship, 246 were from Fujian province, the source of most Chinese restaurant workers in the United States over the last few decades (2009: 113). Lee concludes by pointing out that, while American corporate food lore is filled with figures such as Ray Kroc of McDonald's, Howard Schultz of Starbucks, and Asa Griggs Candler of Coca-Cola, "Chinese food in America has no such dominant figures, yet it is no less a powerful presence in Americana," populated with micro-personalities such as Misa Chang, who redefined take-out and delivery,

Edward Louie, who mastered the fortune cookie-making machines, chefs Wang and Peng, who fabricated General Tso's chicken, and "the mysterious Lem Sen of chop suey" fame (2009: 272).

Chinese restaurateurs and workers, go as far back as 1849—the opening parenthesis of my analysis based on two sets of sources, the Census of Occupations and the print run of major American newspapers—have been acutely under-represented in the discussion on American taste. Heather R. Lee's work on "Entrepreneurs in the Age of Exclusion" shows how even within the constraints of the Chinese Exclusion Act of 1882, until its repeal in 1943, Chinese restaurateurs found a way around the legal classification of coolie labor—as restaurant and laundry entrepreneurs—to generate a remarkable wave of entrepreneurship that may have been paradoxically incentivized by the very act of excluding Chinese labor (Lee 2013: 53–77).

In Lily Cho's pointed post-colonial critique of misplaced requiems, she notes that neither have small-town Chinese restaurants died, nor have all the diasporic populations vanished into exotic Chinatowns. Cho's *Eating Chinese* produces an alternative history of suppressed immigrant agency. These ubiquitous small-town Chinese restaurants and their menus, with their egg foo young, chow mein and chop suey, attest "to a self-conscious and utterly aware production of fictive ethnicity," where the diasporic subject exploits "the menu's capacity for the reproduction of a cultural space in order to produce an ethnicity that can be made palatable" and yet frustrates the fierce white pursuit of a "knowable authentic Chinese subject" (2010: 71). In contrast to the piercing Anglo gaze that seeks to pin down authentic Chineseness once and for all, she posits an alternative possibility.

Her research shows that small-town Canadian Chinese restaurants were de facto community centers where "people went for their morning coffee, or after the hockey game, or for a first date, or for sodas after school" and which developed this "curious intimacy between its proprietors and its patrons" (2010: 80). Yet, small-town Chinese restaurants are often spaces of white nostalgia that consolidates white subjectivity through the production of manageable otherness, which is why we see so much writing and singing (Joni Mitchell's "Chinese Café/Unchained Melancholy" and Sylvia Tyson's "The Night the Chinese Restaurant Burned Down") about them. Cho argues, with a tincture against sentimentality, that such celebration of the Chinese restaurant is a form of rationalization of domination under the guise of inclusion. Just as there would be no "Habermasian public sphere without a plantation economy," the significance of the Chinese restaurant in white Bildungsroman sentimentality is a "barbed assertion of diasporic presence in the absence of any mention of diasporic subjects" (Cho 2010: 101, 103).

Then again, not all nostalgia is the same. Cho asserts that it is equally necessary to recuperate nostalgia from the strictures of white sentimentality, where "the small town Chinese restaurant is . . . a testament to the power of diaspora to be a force of emplacement" (2010: 108). She then goes on to discuss how small-town Chinese restaurants created a space that addresses "the strangeness of dominant culture through an invitation to sit down, to open up the menu, to consume something familiar and different" (2010: 113). As a result they successfully turned their familiar foreignness into an object of desire against the dominant rules of good taste, a counter-poetics of pleasure and sensuousness within the grammar of displacement.

Yet she insists that we be aware that "memorializing the Chinese restaurant from only one side of the counter risks occluding the significant contributions of the activities on the other side—in the kitchen, behind the cash register, at the coffee machine, spaces where one is more likely to be standing than sitting" (2010: 115). Such complex, exasperating accusations are typical of post-colonial theorizing, and Cho does a good job of unsettling the reader through high theorizing and beautiful writing, and sparse evidence of a few menus, a couple of photographs, and a handful of songs. Most importantly, her larger arguments about the ethnic invisibility of the entrepreneur are right on the mark and the dialectic of ubiquity but invisibility that she records is even more acute for another group of immigrants.

The unseen Latino cook

Recent migrations from Latin America have drawn attention to one of the largest groups of immigrants with the longest history within the United States. Often, that very contemporary inflow is what erases evidence of their ancient presence in the American imagination. As Zilkia Janer notes, "The cultural continuity between the two sides of the Mexico–United States border predates the arrival of Europeans and the birth of both countries" (2008: 1). The Treaty of Guadalupe Hidalgo (1848) not only transformed one-half of Mexican territory into the United States but stranded a large number of Mexicans on the wrong side of the border. Among them were ranchers, landowners, and rural workers, for whom southwestern ranch style cookery was the norm, with dried beef, fruit and vegetables, curds and fresh cheeses, pork cracklings, slow-cooked stews (adobos of vinegar, garlic, and spices), and barbecues. Spanish and Native American fry breads, stews, and sausages were adopted quite early into their repertoire. And by 1895 we find evidence of food sellers "serving tamales, tortillas, chiles rellenos (stuffed chilies), *huevos revueltos* (scrambled eggs), *lengua lampreada* (beef tongue with salsa ranchera), *pucheros* (soups), and *ollas* (stews) in a plaza in San Antonio, Texas" (Janer 2008: 9). This is also about when Tex-Mex food, with its chili con carne and combination platters of tamales, enchiladas, rice, beans, and melted cheese, became reductively associated by Anglos with working-class Mexican restaurant fare, dominated by the flavors of ground chilis, cumin, oregano, and black pepper.

By 1898, Encarnación Pinedo was already struggling to free Mexican food from a virulent stereotype by calling her cookbook *El cocinero español* (*The Spanish Cook*), one of the earliest Spanish language cookbooks published in California (Janer 2008: 9). The popular guidebooks produced by the Federal Writers' Project's (FWP) in the 1930s and 1940s and the archives of the America Eats project reveal substantial presence of "Spanish-Mexican food" (Bégin 2012). Bégin writes that the taste of race informed the taste of place as American gastronomic discourse, inscribed in printed guidebooks for the newly emergent tourist trade, established Mexican food as a southwestern regional American cuisine which "offered the sensory opportunity to perceive the race of a conquered people." She avers that "A potent gender dynamic also animated the sensory construction of this domestic yet exotic taste. Daring to eat the spicy dishes prepared by Mexican women was a central experience of white male culinary tourism" (Bégin 2012).[6]

From the early decades of the twentieth century, when more than a million migrants came to the US, Mexicans became increasingly central to working the American food system, from the agricultural laborer to the dish washer and the cook. Even at the cusp of the current recession (2008–2012) it was estimated that 7 million Mexican workers were in the United States, most working in construction and service occupations, particularly as farm labor and restaurant worker (Pilcher 2012: 187). While Mexicans became ubiquitous to the food system, their food was invisible to most Americans. A study of Omaha, Nebraska, found that Mexican food remained confined to the immigrant community until the 1950s, but then it leapt ahead of the immigrant population. Nationally, the number of Mexican restaurants took off in the 1970s, which *preceded* the great northern migration of Mexicans by about two decades (Pilcher 2012: 179).

Mexican food was for a long time hidden in plain view among the migrant and expatriate population as one of the oldest regional cuisines of the southwest, from its distinctive avocados, sprouts, and sour cream at the western end of Hispano-USA, to cactus fruits, green chilis, blue corn, and *pozole* around Sante Fe. The reductive archetype of Mexican food is just beginning to dissipate in the eyes of many Americans. Today, Los Angeles, Chicago, and even New York City are beginning to see a varied Mexican regional—such as Oaxacan and Poblano—and Latin American food at restaurants, in markets, and on pushcarts populating the edges of soccer fields and street fairs (Janer 2008; Zukin 2010; Pilcher 2012).

Wilber Zelinsky's 1980 survey based on telephone directories found that the three most popular cuisines were Chinese, Italian, and Mexican, making up 70 percent of ethnic restaurants in the United States. In that study there was an uneven regional distribution, with Mexican cuisine radiating out from the Southwest (Zelinsky 1985). Jeffrey Pilcher's study based on 2010 data shows the continuing popularity of Mexican food in the Southwest and the West, followed by the upper midwestern cities such as Chicago, and finally the cities of the eastern seaboard. By his estimate there were about forty thousand Mexican restaurants in the United States by the year 2010, which is remarkably similar to the estimates of Chinese restaurants (out of a total of 579,102 restaurants nationally).[7] We are just beginning to record the current material transformation of American food reflected in books and articles on Latino cuisines (Abarca 2006, Janer 2008, Pilcher 2012).

Yet, "One point of commonality between Mexican and U.S. versions of the [more prestigious] nueva cocina has been the marginality of Mexican Americans and indigenous Mexicans" to that haute cuisine and those professionalizing moves (Pilcher 2012: 176). Notwithstanding the popularity of the food, very few Mexican restaurants can command the price and prestige (as shown in Table 3.3 previously) associated with western European cuisines such as French, Italian, and Spanish, or Asian cuisines such as Japanese, revealing a deep-seated and insidious relationship between taste and domination (Janer 2006). In that complex sociology, the rise in prestige of Italian regional cooking since the 1980s adds another layer of argumentation, which underlines at least two interesting peculiarities of Italian food in the eyes of American taste makers.

The valorization of Italian-American food: White but not quite

In 1889, when Alessandro Filippini, the chef at Delmonico's, published his cookbook *The Table*, there were no distinctively Italian recipes in it. Half a century later, James Beard's list of favorite restaurants in 1955 included Quo Vadis in New York and Perino's in Los Angeles, two restaurants that were owned by Italians but didn't offer much of their cooking. Beard could dismiss Italian cooking with the following words, written from France in 1955:

> My opinion of Italian cookery is not too high . . . And getting my first piece of French bread on the train yesterday made me realize again what masters the French are at the art. It seems to me that even the food on the wagon-lit restaurant was better than all the food of Italy (quoted in Kuh 2001: 61).

Addressing what appears today to be the inexplicable disrepute of Italian cuisine, Patric Kuh notes:

> The tenets of haute cuisine of limpidity, distillation, and smoothness stand in direct opposition of those of Italian *cucina*. Where the Italians might grill a whole fish over dry vine shoots, the French must pass a fish mousse twice through a *tamis*. Where the French must chop their parsley to its finest consistency, the Italians might add their herbs whole or cut fairly large . . . The problem for Italians was precisely that their best food stood in direct contrast to the aesthetic of refinement that was the ideal throughout the 1940s, 1950s, and 1960s (Kuh 2001: 180).

Sometimes, aesthetic evaluations of food have nothing to do with the nature of the food or the skill involved in producing it. The Italian misfortune—at least in American eyes—may have been that Italian-Americans were poor and derided, and hence their food was dismissed for those reasons, rather than for any substantive evaluation of their cuisine. When American Italians climbed out of the ghetto and into sports arenas, corporate offices, governor's mansions, city halls, and movie studios, Italian food was re-assessed in the American imagination.

The story of Italian food in America gets more complicated if we get closer to the material and expand our time horizon. There are cycles of rise and fall within longer cycles. Paul Freedman shows, in his detailed study of menus of elite restaurants in the middle of the nineteenth century, how versions of macaroni and cheese (such as "macaroni au gratin," and "macaroni au Parmesan") were the most commonly found, followed by escalloped oysters, baked beans and pork, oyster patties a la Béchamel, and fricassee of chicken (Freedman 2011; Clarkson 2009). Thomas Jefferson had already popularized macaroni and cheese at the end of the eighteenth century. From that high perch in prestige, where northern Italian regional foods were seen as analogues to the Grand Tour, Italian food would be dislodged by the entry of new southern Italian immigrants between 1880 and 1924 who were numerous and mostly poor, hence derided by the taste-making elite.

That disdain spread down the class hierarchy. An Irish woman conceded that although she had no prejudices against her Italian neighbors, the smell of garlic made proximity difficult (Cinotto 2013: 85). Italian Harlem carried the stench of poverty for middle-class visitors. By the end of the nineteenth century, northern Italians had already played a part in racially denigrating the diet of their southern compatriots. One of the earliest references to Sicilian pizza is by Carlo Lorenzini (pen name Collodi), the Tuscan author of *Pinocchio*, who wrote in 1886, "The blackened aspect of the toasted crust, the whitish sheen of garlic and anchovy, the greenish-yellow tint of the oil and fried herbs, and those red bits of tomato here and there give pizza the appearance of complicated filth that matches the dirt of the vendor" (Capatti and Montanari 2003: 27). The reputation of Italian food recovered a little in 1930s NYC, with the furious ascent of Italians into white racism as they sought to distance themselves from blacks and Puerto Ricans in East Harlem, with their rhetorical embrace of *la famiglia* to stem the tide of imagined normlessness among underemployed colored households (Cinotto 2013: 76-86; Gugliemo and Salemo 2003). Yet, that kind of rhetoric did not vaunt them into the elite; it just kept them treading water above the color line.

Nothing devalues a cuisine more than proximity to subordinate others. That explains not only the rise, fall, and rise again of Italian cuisine in America, but also the difficulty of Chinese, Mexican, and Soul food to break away, in dominant American eyes, from the contamination effect of low-class association. Poor, mobile people are rarely accorded cultural capital. The circulation of taste through the social architecture of class and race allows for the creation of a subcultural niche, say for the best taco, genuine dim-sum, or most authentic fried chicken, yet rarely assures a position among elite food cultures.

It is also a matter of timing. The prestige of Italian food could fully recover only by the 1980s, after the bulge of poor immigrants had dissipated over three generations. Per capita income among Italians in NYC in 2010 as the last white group, below those of English, German, Russian, French, Irish, and Polish ancestry, in that order, and above Filipinos, Koreans, Asian Indians, etc., places them just at the right spot to both supply entrepreneurial sweat capital today and shape taste via demand and commentary (New York City Department of City Planning 2010). Italians are also a very large demographic group that carries substantial weight in the marketplace of commodities and commentary. Nevertheless, expensive Italian restaurants and high-end chefs had to position themselves rhetorically against what they disdainfully identified as Italian-American, checkered-tablecloth, red-sauce institutions (Leschziner 2012). The rising prestige of Italian food in America might show us patterns of upward mobility among other ethnics. Analogously, in twenty years from now Chinese food may be able to climb in American estimation, but that depends on a lot, including the continuing economic rise of China and the decline in the flow of poor Chinese immigrants into the United States. Here, depressingly, culture merely follows capital.

Setting his sights on the role of race in the evaluation of taste, Simone Cinotto demonstrates how color was the single most important factor in the consecration of Italian tastes in America (2012). He bleeds the story of the self-congratulation of an upwardly mobile group. He does that by taking a scalpel to an industry—Napa valley wine—that Italians are credited to have almost single-handedly transformed "from a reserve of immigrant groups and urban Europhile elites into a mass national market." In the process he illustrates how the work of David Roediger (2007), Matthew Frye Jacobson (1999), and Michael Omni and Howard Winant (1994) can be deployed with empirical and conceptual subtlety to explain both the centrality of the wages of whiteness in the story of Italian winemaking, and the apparently contradictory power of the margins, to explain the remarkable successes of Piedmontese wine-makers.

Just as the Chinese laundryman or cook did not learn his trade in China to then specialize in cooking and cleaning in California, the successes of Italian wine-makers had very little to do with the so-called Mediterranean ecology of California or with the immigrants' wine-making skills. Here Cinotto deals a devastating blow to the historiographical and popular claims of the successful transplantation of an Old World culture and practical expertise to the New World. That sentimental comparison he shows is the product of a fallacious touristic gaze on a landscape that hides the labor of Asian, Latino, and poor Italian co-ethnics in the laborious transformation of the soil, water, hills, and valleys that made the topography fit for the vine.

Yet these Piedmontese entrepreneurs were great innovators in terms of product development, advertising, marketing, and packaging, precisely because they had very little baggage in terms of Old World traditions. From the giant size of their storage tanks that allowed them to bear the fluctuations of the market better, electrically powered grape-pressing, portable kerosene heaters to ward off nighttime frost, the use of sulfur dioxide to counter the effects of yeasts and stabilize the wine, to industrial refrigeration, they understandably led the market. Here he breaks down another myth—of the tradition-bound Italian. What is even more counter-intuitive is how Cinotto shows that apparently negative developments such as the First World War and Prohibition were turned to the advantage of the Italian wine-makers of California by way of subterranean ethnic networks of support and distribution. Cinotto's work nicely illustrates the play of structure and contingency, race and ethnicity, culture and subculture, in the making of a self-conscious American food culture with complex routes of consolidation.

In his next book, *The Italian American Table*, Cinotto brings us back to Manhattan where I began this chapter. Instead of the tenements of 97 Orchard Street he takes us to the East Harlem of the 1930s, where Italians were beginning to forge a gustatory identity in the crucible of race and ethnicity, setting the table to becoming white so as to relish its privileges of inclusion and exclusion. That process would be completed only after substantial upward mobility, not only of Italians but of Jews, who, due to higher literacy rates and better credentials, would quickly exit the food business, but become the crucial outside boosters for urban Italian cuisine as professionals. The role German restaurants played for Anglo Bohemians in the nineteenth century would be played by Italian and Chinese restaurants for the Judeo-Bohemian intellectual avant-garde.

Today, Italian food is everywhere—not only in "Italian" but also in self-described "American" restaurants. The menu from an "American" restaurant, where the chef describes his cooking as a blend of "a variety of international flavors including Asian, Southwestern and Italian, with classical French technique," includes appetizers such as calamari tempura, a French soufflé, and Vietnamese spring rolls, along with potato gnocchi. The entrées are primarily French- or Italian-inspired, such as olive oil-poached salmon, a grilled red snapper with lemon and herbs, coq au vin, steak au poivre, etc. Sometimes they acquire a distinct Asian, Latino, or Caribbean inflection, with wasabi aioli or fried plantain. The menu lists a separate pasta section, with Uncle Vinny's special rigatoni, gnocchi with tomato-vodka sauce, bowtie pasta with sausage and broccoli rabe, and linguini with saffron-tomato sauce and seafood.

We can see a similar pattern of change in the menu of the restaurant that has become a paradigm for the Third-Wave American restaurant—*Chez Panisse*.[8] Although from the very beginning Alice Waters was drawn to the Mediterranean coast, Italian food and techniques have burrowed deeper into the *Chez Panisse* canon, at least since the time of chef Paul Bertolli. On a recent six-day weekly cycle one can clearly identify strong Mediterranean elements: on Monday, we have ricotta and wild green ravioli, and Brasato di Anatra with house cured pancetta; on Tuesday, butternut squash ravioli, olive oil and broccoli rabe; on Saturday a chanterelle and butternut squash risotto. Menus from other seasons show evidence of grilled vegetables, sweet pea salad, artichoke ravioli, lamb-loin Pecorino-fried chop, bagna cauda, saffron brodetto, pork loin grilled with rosemary and sage, tangerine gelato, orange and celery salad with sheep's milk ricotta, yellowtail jack carpaccio, etc.

By the early years of the twenty-first century, Italian cooking had also embedded itself into the curriculum at the leading cooking school—the *Culinary Institute of America* (CIA). By 2001, the CIA had four full-service restaurants, which were a part of the curriculum. They were: *Escoffier*, the French restaurant, that opened in 1973 (now closed and redesigned as *Bocuse*, discussed in the next chapter); *American Bounty*, serving regional cuisines of the US, which opened in 1982; *St. Andrew's Café*, which opened in 1984 in the wake of concerns about health and early signs of obesity; and *Caterina de Medici*, the Italian restaurant that opened on a small scale in 1984 and was moved to its own independent building in 2001 to become the largest, most popular, and the only profitable restaurant on campus.

The curriculum at CIA was expanded and "The Cuisines of Europe" was changed to "Cuisines of Europe and the Mediterranean," underplaying the previously hegemonic Germanic cuisine of spätzle, sausage, pork chops, dairy, and cabbage, and highlighting the cuisines of Italy, southern France, and North Africa. One special unit in the "Mediterranean" curriculum exclusively focused on pastas—including the making of fresh pastas such as tagliatelle, tortelli, fettucine, cavatelli, orecchiette, tagliarini, garganelli, and farfalle (Rascoll 2004).[9] The fate of other cuisines has been more complicated.

The 1983–84 Catalog of the CIA for the first time identified "Oriental Cuisine" as an area of study separate from "International Cuisine." It included Chinese, Japanese, and Polynesian. By the 1985–86 academic year, Polynesian had dropped out of the curriculum. The 1992–93 Catalog identified "Oriental" cookery with Chinese, Japanese, Thai, and Vietnamese cooking. In the 1996–97 Catalog the "Oriental" kitchen was renamed the "Asian" kitchen and in the 2001–02 Catalog the title was changed again to "Cuisines of Asia" to include Chinese, Japanese, Indian, Korean, Thai, Malaysian, and Vietnamese cooking. This was also when the Asian cookery curriculum was expanded to three weeks from two weeks, partly by eliminating a separate class on forced meats. In a presentation to the faculty in 2005 on the future of American restaurants, CIA's current President Tim Ryan noted the growth of American, Italian, Latino, and Asian cuisines and virtually ignored the French, which is remarkable given that the CIA's curriculum is still structured around French techniques. That is changing too under pressure from Third-Wave (after *Chez Panisse*) and Fourth-Wave (after El Bulli and Momofuku) haute cuisine restaurants, as we will see in the next chapter.

Major surveys of American restaurants also reflect changes in the same direction. In Table 3.4 we have the percentage of ethnically and nationally marked eateries as listed in Zagat's decadal surveys of NYC restaurants. Since 1982, when Zagat began to publish its New York City survey, Italian cuisine has maintained its popularity (in spite of increasing variety due to omnivorousness) among the fine-dining clintele. Continental cuisine, so derided by Calvin Trillin (1994), has effectively vanished from the scene over the last three decades.

Japanese makes a consistently strong showing of 4–7 percent of marked restaurants, while every other notable cuisine—Mexican, Indian, Thai, and Vietnamese—ranges between 2 and 7 percent. Interestingly, the popularity of Chinese has been falling in estimation from a high of 6 percent. Yet Chinese ingredients such as bok-choy and Sichuan peppers, and techniques such as stir-frying, steaming, and wanton-wrapping, are becoming more common in "New American" restaurants. Thai, Vietnamese, and Nuevo-Latino cuisines are showing promising signs of growth (as restaurant reviews in major American newspapers show) but they had not yet registered numerically. I suspect their numbers are going to increase in the near future. The Italian influence is even more marked when we acknowledge that the New American cuisine—which is also increasing in popularity—is strongly shaped by it, as shown previously.

Data from the annual survey of the National Restaurant Association (Table 3.5)—which, unlike the previous material, includes "Fast Food" establishments—shows that Italian eateries do even better as check averages fall under $25. There are hardly any French restaurants under that figure. The

TABLE 3.4 Zagat survey: New York City restaurants at the decadal benchmark

Cuisines	1990 %	2000 %	2011
Italian	23	22	20
Northern Italian	(73)	(41)	n.a.
Southern Italian	(16)	(10)	n.a.
Unspecified/both	(11)	(50)	n.a.
Pizza	2	3	8
Mediterranean	2	3	3
American (New)	below	10	below
American (Trad.)	15	6	21
Cajun/Creole	1	1	n.a.
Soul/Southern	2	2	4
Other Regional American	2	1	n.a.
French	15	13	7
Continental	5	2	1
Asian	-	1	n.a.
Chinese	6	4	4
Noodle shops	-	1	n.a.
Japanese	4	5	7
Korean	0	1	1
Thai	2	2	3
Vietnamese	0	1	1
Indian	2	2	4
Mexican	4	2	7
Nuevo Latino	-	0	n.a.
Tex-Mex	above	above	0
Spanish	1	2	2
Greek	0	1	2
Other	14	15	5
TOTAL	**100**	**100**	**100**

[1] Source: Zagat 1989, 1999, 2010.

[2] Number of restaurants counted multiple times under different cuisines.

TABLE 3.5 Menu theme as percentage of all restaurants in the National Restaurant Association sample (1984–2010)

Menu Theme	1984	1991		2000			2010		
	Restaurants with food & beverage %	Full Service %	Ltd Service %	More than $25 (ave. check) %	Bet. $25-15 (ave. check) %	Less than $15 (ave. check) %	More than $25 (ave. check) %	Bet. $25-$15 (ave. check) %	Less than $15 (ave. check) %
Steak/Seafood	25	17	-	38	26	8	23	18	1
American[2]	25	35	-	26	47	57	38	42	57
French/Continental	10	10	-	13	3	Other	Other	Other	Other
Italian	5	6	19	9	6	5	8	6	1
Pizza	3	n.a	n.a.	2	Other	3	2	3	6
Mexican	n.a.	n.a.	n.a.	2	2	5	1	6	5
Asian	n.a.	n.a.	n.a.	n.a.	n.a.	n.a.	3	6	3
Others[3]	32	32	81	12	18	22	26	19	27
TOTAL[4]	100	100	100	100	100	100	100	100	100

[1] Source: National Restaurant Association's *Restaurant Industry Operations Report* (Yearly). The Restaurant Association data has comparability problems over the years as the categories have been changing. Percentages are rounded to eliminate decimals.

[2] "American" includes American, chicken, barbeque, family style and variety.

[3] "Others" as a category here is expansive and includes Hamburgers, Sandwiches, and for the earlier years Mexican, Asian, Other Ethnic, and a number of Unspecifieds.

[4] Due to rounding, not all columns add up to 100.

"American" category increases to almost 60 percent as check averages fall to under $15—mostly hamburger joints, steak houses, and seafood places. Between 2000 and 2010, French/Continental restaurants fell from 13 percent in the class of the most expensive restaurants (where the French have always done the best), to below 2 percent, where they had to be subsumed within the "others" category.

Nevertheless, French restaurants do much better in Zagat's national survey of "America's Top Restaurants" (Table 3.6), in which between 19 and 25 percent of the restaurants serve French foods of various kinds, from Bistro to Classical French, with the former increasingly replacing the latter in popularity. Over

TABLE 3.6 Zagat: "America's Top Restaurants"

Cuisines	1992 (%)	2000 (%)	2010 (%)	2014 (%)
American	22	32	37	32
French	25	26	24	19
Continental	12	6	4	2
Italian	18	14	15	19
Asian	-	3	3	-
Chinese	5	2	2	1
Japanese	4	4	7	13
Mexican	3	2	1	2
Indian	1	1	1	1
Thai	2	1	1	2
Vietnamese	1	1	1	1
Cajun/Creole	3	2	2	2
Other American Regional	4	6	2	7
TOTAL	**100** (N=722)	**100** (N=883)	**100** (N=1,532)	**100** (N=1,478)

[1] The category of America's Top Restaurant was begun in 1992, hence that is the first year listed.

[2] Pizza included within Italian.

[3] When a restaurant is listed as Chinese and Vietnamese it is counted twice.

[4] Includes only those diacritically marked with ethnicity, nationality, and regionality. Does not include steak houses and seafood restaurants.

the years since Zagat began its list of America's Top Restaurants (1992), the number of Italian restaurants on that list hovered around 15 percent until 2014, when they caught up with French restaurants. The most dramatic improvement has been in the fate of "American" cuisine, especially the New American cuisine, with over 30 percent of diacritically marked restaurants identified within that category. Very clearly, a self-consciously American haute cuisine has been born in the last two decades, and interestingly at the same time it has begun to regionalize, notably into Louisianan, Californian, Southwestern, and Northwestern variants, especially in the leading cities of these regions, such as New Orleans, San Francisco, Phoenix, and Seattle respectively. In recent years, those regional variants have begun to settle under the category New American.

Astonishingly, only 3 Chinese restaurants and 7 Mexican restaurants are counted by Zagat among the top restaurants in the USA in 2014, compared to 59 Japanese, 84 French, 85 Italian and 139 American. There is not one Chinese or Mexican restaurant among the top in Los Angeles, San Francisco, New York, or even in San Antonio, and only one elite Mexican restaurant in Houston. It could be argued that Zagat is never very cutting-edge and is, in fact, behind the times. It is true that Zagat is the bearer of middle-brow taste among the professional middle classes, but that is what pays the bills of upscale restaurants in terms of volume and value. Given the economics of restauranting, that is the taste that counts, which makes the limited number of ethnic referents a relatively narrow distillation of a hierarchy of taste.

A reprise

If we paint the picture with the broadest brush-strokes, the changing accent of American cuisine can be explained by immigration patterns. We can identify three waves of migrants into the United States, totaling about 77 million until 2010. Looking at the picture from a high level of abstraction, hence ignoring the details and nuance, we can say that the dominant template for American food was provided by the first 20 million northern European immigrants, as can still be seen in the meat-and-potatoes complex, along with the hot dog, hamburger, dairy, sauerkraut, steak, pies and beer variant. Within this pattern, the distinctive food of the ethnics (defined as other peoples' food) such as the Germans, the Irish, and the Scandinavians was melted out of the national discourse. German, Irish, and Scandinavian gustatory identity was submerged in a white, Anglophone text, that was a hybrid for its time, but flattened out in posterity's view, so much so that we cannot much recall (from the vantage point of 2015) their distinctive foods anymore, other than as caricatures of excessive drinking—difference became drunkenness (in the case of the Irish). With some regional exceptions—small, local traditions such as pasties in the Upper Michigan peninsula, and Pennsylvania "Dutch" food—a relatively uniform national text was created by writing out the Native American and African-American gustatory experience.

Then came the next 20-odd million "ethnic" immigrants—Italians, Slavs, eastern European Jews, and Greeks—who wouldn't melt away. This was not because they were any more insistent than the first wave, but partly because of their sheer volume and concentration both in terms of space (northeastern cities) and time (1880–1924); equally because of their gravitation towards long-lasting ethnic enclaves; and to some degree because of their temporal proximity to our own times (so we can still see them as distinct). In addition, they retained their ethnic identities because just as their difference was about to be erased due to upward mobility and assimilation, their sectional identity was revivified by the ethnic resurgence that followed the Civil Rights Movement, both as a cultural ideal and as a retort to blackness. Americans discovered the virtues of quintessentially ethnic food—pizzas, pirogues, gyros, and bagels. They would eventually become so popular that new forms of corporate cuisine would be built on them. These immigrants would be absorbed into a different kind of whiteness—tamed but flavorful. In this story, Cajun/Creole cuisine would play a role in the symbolic reconciliation, on one hand, between an imagined national uniformity and regional particularity (often mediated through urban versus rural consciousness in the fraught contestations around the category of Creole, for instance), and on the other hand, between Black and White identity. The rest of America—including Zagat surveys—continues to conflate the polarities of this idealized reconciliation, of Cajun and Creole cuisines, to the great consternation of many a Louisiana local.

Interestingly, the cuisine of two racially marked groups, Chinese and Mexicans—two of the oldest "ethnic" groups in the USA—would both become ubiquitous and yet remain classified as permanently foreign foods, unlike pizzas or bagels. A survey of ethnic restaurants conducted by the National Restaurant Association in 1999 identified twenty different cuisines that Americans consider ethnic. Pizza places were excluded from the survey for having lost their ethnic affiliation. It also noted that "[s]ome cuisines are becoming so in-grained in the mainstream of US culture that they are hardly considered ethnic any more. This applies especially to certain forms of Italian, Mexican, and Chinese (Cantonese) cuisine" (NRA, 1999: 5). That is an optimistic view, because Americans might have trouble there both with race and with ideas about essentially different cooking—think pasta and *lomein* and their resonances. Difference could be disenfranchised even in the post-1960s world.

From 1924 to 1965—that is, for two generations with relatively few immigrants coming in (about 7 million over four decades compared to four times that figure before and after that period)—Americans would elaborate a naturalized and standardized American cooking, with the help of a new kind of mass media—radio and television. It is the food of this period that most Americans today would come to identify as unambiguously American food—Germanic food, often delivered by corporations, with a few ethnic accents. *Cuisine*, on the other hand, would be Continental, which would be a vague shorthand for the imagined food of European elites.

The next group of migrants—another 30 million or so—this time from the very places blocked by racialized laws of the pre-Civil Rights era, such as Asia, and driven by dispossession, such as in Latin America, would reach the American shores, destroying the layered sedimentations of the first and the second 20-millions. This would be the death of American food as we know it. Since we are still in the midst of this transformation, it is not yet normalized into a paradigm. The breaking of the established American mold would also allow the food of the ultimate racial Other—African-Americans—to be reinvented as Soul food. The ferment at the bottom would finally bubble up to the top to inflect American cuisine and destroy the established template (as I will elaborate in the next chapter). Difference would be democratized. In the process, Americans would find themselves in the midst of a reconfiguration of the culinary canon and Italian-Americans—ethnic but white—would play a crucial role in their reimaginings.

Italians and eastern European Jews, along with Greeks, Poles, Hungarians, and Southern blacks, have provided an opening for more recent ethnic groups to make their mark in American haute cuisine. In that sphere the importance of the Civil Rights Movement that taught Americans both toleration and the pleasures of cultural miscegenation cannot be underestimated. That movement is the single most important reason that Americans see so many Asian and Latino migrants in the United States today—a movement that made it impossible to discriminate on the basis of race in immigration laws. Now these newer immigrant groups have become the source of substantial innovation in American cuisine—mojitos, tacos, wraps, wantons, wasabi, and beyond. The Civil Rights Movement provided the cultural and legal opening, while Italians and Jews provided the networks and institutional opening in terms of establishing restaurants and producing their clientele and critics.

The demand for a new haute cuisine at the end of the twentieth century was met by a supply of entrepreneurs and workers from the segmented labor market that was patterned around ethnicity. For a long time, expensive American restaurants were run by French or German chefs partly because of the reputation of French and especially "Continental" cuisine. Neither of these groups could supply enough chefs to satiate the feeding frenzy of the last quarter of the twentieth century. As the French and German economies recovered from World War Two, the pool of emigrants dried up. New immigrants, old ethnics, and white American boys poured into this opening, often trained in the mushrooming cooking schools run by German transplants (Culinary Institute of America) and French expatriates (The French Culinary Institute, now ICC).

The United States had two dramatic advantages over almost any other nation, first, in terms of supplies of downscale ethnic talent that could be upscaled, and second, in the re-telling of their own national story as a history of immigration, which Handlin (1951) most clearly delineated. American history would be re-oriented from the frontier towards immigration, and in the process American culture would be reimagined as an immigrant one, where foreign cultures are seen to be absorbed into and radically transform American taste. That is a rare script of self-understanding in global comparative terms. It is rare to find the natives of another nation—including their historians—who are willing to see their own culture as a relatively recent foreign one. Other national narratives are much more grounded in their rooted imaginations, often ignoring migrant cultures. Which is also why literal taste, in those national domains, is separated from aesthetic taste, to insulate the latter from the cross-border contamination and the groundswell from below.

One group of ethnics in the USA was particularly well-positioned to take advantage of this opening—Italian-Americans. Italian food was slowly rediscovered in America by way of northern Italy, which followed Milan's and Florence's style-setting standard in the world of haute couture, and was aided by the upward mobility of Italian-Americans. The resurgent reputation of Italian food was only one half of the equation. There had to be a supply of chefs. And not everybody was willing to be a chef, not yet.

American Jews had climbed up and out of the business of feeding others that they had mastered at the end of the nineteenth century in the delicatessens (where they had succeeded the Germans) and the hot dog stands. Because of much higher rates of literacy, second- and third-generation Jews quickly moved into City College and out of the delis. They entered the retail trades of healing and litigation, which were now closed, college-certified professions (Steinberg 1989).

Italians moved in to replace the Jews, the Germans, and the occasional French. As professionals, particularly in trend-setting eastern cities such as New York, the Jewish cohort moved quickly from being suppliers of ethnic food in delis and at hot dog stands, to consumers of the cuisine of others, such as Italians and Chinese. Italians, on the other hand, burdened as they were with much lower rates of literacy and with a rural background, continued to be the producers of some of the best American food and wine. There would be no renaissance of American haute cuisine without Italian suppliers of California wine, local herbs, and produce, or as producers of transplanted regional Italian cuisines in American cities. Nor would there be an American cuisine without Jewish consumers, including food writers, commentators, and restaurant critics (Steinberg 1989).

Chinese, Italians, and Greeks could dominate certain niches of the food-service market because of ethnic ties in the labor market. These three ethnic groups included large numbers of male sojourners, who created both a high demand for eating places and a willingness to do the necessary jobs. Some, like the Forty-Niner Chinese in California, had been driven out of other spheres of profitable economic activity, such as gold-mining and farming, by violence and race-based legislation, leaving them to cook and clean for male, white miners who were willing to concede such feminized functions to the Orientals. Therein hangs a fascinating tale of the Chinese take-out and the laundry.

For much of the twentieth century, the American restaurant world appeared to prefer French chefs and Italian maîtres d'hôtel, often working for Italian owners made invisible by the French names of their restaurants—a tradition that would slip into the twenty-first century with Sirio Maccioni's *Le Cirque*; a tradition akin to Chinese owners of sushi establishments today and Bangladeshi proprietors of Indian eateries. The clientele could not figure out the difference, and the prestige of French, Japanese, and Indian food was higher, mostly for non-culinary reasons. Yet it was much more expensive to hire a French, Japanese, or Indian chef because of the demographic profile of immigrants from these nations. In contrast, a poorer, working-class migration from Italy, China, and Bangladesh fed the supply side of the labor market equation for these establishments.

Yet many ethnic eateries are unsuccessful in remaining in business for long because they are under-capitalized and cannot weather the inevitable fluctuations of the market, and they often run out of luck on the fragile wager on endless over-work and perpetual good health. Those who succeed, such as Muhammad Rasool (introduced in Chapter 2), send their children to college who, on completion, are unwilling to accumulate sweat capital because of better credentials. If they stay in business it is because they have better connections, English language capability, and assets to trade in, creating a more upscale business where returns are greater. A typical route is from the successful pizzeria or diner to a white tablecloth restaurant.

The nature of the American economy is such that it is fed by a workforce both at the bottom as dish-washers and farm-workers and at the top as physicians, software engineers, nurses and professors. These new American immigrants are numerous, they come from many more places, with many more cultural tools, and some come with much more class power along with their professional skills. As they enter a relatively democratic cultural landscape after the Civil Rights Movement, it is easier for them to make a mark quickly than it was for, say, Italians, Jews, or Southern blacks in northern cities at the beginning of the twentieth century. Many of these professionals not only have money but are also Anglophone, a major advantage in the cultural dog-eat-dog of ethnic succession.

I have made a handful of points in this chapter. First, I have sought to enumerate the changes in American cuisine, specifically the rise of Italian-American food, by counting what can be counted. Second, changing sources of migration have both changed the supply of cooks and transformed our palates. I have identified a pattern of ethnic succession in food work. I have also noted that too much or too little upward mobility is bad for leaving a mark on American fine dining.

Entrepreneurial activity in the food business is particularly amenable to the theory that the economic system is embedded in the larger normative networks that Karl Polanyi (1944) drew our attention to. Ethnic entrepreneurs buy and sell stuff that makes no sense without the cultural envelope. Edible commodities in particular have elaborate social lives. That is an insight reaffirmed by cultural anthropologists working on material culture and the social life of things (Miller 1987; Appadurai 1986).

Finally, to begin to understand the changing resonances of ethnicity and race, and hence ethnic food, one has to understand these classification systems—race and ethnicity—as discursive fields, where for instance the Irish did not change their color but did become white in the course of the Civil War (Ignatiev 1995) and hence never developed a gustatory identity distinct from the normative white culture (see Diner 2001; Ray 2004: 101–14). While Jews, once considered a different race because of their religious identity, are in the process of becoming white (Brodkin 1998) and due to rapid upward mobility (thus uninterested in the investment of sweat capital in running a restaurant) are losing their capacity to retain their culinary identity as a mark of difference, while Italians continue to bring a different kind of whiteness to bear on their food, which has as much to do with class as race. The demographic weight and the middleness of Italian migrants, as white but not quite, plays well in the current contours of the fine dining market. With time, that will pass too.

Immigrant restaurateurs have been crucial to the changing transaction in taste in American cities, although they have often found the hierarchy of taste, based on notions of race, nation, and ethnicity, insurmountable. Culture, it seems, follows global and social capital, and flees from the contamination of labor. Yet, it is also clear that American tastes have been opening up, and that has led to important changes in haute cuisine (as we will see in the next chapter). The question remains whether palatal taste will be a carrier of more durable progressive changes, as the domain of music (aural aesthetics) was to social movements of the last century.

Notes

1. For robust epistemological questions about big data, small data, and no data, and ways of using and accessing them see Moretti 2013 and Borgman 2015.
2. According to Andrew Smith in "1900 there were 42,700 tenement buildings in New York, housing almost 1.6 million people" (2014: 133).
3. "Ethnic restaurant" can be found 273 times in all documents in *The New York Times* from 1851 to 2013, including classifieds, articles, reviews, etc. On the other hand, if we limit the search only to articles and reviews we get fifty-one hits.
4. "Ethnic food" appears 631 times in all documents, and on 368 instances in articles and reviews, from 1851 to 2013.
5. Per capita income, rounded to the thousand, by ancestry in NYC in 2010 was, from the top: English $70,000, German $60,000, Russian $55,000, French $54,000, Irish $50,000, Polish $50,000, Italian $40,000, Filipino $35,000, Korean $33,000, Greek $33,000, Asian Indian $28,000, Arab $28,000, West Indian $24,000, Colombian $22,000, Chinese $22,000, Puerto Rican $18,000, Dominican $14,000, Mexican $13,000, etc. (New York City Department of City Planning 2010).
6. In the rest of this section, due to constraints of space, I am only going to address Mexican immigrants and their food, with almost nothing to say about other Spanish-speaking Caribbeans such as Puerto Ricans, Cubans, and Dominicans, with their distinct cuisine of plantains, yucca (cassava), pork, and rice and beans; their domination of the bodega business in New York City; and the *cuchifritos* (snack stands) and *La Marqueta* (covered food market) of *El Barrio* or Spanish Harlem. Janer (2008) notes that a number of things are transformed with Latino food businesses in the United States. First, specialized food stores such as Mexican bakeries tend to broaden their offerings to include Salvadoran and Guatemalan breads and pastries to expand their market. Second, what are often considered street foods such as Puerto Rican fritters like *bacalaítos* and *alcapurrias* appear as appetizers at lunch counters and restaurants. Third, elaborate and occasional dishes such as complex moles and rich desserts, often prepared only for Christmas, Lent, and family celebrations, are available all the time in the post-migration context. These three directions of change are, she argues, what gives the appearance of unhealthiness of many Latino diets, along with the excessive use of soft drinks in place of fruit juices (Janer 2008: 102, 142).
7. Jeffrey Pilcher, personal communication, October 14, 2012.
8. The First Wave begins with Delmonico's; the Second Wave with Le Pavillon; the Third Wave with *Chez Panisse*; and the Fourth Wave, internationally, with El Bulli, and nationally, with Momofuku.
9. Thanks to CIA archivist Christine Crawford-Oppenheimer and chefs Eve Felder and Charles Rascoll for explaining the fine points of the changing curriculum to me in 2004.

4

Extending Expertise: Men in White at the Culinary Institute of America

Ethnic food is the shattered mirror of haute cuisine. To comprehend the disparate, fragmented domains of ethnic food, which has no center other than its difference from the consecrated cooking of professional experts, it is necessary to hold up that mirror of difference. The divergence between native cooking and expert training is what provincializes one and universalizes the other. Such difference is shaped by the very structure of the modern world along lines of race, gender, and nation. To produce a profession it is necessary to ensure a tightly coiled, small world that is heavily networked with strong ties, well policed along its boundaries, and good at excluding others who might be engaged in similar activities as seen from the outside, but will be perceived as dramatically different from the inside. So let us take a look at the small world of professional chefs, the mirror-image of the ethnic cook and the home cook.

On November 18, 2013, chefs David Chang, Alex Atala, and René Redzepi graced the cover of *Time* magazine under the title "The Gods of Food".[1] The lead article "The Dudes of Food," sketched elaborate family trees of chefs that did not contain a single woman. Of the fifty-eight named chefs on those family trees, fifty-four are European, American, or Australian, one Japanese (Seiji Yamamoto of Nihonryori), one Mexican (Enrique Olvera of Pujol), and one Chilean (Rodolfo Guzman of Boragó).[2] Similarly, the top ten chefs among the 50 Best Restaurants in the World selected by San Pellegrino in 2013 were all white men (with the exception of Elena Arzak Espina, who is co-listed with Juan Mari Arzak).[3] At number twenty on the San Pellegrino list we have the first non-white face, Yoshihiro Narisawa, who cooks French-style food in Tokyo, and then at number twenty-two we have Seiji Yamamoto cooking real Japanese food at Nihonryori RyuGin in Tokyo. Narisawa also leads the San Pellegrino list of Asia's 50 Best Restaurants, where French techniques are celebrated with Japanese ingredients, according to the *Wall Street Journal* (Chow 2014). In the same way, the Culinary Institute of America's ProChef Smart Brief news feed repeatedly engages with the Asian culinary scene, especially highlighting chefs from Japan, Hong Kong, and Singapore, yet rarely extending that attention to China, Indonesia, the rest of Southeast Asia, India, or all of Africa, partly because chefs from those regions have been unable or unwilling to pull themselves into the global hierarchy of dominant culinary discourse. With token exceptions, those regions do not play in the global culinary discourse because they cook and talk differently from what counts in the social field of culinary capital. Similarly, none of the showcased chefs on the 2014 San Pellegrino's 50 Best Restaurants in the World list are African, New World Black, Indian, or from the Chinese mainland—that is, a population base of about 3 billion people—and only two of the listed chefs are women, always paired with a man.[4] That is an astonishing distillation of the heights of a social field. Yet, that kind of narrow multi-nationalism standing in for the whole world isn't substantially different from, say the world literary space as structured from the sixteenth- to the twentieth century, centered on Paris and delineated by Pascale Casanova (2005b; on films see Schwartz 2007). The elimination of women from such a pantheon is not accidental. It is constitutive of professionalizing moves in an emergent field as I will show below. What is equally interesting is not only those who are excluded but the difference that is systematically included.

The Time Magazine controversy comes years after Charlotte Druckman's pointed observation in *Gastronomica* titled "Why Are There No Great Women Chefs?" which begins by quoting the art critic Linda Nochlin on "Why Have There Been No Great Women Artists?" that things are in art as they are in a hundred different areas, excluding and discouraging all those "who did not have the good fortune to be born white, preferably middle class, and above all male" (Druckman 2010; Nochlin 1971). The matter hinges on how "great" is defined and by whom, and in doing so affirms what Nochlin already suspected in posing the question. Druckman noticed that *Food & Wine*'s annual roundup of ten Best New Chefs always listed one token woman. It took fifty-five years for Michelin to offer the third star to a woman chef, in 2007 (to Anne-Sophie Pic). It is a remarkable delineation of the chef's world that apparently counts in the world of chefs today (and in numerous other professions). Julia Moskin notes that "All groups except for white men are underrepresented at the top of the profession" (Moskin 2014: D6). By one account, at the Metropolitan Museum, "5 percent of the artists in the Modern Art sections are women, but 85 percent of the nudes are female" (Eberstadt 2014: 1).

For a decade, the top of the field was occupied by Ferran Adrià and his restaurant El Bulli. In 1996, Joël Robuchon, often counted as the top chef among professionals, named Adrià as the best chef in the world, sending ripples through the French establishment. El Bulli itself is an older restaurant, established in 1961. Adrià was picked to run it in 1987, garnering three Michelin stars by 1997. *Restaurant* magazine listed it as the number one restaurant in the world in 2002. In 2003, Arthur Lubow consolidated Adrià's position with the cover story, "The Neuva Nouvelle Cuisine: How Spain Became the New France," in which he quoted Charlie Trotter saying "Spain is where the zeitgeist has shifted" (Lubow 2003). Adrià, born in Barcelona, is a cerebral-celebrity chef. "But, if you deconstruct him the way he deconstructs food, you discover that he is also an artist, a scientist, an inventor, a stage director, a designer, a philosopher, an anarchist and, to a degree that some of his more solemn admirers maybe fail to grasp, Coco the Clown" (Guardian 2006). An illustration of his much talked-about technique is the way Adrià breaks down a Spanish omelet into eggs, potatoes, and onions, and then reconstructs it into a layered potato foam, onion purée, and egg-white sabayon, topped with deep-fried potato crumbs, served inside a sherry glass, ironically and evocatively named tortilla español. Molecular gastronomists' ability to deceive dinners with professional excellence and artifice is a deliciously baroque counterpoint to the demands for transparency, authenticity, and honesty—which we can name as the *Chez Panisse* Paradigm—that have become the orthodoxy in the new haute cuisine, returning us to the trade's Early Modern conception of artistry as artifice (Davis 2013: 13).

This kind of reconstructive-cerebral cooking is shaping even so-called traditionalists. That attitude, if not those techniques, are becoming *de rigueur* for inclusion in the field as players. Massimo Bottura, chef-owner of the three-Michelin-starred restaurant Osteria Francescana in Modena, Italy, and listed as the number three restaurant on the World's Best Restaurant List (such improbable lists are signs of the times), underlines that it is his friendship with top chefs around the world that is forcing him to open up his mind without losing his footing.

> When I'm in New York, I go to my friends' restaurants—people like David Chang, Daniel [Boulud], Mario [Battali], Wylie Dufresne, the Torrisi brothers and [Alain] Ducasse if he's in town. Things have changed over the last ten years in gastronomy—chefs don't close their kitchens to other chefs anymore. It's about sharing. We travel all over the world and share techniques, experiences and ideas with one another . . . Contemporary cuisine is not just about the ingredients—it's also about the quality of the ideas. At Osteria Francescana, I look to the past all the time, but not in a

> nostalgic way—in a critical way, to bring the best from the past into the future (Silberman 2013).

Most importantly, the contemporary chef that counts is the one in the network of chefs who references others (as peer reviewers), and that is a miniscule and uneven network in global terms.

In 2010, Noma, René Redzepi's restaurant in Copenhagen, Denmark, replaced El Bulli at the top of *Restaurant* magazine's San Pellegrino World's 50 Best Restaurants, which is determined by "800 international leaders in the restaurant industry, each selected for their expert opinion of the international restaurant scene" (San Pellegrino 2010). As in the fashion world it is a very competitive field, with new restaurants replacing recent brands and icons. In some ways Noma can be considered the anti-El Bulli, with its intense attention to micro-locality and seasonally attuned produce such as truffles from Gotland (a region of Denmark), "woodruff, beach mustard and Caldonia lichen" (Redzepi 2010), often served on rocks to further authenticate a Nordic landscape—food closely tied to its time and place, instead of the transnational technocuisine of foam, liquid nitrogen, and deconstruction. Yet, Noma and El Bulli are a pair from the same small universe.

Judgments of good food in these instances, as in analogous aesthetic fields such as book reviewing and art criticism, are determined in small circles through processes of "double-reading," first as a civilian with a gut reaction, followed by an analysis of technique, skill, and innovation where the emotional response is turned into an object of scrutiny with distancing criticism, recursive evaluation, and evidence-based reviewing, borrowing protocols from a science of subjectivity (Shapin 2012; Leschziner and Green 2013; Chong 2013). Ashley Kosiak, a student of mine, noted, "Similar to clothing fashion, in haute cuisine the chef replaces the designer, is praised by the expert critic (analogous to *Vogue's* Anne Wintour), and is discussed and coveted by the general audience. Just as I will not be eating at Noma, I cannot afford the latest items from new designers such as Zara Gorman and Nabil El-Nayal. Yet they do shape the limits of my horizon" (Kosiak 2011).

El Bulli (now closed) and Noma represent the changing shape of the field on which the chef now plays in global cities; as entrepreneur, technician, ideologue, aesthete, moralist, artist, artisan, and a designer in the current language of haute cuisine. The new American chef occupies as spectacular a position in the field as an Adrià or Redzepi, in a quickly re-configuring domain headed by figures such as Thomas Keller, Wylie Dufresne, and David Chang (as I will elaborate on in the next chapter). As in any overheated and fashionable field, the list is outdated as soon as it is made. That, in fact, is a sign of a field in upward motion in the social world. Yet, this tide is not lifting all boats.

Alan Richman has noted in *GQ* that this new-style cooking is "entirely male" (2014). "I found no exceptions," he writes,

> Not once have I seen a female chef prepare such food. Men have always dominated restaurant kitchens, but I don't recall ever encountering such gender-specific cooking. The chefs work with like-minded discipline, hardly ever haunted by doubts, seemingly in possession of absolute confidence, to say nothing of the adoration of customers. Nobody is telling them what they might be doing wrong. The food is intellectual, yet at the same time often thoughtless (Richman 2014).

As Roosth shows in her ethnographic work in Herve This's laboratory in "Foams and Formalisms" (2013), when the terms of aesthetic judgment shifts to molecules and chemistry from culture and practice, we have the accentuation of scientism (which is more than science), masculinization, and demonization of "old wives' tales"—a not so subtle reference to outdated practices of old women, who are incidentally the very people who do most of the cooking in the world, everywhere. This masculine scientism of molecular gastronomy takes to the limit and essentially differentiates the gendered address of those involved in cooking and care-giving (for analogous analysis of birthing and cooking, see Katz-Rothman 2016).

The new American chef is born in spaces between three positions: the (female) domestic cook, the (colored male) ethnic cook, and the (white or Asian male) professional chef. In the public domain the untrained cook and the school-trained American chef are precise foils of each other. Interviews with immigrant restaurateurs working in the domain of "ethnic cuisine" underline that they do not inhabit the same field as American chefs in the making, which leads me, in the next section, to re-interrogate the struggle for professionalism at the institutional heart of American haute cooking. This community of insiders, that some immigrant cooks with haute aspirations struggle to be admitted into, as we will see in the next chapter, is in itself a work in progress of extending expertise most typically for white American and Asian-American men. Institutional standards of cooking and critical analysis, along with criteria of social judgment, are built within its perimeter boundaries and internal hierarchies at the Culinary Institute of America (CIA), which is one exemplary institution where American cooks become chefs by acquiring new tastes, obtaining fresh words to articulate them, gaining novel cooking skills, attaining new morals and identities. It is at the CIA that working-class white men often acquire unaccustomed social demeanor that marks them as radically different subjects from housewives and ethnic cooks.

Cooking skills and confidence

Chef Tim Ryan, the current President of the CIA, noted that by 1996 he was wondering whether it was time to update the curriculum: in particular, if it was still useful to teach the classical French mother sauces. Yet, as he surveyed his friends and colleagues in the restaurant industry, he said, they were unanimous. He doesn't recall a single person who believed that the training at the CIA ought to change. Each asserted that the skills associated with mastering Carême's and Escoffier's mother sauces were essential (Ruhlman 1997: 262; personal conversations with Ryan).

Celebration of mother sauces has a long history in gastronomy. French journalist Curnonsky (born Maurice Edmond Sailland), author, with Marcel Rouff, of the authoritative thirteen volume *La France gastronomique* (1921–8), and perhaps the most celebrated gastronomic writer of the early twentieth century, had declared "Sauces comprise the honor and glory of French cookery. They have contributed to its superiority, or pre-eminence, which is disputed by none. Sauces are the orchestration and accompaniment of a fine meal, and enable a good chef or cook to demonstrate his talent" (Lang 1988: 939). In the *Guide Culinaire*, August Escoffier, noting the importance of stocks and sauces made from them, states "Indeed, stock is everything in cooking, at least in French cooking. Without it, nothing can be done" (Escoffier 1989: 1). The famed French sauces under discussion here had superseded the spiced sweet-and-sour medieval sauces based on verjuice and wine that often relied on garum, spikenard, cloves, etc.

According to the fifth edition of *The New Professional Chef*, which was being reworked with precise and painstaking detail by the CIA staff during my tenure there, the "grand sauces—demi-glace, velouté, béchamel, tomato, and hollandaise—were once referred to as the mother sauces, to indicate that from these basic sauces many others were created" (CIA 1991: 297). It noted parenthetically that "Although they may not be relied upon as heavily as in years past, the grand sauces are still important in a contemporary kitchen" (CIA 1991: 297). Then it goes on to show how demi-glace (a brown sauce, itself made from sauce Espagnole), for instance, can be the root of numerous other sauces such as poivrade (with a red wine reduction, peppercorns, and butter), chasseur (mushrooms, shallot, white wine, tomato glace), Robert (with white wine, onions, mustard, and butter), charcutière (Robert sauce plus julienne of gherkins) and so on. Sauce Espagnole, the root of the root in this case, is made by sweating a mirepoix of one portion of onions, and one half portion of carrots, one half portion of celery, and tomato puree, sautéed lightly until caramelized. Then brown roux is added, brown veal stock thoroughly incorporated, simmered up to three hours, skimmed, strained, cooled, and stored for later use. By the eighth edition, *The Professional Chef* allows that

"Not all commercial kitchens prepare stocks today, either because meaty bones and trim are not readily available on a consistent basis or because they do not have the space or manpower to successfully prepare and hold stocks" (CIA 2006: 350). After recommending evaluation of commercial sauces (called bases) centered on flavor, saltiness, balance, and depth, it provides short cuts to deepen their flavor by sweating or roasting vegetables and simmering them in diluted bases, "perhaps along with browned trim, to make a rich brown sauce" (CIA 2006: 350).

By 2006, CIA's President Ryan would change his mind (a little), in terms of the necessary techniques of sauce-making, with new focus on Asian and Latin American ingredients, techniques, and grammars of cooking. The 2006 edition of *The Professional Chef* devotes three extraordinary chapters to various regions outside the typical focus of Francophile cuisine. Chapter 5, titled "The Americas," includes ingredients, recipes, and cuisines of various regions of the USA, Mexico, and South America. Chapter 6 attends to the special ingredients and techniques from various parts of Asia such as China, India, Japan, Korea, the Middle East, and Southeast Asia. Chapter 7, "Europe," begins with France and Italy, but extends to other parts of the Mediterranean, eastern and central Europe, Spain, and Portugal. By 2006, robust new recipes are added, such as for dashi stock, as one of the foundations of cuisine, while pestos and pastas proliferate, as do more down-home American cooking such as ham bone and collard greens. Daring new soups are added to the repertoire such as the Chinese *suan la tang*, Korean *yukkaejang*, Japanese miso, Thai chicken soup with coconut milk and galangal, wonton soup, and Vietnamese pho, as well as newer regional Italian variants such as minestrone *alla emilia*, and Tuscan white bean and escarole soup. The Mise en Place section by now includes not only the *fines herbes* (chervil, chives, parsley, tarragon) and *quatre épices* (black peppercorns, nutmeg, cinnamon, cloves), but also a variant of garam masala (cardamom, coriander, cumin, cinnamon, cloves, black peppercorns, nutmeg, and bay leaves), Chinese five-spice (star anise, fennel, Szechuan peppercorns, cloves, and cinnamon), barbecue spice mix, chilli powder, curry powder, red, green, and yellow curry pastes, and various Asian-style marinades. Yet nouvelle French cuisine techniques remain the anchor of the curriculum.[5] And that is because those procedures belong to the very language of American haute cuisine, in spite of some new skills, new ingredients, and new kinds of people that have forced their way into the field. To insiders it looks like epochal change, to outsiders a mere ripple.

Most importantly, a specific set of technical standards are developed, formalized, and replicated at an institution such as the CIA. Let us take the example of a consommé. I stumbled right at the gate as I started work with a young, widely respected, and talented chef at the CIA. First, I did not know that a consommé is really a double consommé, as it is the reduction and clarification of a stock (which is a kind of a consommé). We began with a gallon of brown stock (made from browned veal bones, water, standard mirepoix—onion, carrots, and celery—tomato puree, salt, and the standard sachet d'épices containing parsley stems, dried thyme leaves, bay leaf, cracked peppercorns, and crushed garlic cloves) intensified and reduced to a quart. We made a small onion brûlé (a caramelized onion half), chopped up another round of mirepoix, and added eight ounces of ground beef-shank, three beaten egg whites, and four ounces of tomato concassé to the stock, sprinkling it with salt and milled cracked pepper. The fire was turned up and the contents stirred, but just before boiling-point was reached—measured by intermittent lazy bubbles reaching the surface—left to simmer on low heat for a good hour (note that the stock had already taken about eight hours to make the previous day). As if that wasn't subtle enough the chef insisted that much depends on whether the tomatoes were fresh or canned. If they were hothouse tomatoes in the winter, they wouldn't have adequate acidity, so he used canned tomatoes, and perhaps even added a little white wine or lemon juice to accentuate the acidity. Midway through the process of making a consommé, a mess of muddled beef, egg whites, and mirepoix floats up to the top of the cooking stock as a raft. That is about halfway to the concentration of flavor. Eventually, the raft is removed and the remaining stock strained to be served as consommé in beautiful china with a soup spoon.

The standard for a legitimate consommé is clear. "Rule of thumb: you can read the date on a dime at the bottom of a gallon" (Ruhlman 1997: 40). This kind of stringency, specificity, replicability, is what is central to haute cuisine and unnecessary and unimaginable for everyday home cooking. That stringency of standard and hence evaluation goes hand in hand with accentuating skill. Any form of doing that exits the household to become a specialized task conducted in a specialized institution and remunerated, as has happened with spinning, weaving, cooking, childcare, elder care, and health care, leads to the development of new techniques in that field precisely because of specialization (focus, attention, resources) and competitive concentration from other professionals, which is at the very heart of any specialist "field." So as cooking leaves the domestic kitchen and the cookshop, the skills required to cook also change, along with the gender and ethnicity of the cook.

Pierre Franey, arguably the American century's original foreign-born celebrity French chef, asserts that on May 9, 1939, he was extremely confident, at the opening of the World's Fair in Flushing Meadows, Queens, New York, when he, along with a dozen chefs, launched the Restaurant Français at the Pavillon de France:

> Marius Isnard, the *chef de cuisine*, was calm. The sous-chefs and the *chefs de parties* at each station were in their element. As were we all. When you

> learn to work in a French restaurant, you submit to a militaristic organization. Even with a team of 150 workers, most of whom had not worked together before, the assignments were so well defined that we knew precisely what to do and how to behave (Franey 2010: 79).

This feeling of confidence and calm in the most overheated haute kitchen in New York City, shared by the son of a village blacksmith, a self-declared "rube" from St. Vinnemer in Burgundy, is extraordinary. The confidence did not come easily or naturally. It came after decades of hard work in kitchens and the embodiment of national propaganda about a cuisine. Much social work had to go into it. First, the very idea of France and its productive provinces had to be consolidated. French cuisine had to become a hegemonic practice in the profession. Most importantly, the required skills, shared nomenclature, and evaluative criteria of an established and consecrated practice had to be embodied.

The confidence was a by-product of the competence to produce and evaluate a shared repertoire of cuts, stocks, sauces, braises, roasts, and desserts. Among these was the skill of clarification of the consommé: basic work repeated by every commis and trained chef until it is internalized, but which is almost never demanded in any institution other than the haute French cuisine restaurant. Franey had done the work of clarifying the stock every day since he joined the staff at Thenin, a Parisian restaurant, at age fourteen in 1934. The cold beef or chicken stock would be poured into a four feet high pot. It would be heated and stirred, adding a mixture of egg whites, carrot trimmings, leeks, crushed eggshells, bones, herbs, and spices. He spent hours stirring and scraping the mixture with a ladle. Three hours later, drawing the consommé out through a spigot at the bottom of the pot, he would leave the floating impurities on top. He would learn to produce, evaluate, and affirm that the consommé, which "is one of the glories of French cooking," is pure "artistry and perfection" (Franey 2010: 40–1). "A consommé cannot have the slightest hint of cloudiness; it must be rich in flavor, even though it is so light in its appearance. A splendid consommé, perhaps garnished with diced vegetables, serves as the opening act for the rest of the meal" (Franey 2010: 41).

A generation later, coming up through the ranks of a three-year apprenticeship, Jacques Pépin's scandalous error at Le Grand Hôtel de l'Europe was to stir a ten-gallon pot of consommé barely simmering in the back of the kitchen, catastrophically muddying it (Pépin 2003: 56). By his seventeenth birthday, barely six months out of his apprenticeship, Pépin would nevertheless acquire the "confidence" to run his own restaurant at L'Hôtel Restaurant de la Paix at Bellegarde, twenty miles west of Geneva at the foot of the Jura Mountains, due to his mastery of standard culinary fare, all culled from his "Bible" of *Le Répertoire de la cuisine*, first published by Gringoire and Saulnier in 1914 and containing more than seven thousand classic recipes of the pre-nouvelle French cuisine (Pépin 2003: 69, 99).

Almost a century later, students at the Culinary Institute of America would effectively have the same sort of training, evaluative schema, and ideological posture towards the consommé. It would be one of the bases upon which a profession and its shared standards would be built. Franey could have been extremely confident only because on the first night of the World's Fair in 1939 the menu at the Pavillon de France restaurant opened with a double consommé de viveur, followed by Paillettes dorées, Homard Pavillon de France, etc. (all written in restaurant French). On that list was everything he had made before, at least a thousand times, even though he was only an eighteen-year-old cook in a foreign land where his mother tongue was otherwise useless. By the end of that opening season he would have served 136,261 customers precisely. Two other stepping stones would send him careening on his way to stardom. One would be a network of elite regulars at Le Pavillon and Le Côte Basque—American restaurants born from the French Pavilion at the World's Fair—such as the President of the American chain Howard Johnson, who would hire him as a Vice President and assign him their test kitchen, and another his friendship with *The New York Times*'s first full-time and consecrated restaurant critic Craig Claiborne, a little under twenty years after the opening of the World's Fair. The chef needed the right patron and media exposure to become one.

Skills have to be learned, palates developed, criteria for evaluation established, and bodies trained to cut, chop, and roast, in the process altering posture, gesture, language, and demeanor. An ethnic cook by definition does not play in the same field with the same tools or shared evaluative schema. He belongs to smaller, fragmented, incommensurable, unregulated culinary domains that are unaccounted for, which is precisely what makes him ethnic. He also does not belong to the same networks of patronage and media coverage.

Chef Eve Felder, one of the leading visionaries at the CIA, now the Director of their Singapore campus, and a remarkably talented chef from that Third-Wave temple of new American restaurant cuisine, *Chez Panisse*, is clear that teaching professional cooking is about instructing students on ingredients, ratios, and techniques. Techniques include knife skills, butchery, stock and sauce making, cooking proteins just right, mixing flavors, counterposing textures. The object is to do all that according to standards agreed upon by professional chefs playing in the field of haute international cuisine, formalized in the early years of the twentieth century by French practitioners and ideologues such as August Escoffier. They were updated in the second half of the twentieth century by Paul Bocuse, the Lyonnaise chef, who is often considered the father of the last influential wave of nouvelle French cuisine (with a strong Japanese inflection, especially in plate presentation) that has rippled through the world of professional cooking (see Ferguson 2004; Rao, Monin, and Durand 2003; Ferguson and Zukin 1998; Fischler 1989, 1993).

Escoffier's cookbooks present what has been done or what ought to be done; a constant need to play by the book, nothing outlandish, and to perpetually aspire to perfection (Schmidt 1974: 184). For a quarter century now, Escoffier has been replaced by Bocuse, but the aspiration to a perfect world is as insistent. Perfection can be the horizon only in a profession, real to the field of ambition, delusional in terms of real life. We will return to this point with Thomas Keller in the next chapter.

Bocuse's oeuvre is being overtaken right now, which makes it the precise moment to institutionally commemorate his location in the genealogy of the profession. That transition is marked at the CIA by changing the name of the flagship French restaurant, from Escoffier to Bocuse (on February 22, 2013). It bookends the last transition, just as the Escoffier Room was born in 1974, precisely when Bocuse had already replaced Escoffier as the new ideologue of the profession. The Bocuse—the new restaurant at the CIA—was designed by Adam Tihany, transforming an outdated, classically oriented space that students referred to as the E-Room, into a sharply modern twenty-first-century restaurant that looks a lot like a Per Se or a Daniel. Mark Erickson, the institute's provost, noted that in the new kitchen, old hierarchies and "separation of the classic stations of the original Escoffier" would no longer be maintained, and that at "Bocuse, sauces, sautéing and vegetable preparation will be done at several stations, and there will be much more collaboration among the cooks" (Collins 2012). The relationship between ingredients and menus is reversed now, where seasonal ingredients, the newly canonized ideology of the profession, determines the menu, rather than the dynamic of "old times" when menus demanded canned asparagus to showcase the hollandaise. Today, there is no out-of-season asparagus. Yet, not everything echoes the new agrarian ideal. Newly ascendant techno-emotional cuisine with its distinctive foams, spherifications, gels, crumbs, powders, etc. also registers at the CIA, especially in the new Bachelors of Professional Studies (BPS) in Culinary Science (since 2013). As a result, The Bocuse restaurant accommodates a new brigade station with the sous vide, a technique of cooking at steady low temperatures in sealed vacuum bags, marking the current concordat between technological triumphalism, scientism, new urbanity, and re-configured rurality.

Teaching professional cooking in New York means reiterating and reinterpreting institutional standards of various nouvelle cuisines that have emerged in dialogue and disagreement with Escoffier's institutional standards over the long-twentieth century (ca. 1880–1999) in various waves of novelty. It also means repeating the dishes and techniques over and over again to make such standards a habit, second nature, even while developing new translations of old principles and practices. That is an exercise that can go awry without discipline.

An important but understudied aspect of teaching professional cooking in the US is to address the social dimension of professional cooking embedded in broader hierarchies of class, gender, race, and ethnicity. In a sense students are trained by routines that turn them into chefs and particular kinds of men and women. In the following pages I will develop the connection between cooking and social hierarchies. As a result I will retrace the pedagogical processes of producing such functioning bodies at the heart of American institutional haute cuisine, with particular attention to what has to be excised, excluded, transcended, and inculcated to make the new American chef, who is the foil for the ethnic cook and the home cook. The discourse of haute cuisine and the practice of restaurant cookery overwhelmingly produce male, white, international chefs, where "international" is the opposite of the domestic ethnic. Here power is productive: both within institutions such as the CIA and outside of them, it produces skilled hands and certain kinds of social subjects. Skills come implicated in normative hierarchies.

Yet that is not the whole story. The nature of professionalization depends on time and place: the sociocultural ecology, so to speak. Masculine and racist scripts that worked, say, for American physicians at the end of the nineteenth century, could not work for chefs at the end of the twentieth century, because the legal and cultural context had changed. That is an important difference. It is a subtle act of normalizing and neutralizing race and gender, as is the demand in every profession today. As the world around the CIA has been changed by waves of feminism and civil rights movements, excessively grandiloquent versions of white masculinity have become impediments to the upward mobility of chefs. Organizational leaders at the CIA have been struggling to change the character of the chef-in-making and his associated habitus. The rest of this chapter is devoted to that enterprise of extending technical and social expertise of a class of people who historically come from the working class but ideologically and materially serve the upper classes.

Teaching at the Culinary Institute of America: Disciplining bodies

When I began teaching at the CIA in 1995, two things intrigued me about the place. First and foremost, it was the surprising ubiquity of the word "professional." The most disparaging thing one could say about a colleague was that he was being unprofessional. If you asked anyone, as I did, what that meant, they would list the things one should not do as a professional, such as swearing, sexual harassment, dress code violation, violence, shouting, drugs, too much alcohol, smoking, etc. Such excesses were read as markers of untamed working-class masculinity in a world where the domain for such idioms was shrinking dramatically in legitimacy. The characterization was powerful precisely because it was nebulous, analogous to an aroma, which is precisely why it evoked a whole structure of feeling. What was intended was mostly left unsaid. Relatedly, I was fascinated by the religious aura surrounding issues of comportment and manners, made visible by the dress code, where the official code outlines the color of underwear allowed under chefs' whites. Conversations at the faculty table almost always veered towards complaints about declining standards of dress and demeanor among the students. Why this focus on middle-class, almost Victorian, models of discipline, character, and propriety?

Yet, I was also surprised by the aggressive masculinity of the place. Everyone had learned to acknowledge the presence of women amongst them, but there was the residue of an assumption that only real men could be chefs, the rest merely cooks, or worse still housewives. Why was this sense of masculinity so pervasive in spite of the institutional attempt to neutralize it? Such questions led to others: Why were only a small percentage of the cooking students (in contrast to Baking and Pastry), and the faculty and administration, female? Why did many women find it a difficult place in which to work and learn? Was the institution changing in its gendered demeanor? To what purpose?

As Fred Katz noted long ago, with the profession of nursing in mind, "Few professionals talk as much about being professionals as those whose professional stature is in doubt" (1969: 71). To better understand these anxieties I needed to contrast the culture of the institution with a comparable one, preferably the culture of an emergent profession. To do that, I needed to look at other professions, specifically something born from women's nurturant work, but turned into a man's career (Litt 2000). So I develop the analogy below, conducting a thought experiment, with medicine in mind at the end of the nineteenth century.

The first great transformation of American medicine into the modern professional field that it is today happened between the Civil War and the First World War—let us call it First-Wave Modern Biomedicine—and it fundamentally changed the character, training, skills, and returns to the profession. That is the analogic moment in the life cycle of professional cooking today: physicians then (ca. 1865–1914) and chefs today (ca. 1970–2000). Medicine is currently going through its next great transformation, producing Second-Wave Modern Biomedicine, with its focus on outcomes-based research, double-blind studies conducted by for-profit drug companies, not-for-profit universities, and teaching hospitals, governed by state bureaucracies of health and human services, and statutory institutions, such as National Institutes of Health in the USA. Absorbing technological changes in computing, biostatistics, scanning, molecular biology, pharmacology, and genetics, a newer kind of medicine is emerging all around us that has been interrogated by anthropologists and sociologists (Clarke, Shim, Fosket, Mamo, and Fishman 2003; Berg 1997). This Second-Wave Modern Biomedicine has far outstripped the valence of even the most high-tech molecular gastronomes and celebrity chefs. So, to make it clear, I am not comparing the processes of profession-making in the fields of current biomedicine and current professional cooking. I will pay attention to the analogic moment of medicine more than 100 years ago at the beginning of the long twentieth century and chefing today to illuminate the comparative moment of early, insecure professionalization.

First-Wave Modern Biomedicine provides an instructive comparative framework for professional cooking because that is when physicians reinvented themselves as an occupation that superseded the vocations of the *ancien régime* in theology, philosophy, medicine, and law, and they did so by clearly separating themselves from informally trained, experience-based, care-givers, medics, midwives, medicine men, and apothecaries. The First Wave came at the end of the nineteenth century in the US. Subsequently, all aspirants to the modern title of a professional have had to measure up to the trajectory of physicians, with their claims of cognitive exclusiveness, scientific expertise, and success at occupational closure. In the following pages I develop the analogy of professional cooking not only with First-Wave Modern Biomedicine, but also with analogic moments in other professions such as law, dentistry, and school and college teaching.[6]

Scholars such as Andrew Abbott (1988) have shown the importance of the ecology of professions and semi-professions within which a vocation is embedded. He illustrates how the pushing, pulling, elbowing, between various professions and sub-professions keeps an emerging profession in dynamic tension with its neighbors, and can explain much about any single profession. Strife between professions produces their social location. Physicians, nurses, dieticians, lab technicians, phlebotomists, produce each other by fighting for turf and marking out their domain, a fight which is never settled for good, although it is crystallized by legal monopolies such as the right to prescribe medicine.

On the other hand, depending on a theory of essential features, other scholars have tried to identify professionals by isolating some of the characteristics of exemplary occupations (Hughes 1958; Etzioni 1969; Johnson 1972). For instance, Etzioni (1969) defines a profession by the length of training. According to her a professional is one who is specifically trained for his occupation for a period of over five years, while a semi-professional is one who is trained for under five years. I synthesize both these perspectives, which transforms the relational and essential prognosis into a dynamic morphogenetic process. The point is to pay attention to the life cycle of a profession and the context that allows certain kinds of people into the cohort and excludes others by legal fiat, culture, capital, or convention. Let me explain what I mean by that.

Liberal arts: Curricular strategies of inculcating gentlemanliness

After the advent of First-Wave Modern Biomedicine, a broad liberal arts degree came to be seen as increasingly necessary by those who sought to elevate the class profile of American physicians. Thus a Bachelor's degree became a prerequisite for medical college admission in the USA, without much pedagogical justification.[7] The attempt was to stress the mental aspect of the profession over the physical, hence physicians typically hesitated to touch their patients. Instead, they listened to them. Furthermore, the eminent historian of medicine Roy Porter writes, "By 1900 it was becoming possible to understand a patient not by his story, nor even simply through pathological signs," but by ceaseless physiological monitoring "by the apparatus of numerical and chemical readings" (Porter 1997: 346). Diagnostic tests so transformed First-Wave Modern Biomedicine that by the middle of the twentieth century doctors had to be encouraged to touch their patients again. In the first chapter, titled "Doctor and Patient," in the ever popular manual *Hutchinson's Clinical Methods*, it is advised, "Never underestimate the power of communication inherent in touching your patient. Try holding the hand of a frightened old lady and see how it gives her more comfort than your words of reassurance." It continues, "Gentleness is all important; indeed abdominal palpation, to be successful, must be like a caress . . . It is all part of gaining the patient's confidence" (quoted in Swash 1995: 3).[8] Nonetheless, particularly physical branches of medicine, such as surgery, dentistry, and nursing, were the last to be professionalized (Adams 2000; Etzioni 1969). Eventually, medical diagnostic technologies of the Second Wave of Biomedicine through the twentieth century—of seeing inside bodies, listening to what is invisible, chemical testing and marking, gas chromatography, mass spectrometry, and various modes of imaging from X-Rays to functional MRIs—comfortably separated physicians from laypersons, who could never again threaten the former's expertise.

Cooking schools are facing similar pressures today to those that faced First-Wave Biomedicine: to heighten the chef's profile, where there are no large technological gaps yet between the home kitchen and the restaurant kitchen other than scale, more heat, and more sharpened knives. When I joined the CIA in 1995, as one of the first appointments in an expansive liberal arts hiring project, the CIA had a one-week Introduction to Gastronomy course as the only liberal arts-oriented class in an eighteen-month curriculum. I learned later that the gastronomy class was a product of a "dramatic revision" of the curriculum in 1989, with the addition of courses less closely related to cooking such as Supervisory Development, Management of Wines and Spirits, and Menus and Facilities Planning.

In 1985, President Metz of the CIA and then-Vice President Tim Ryan had, with the backing of the Board, begun making specific inquiries and conducting surveys about developing a baccalaureate program. To test the market, the first survey of 210 students enrolled in the AOS—Associate of Occupational Studies—program at the CIA was completed in June 1985. A July 1989 survey of 941 students and another in January 1991 (N=1175) confirmed the internal demand for a baccalaureate program. Between 40 and 48 percent of the students (in the three surveys) showed interest in pursuing a bachelor's degree. Soon after this, the CIA hired a consultant to interview thirty leading industry executives, chefs, editors, and restaurateurs—"key persons such as Ken Aretsky, Michael Bartlett, Joseph Baum, Jerome Burns, Julia Child, William Fisher, John Farquarson, Pierre Franey, Dan Gescheidle, Richard Melman, Robert Nyman, and Martin Yan" (CIA 1992: 7). Eighty percent of these leaders confirmed what the surveys were showing—the demand and the need for a baccalaureate degree. Other CIA internal studies cited the National Restaurant Association's (1988) *Current Issues Report: Foodservice Manager 2000*, which predicted a need for almost 450,000 new managers by the year 2000, of which 50,000 were likely to be recipients of higher education. The CIA study also cited an article by Wayne C. Guyette (1981), titled "The Executive Chef: Manager or Culinarian?" in *The Cornell HRA Quarterly*, to point to real concerns about the training of chefs. Finally, it referred to a Bureau of Labor Statistics report showing that 22 percent of the total jobs available required a baccalaureate degree, while only 20 percent of the population had such a degree. It optimistically concluded, "clearly, with the growth of the hospitality industry, increasing customer sophistication, more competition, and business complexities, there will be an increasing need and expectation for industry leaders to possess a baccalaureate degree which this program will provide" (CIA 1992: 9).

By 1993, a thirty-eight-month, 132-credit Bachelor of Professional Studies (BPS) course was established, and new fifteen-week, semester-long courses in the History and Culture of Europe, History and Culture of the Americas, History and Culture of Asia, Economics, Composition, Food Writing, Accounting, and Psychology were added to the usual cooking, table service, sommelier, and business classes. That added another seventeen months to the curriculum, which saw some initial resistance from students in terms of recruitment, notwithstanding the optimism of the internal studies conducted earlier.

Liberal arts classes were added not only to the new BPS curriculum but also to the traditional AOS program, which is still the anchor of the CIA. By 2002, a fifteen-week writing class and a fifteen-week interpersonal communication class had been added to the eighteen-month AOS curriculum. There have been a number of curricular strategies used at the CIA to socialize working-class boys and men into middle-class aspirants (a) by developing a palate and a vocabulary akin to the upwardly mobile professional classes, so that (b) they can better serve their upper-class clientele and (c) acquire middle-class wages and status. In addition to technical skills of cooking and baking, students are trained to acquire middle-class styles of being-in-the-world in a number of ways.

For instance, the course "Introduction to Gastronomy" introduces incoming students to great French chefs such as Fernand Point and Paul Bocuse (with Americans such as Alice Waters added in 1996) as a way of encouraging students to recognize the possibilities of prestige within their occupation and producing a preferred genealogy of the profession.[9] Second, entering students were assigned to eat "on stage," where they were served the most conservative of French haute cuisine, with its elaborate paraphernalia of silverware, sauces with French names, and mannerisms most alien to working-class American boys. Here an interesting etymological slippage joined the French word *stage* for artisanal apprenticeship to the architectural site where meals were consumed on a raised stage in the Great Hall, with its chandeliers, stained-glass windows, and flags of wine-producing nations that gave it the fitting air of a cathedral of culture. Students' manners were on display, when they ate "on stage," to the policing gaze of their table service instructors.

Classes in "Interpersonal Communication" (IPC) were established to universalize middle-class ethos, manners, and language (including body language) as the only possible norm for a professional. That was done both by training working-class boys and men to internalize middle-class modes of communication (no shouting, no name-calling, no addressing people in anger) as the only sanctioned style, and by training their eye to catch deviations from that standard as managers in Supervisory Development. All three of these classes—Gastronomy, Interpersonal Communication, and Supervisory Development—also generated the greatest resistance from students and chefs, who, lacking a class ideology, often termed these classes as irrelevant to their technical skills. It was invariably male, working-class students who struggled the most in these non-cooking classes, while the women did quite well. On graduation, according to an internal survey, most students acknowledged the primary importance of "professionalism" in their training, underlining the apparent ideological success of the process (CIA 2003).

Equally importantly, oral and practical exams were increasingly supplanted by written exams in almost every course. Most dramatically, we see the transformation in the Externship Manual, which has expanded to a detailed 100-odd page, twenty-module exercise, worth the most academic credit (six credit-hours) in the whole program. Prior to 1989, the six-week Externship experience was evaluated informally with no required written work. Most culinary students find such written requirements cumbersome. Yet, some students, especially female students, in alliance with their writing instructors have seized the opportunity to publish *Amusé: A Literary Magazine* since 2003, which is in itself a sign of grander aspirations. These are some of the ways in which, to answer the sociologist Gary Alan Fine's question, "how the children of blue-collar workers become socialized to a career that demands knowledge of arenas of cultural capital ('taste') to which they have not been exposed" (Fine 1996: x).

The socialization of students would be incomplete without transforming their chef role-models into epitomes of middle-class sensibility. That has been done by strong sanctions against shouting, cursing, drunkenness, carousing, and harassment of women and minorities, which were painted as crude working-class behavior since the early 1980s. With infinite sensitivity to American impatience with the language of class, this project of inculcating middle-class manners has been called professionalism.

In conjunction with increasing paperwork—in terms of course guides, lesson plans, lecture notes, etc.—and book-learning, which has become a new focus since 1989, this project has generated persistent subterranean tensions at the CIA between chefs in their "whites" toiling away in hot kitchens and "suits" who sit in judgment over them in air-conditioned offices on higher floors of Roth Hall. These "suits" are often seen as paragons of middle-class respectability. Given the institutional discourse on demeanor, the tension is appropriately inscribed on attire. Without a legitimate ideology of their class project, old working-class chefs find themselves at sea in this new institutional culture and legitimately see their control slipping into the hands of "suits," aided by younger cohorts and by painful betrayal by Presidents who are much more attuned to middle-class aspirations and upper-class sensibilities, especially with the rising profile of the chef in American popular culture. As Wilensky notes with regard to all professions, "The newcomers see the old-timers as a block to successful professionalization; the latter see the former as upstarts" (1964: 145).

Some of the expansion of the liberal-arts and reading-and-writing components of the curriculum has come about due to expectations of organizations such as the Middle-States Commission on Higher Education (henceforth Middle-States), which is the accrediting agency for colleges and universities in the mid-Atlantic states of the United States. The CIA sought and successfully received Middle-States accreditation in 2002. For a single-focus institution, such as the CIA (and Julliard for instance), Middle-States expects about 40 percent of the curriculum to be liberal arts rather than profession-oriented. The other source of curricular transformation is internal CIA assumptions about an "educated professional" which, it is argued by its leaders, is the shape of the "future chef." This is in part about the upwardly mobile aspirations of the profession. Middle-States accreditation was sought both to upgrade the profile of the graduating chef and to out-maneuver competitors in the crowded field of more than 500 culinary schools in the USA.

The nature and relevance of the curriculum has been a source of considerable debate within the educational bureaucracy in the US at least since the Civil War. As primary education became free and compulsory in the Northeast and Midwest by about the 1860s and was imposed on the American South in the course of Reconstruction, questions were raised about the relevance of secondary education for working-class Americans. It was argued by some that vocational education that focused on specific technical skills was a productive alternative to the diffused and mostly unmeasurable skills taught in high schools and colleges. But the leaders of American secondary education were hostile to vocational training because in their eyes it undermined the ideals of a culturally socializing education oriented toward liberal arts. More importantly, vocational schools did not flourish for two reasons: first, most of the training for manual labor could be acquired on the job or through apprenticeship; and second, manual education did not provide social mobility into middle-class culture, which would become the dominant paradigm of expectations about careers in the twentieth century. Thus most working-class students either dropped out to pursue a trade or continued to acquire a liberal college education so that they could climb the ladder of social stratification (Collins 1979: 114–15).

The Progressive movement in education made some improvements to the curriculum in terms of relevance, but at the end of the day it was liberal arts plus athletics. Thus, football and fraternities became the salvation of secondary schools and then colleges at the turn of the nineteenth and twentieth centuries, which in terms of specific skills added circles of sociability and class endogamy as the unspoken objectives of college curriculum. The real competition to traditional colleges and universities with their liberal arts curriculum came from professions such as medicine, law, and engineering, none of which required a college education at the end of the nineteenth century.

Universities sought to counter that challenge by opening professional schools and by making the BA a requirement for admission to schools of law, medicine, and engineering. That added four more years of tuition money to the coffers of colleges and created an artificial demand for their own BAs, which by the second half of the twentieth century became a requirement for respectability.[10] That also resolved the crises of over-supply that have haunted American higher education from the very beginning, because of fewer restrictions on educational entrepreneurs who have established more colleges in the US than anywhere else (the US has almost five times more colleges than any other nation in the developed world) (Collins 1979: 121). That very over-supply has also forced American colleges to be less selective by way of not only scholastic aptitude but also denomination and gender, making American colleges more secular and gender neutral (comparatively). Through these transformations a broad liberal arts education has remained the touchstone of the college experience.

In keeping with that trend, the current administration of the CIA has attempted to heighten the academic profile of the institution by hiring PhDs for its BPS program (about a dozen by 2010), and by making a PhD a requirement for continued employment in the department. The President of the CIA acquired an Executive PhD from the University of Pennsylvania in 2003. Compared to the older pattern of listing the chefs under whom they had worked, major companies where they had labored, or famous restaurants where they had worked, increasingly, chefs' biographies in the school brochure list degrees and certifications, many of which are obscure and minor, such as Certified Hospitality Educator.[11] Thus, formal credentials are increasingly replacing personal attributes and patronage. Furthermore, academic paraphernalia such as sabbaticals were introduced in 1997, with the first one granted in 1998. (By comparison, Harvard granted its first sabbatical in 1880, also in the process of professionalizing its academic faculty.) CIA's policy statement on sabbaticals self-consciously notes: "The sabbatical leave is one of the more agreeable customs of an academic career, providing the college educator an opportunity for mental refreshment unique to higher education" (CIA 2003). Subsequently, the sabbatical policy was further amended to allow for individuals with seven years of service to apply for a sabbatical (as both the etymology of the term "sabbatical" required and the practice of universities and colleges pointed to) instead of the previous policy of ten years.

After 2001, faculty development was pursued with greater formalization and accountability, with new forms, annual plans, and written applications, again provoking strong recriminations from older chefs. All three steps cited above—PhDs, sabbaticals, faculty development plans—echo exactly what Mary E. Woolley, the first academic president of Mount Holyoke College (1901–37), did to transform her institution from a seminary established in 1837 to teach young ladies morals and manners, to a first-rate college (Glazer and

Slater 1987: 30–4). As with President Woolley's efforts, these changes have raised the hackles of many an old timer at the CIA, and the administration has been unable to extract a research agenda or a substantial record of publications from the faculty, yet (partly due to a very heavy teaching load).

Character

An important variable in the professionalization of First-Wave Modern Biomedicine was a particular kind of institutional culture, with its minutiae of manners, mores, discipline, and dress code. That is, doctors had to be trained for their upward mobility, which was to make visible their class promotion by way of bedside manners, white coats, and the stethoscope. In a popular advice manual for medical practitioners, *The Physician Himself and What He Should Add to His Scientific Acquirements* (1890, first published 1881), D. W. Cathell noted that conviviality between physician and patient "has a levelling effect, and divests the physician of his proper prestige" (1890: 80). Appearing in shirtsleeves, unwashed and unkempt, was unwise because it would "show weakness, diminish your prestige, detract from your dignity, and lessen you in public esteem, by forcing on everybody the conclusion that you are, after all, an ordinary person" (1890: 83). A way of gathering deference was to mimic the attire of more established professionals, such as when surgeons put on the *faux* academic long gown (Katz 1999: 23; Power 1933: 23). The next step in the sartorial marker came early in the twentieth century, when medicine-men increasingly transitioned from black robes to the white lab-coats to signify their transition from a guild to a scientific profession (Hochberg 2007).

A significant sign of self-consciousness about upward mobility of the occupational group is the very process of identification of the group as a profession. The word "professional" is derived from the old English phrase "to profess a religious belief," which the *Oxford English Dictionary* (OED) dates back to the twelfth century. By the middle of the sixteenth century, the word "profession" came to be used to signify

> the occupation one professes to be skilled in and to follow. A vocation in which a professed knowledge of some department of learning or science is used in its application to the affairs of others or in the practice of an art founded upon it. Applied specifically to the three learned professions of divinity, law and medicine (OED 1989).

The OED cites Francis Bacon in 1605 saying "Amongst so many great foundations of colleges in Europe, I find strange that they are all dedicated to professions, and none left free to Arts and Sciences at large" (OED 1989:

Volume XII, 573). The use of the word "professional" expanded while its scope was narrowed to closed, specialist knowledge, which became quite popular by the second half of the nineteenth century.

In all probability the word "professional" was first used at the CIA in the year 1955 in a brochure about "Courses in Professional Cooking." An identical brochure from 1951 does not contain that word. (Brochures for the intervening period are missing). The CIA has had three incarnations. It began in 1946, with fifty students and a faculty consisting of a chef, a baker, and a dietitian, as the New Haven Restaurant Institute, as a vocational training ground for Second World War veterans. It offered a sixteen-week program featuring instruction in seventy-eight popular menus of the day. Members of the New Haven Restaurant Association sponsored the original school, whose founders, Frances Roth and Katharine Angell, served as its first Director and Chair of the Board, respectively. In 1947 the New Haven Restaurant Institute moved to a forty-room mansion adjacent to Yale University. The school's name was changed then to the Restaurant Institute of Connecticut, and in 1951 it became known as the Culinary Institute of America, with each step expanding its claim to represent a city, then a state, finally a nation.

It was in the 1960s that the school's educational program was expanded to two years. By the time of Roth's retirement in 1965, the school had increased its enrollment to 400 students and operated a $2 million facility. In 1969, double-class sessions (7am–2pm and 3pm–10pm) were initiated to admit more students. Even that wasn't adequate to the ambitions of the school's administrators. Soon after, they launched a search for a new home, and found a five-story, 150-room Jesuit seminary, with eighty acres of land overlooking the Hudson River in Hyde Park, NY. They paid $1 million for it in 1970. Two years and $4 million in renovations later, the new school opened, with its main building renamed Roth Hall (CIA 2015). In 2010 the CIA was training 2,000 degree-acquiring students, almost 6,000 professionals, and another 1,600 food enthusiasts. The main buildings house forty-one professional kitchens and five restaurants and cafés, worked by tuition-paying students. Now the CIA has campuses in Napa Valley, San Antonio, and Singapore, but the Hyde Park Campus continues to be the flagship. The official argument is that this vast and expanding enterprise is tied together by character imparted by professional training.

Outside the CIA, but within the larger emergent field of American professional chefs, "The Culinarian's Code of Conduct" was adopted by the American Culinary Federation (ACF) at its Chicago convention in 1957. The Code has numerous references to the "profession," and its general tenor highlights what appears to be upwardly mobile aspirations of a guild, with proclamations such as, "I pledge my professional knowledge and skill to the advancement of our profession and to pass it on to those that are to follow;" "I shall be just as enthusiastic about the success of others as I am about my own;" "I shall be too big for worry, too noble for anger, too strong for fear and too happy to permit the pressure of business to hurt anyone, within or without the profession;" etc. (ACF 1957). The rhetoric underlines the attempt to shift cooks' orientation from narrow self-interest to the profession. The text is primarily a pledge of loyalty to one's colleagues. Some analysts consider the development of a code of ethics as an important stage in the natural history of a profession (Caplow 1954; Wilensky 1964; Johnson 1972).

The code of conduct appears as one of the longest sections of the *Student Handbook* at the CIA that has remained relatively unchanged over the last decade, under the heading "*professionalism*, uniform and hygiene policy." There the importance of professionalism is underlined in the following way (which I quote at some length as it is the center piece of professional claims made visible). First, it announces that "As professionals at The Culinary Institute of America, we are constantly working to enhance the status of the hospitality industry." Then it asserts that cooking professionally "is an ancient and respected profession," and that it "takes many years of hard work, training, dedication, and tenacity to become a leader in this industry, but it takes only a few moments to dress, act, and think like a professional." Then it lists expectations for "anyone who aspires to be regarded as a professional in the hospitality industry," where professionals:

> refrain from abusive and foul language;
> speak and act without prejudice to race, color, creed, religion, age, gender, disability, ethnicity, veteran status, marital status, or sexual orientation . . .
> refrain from the abuse of drugs and alcohol . . .
> are polite and courteous to all visitors, peers, and colleagues;
> work with a positive attitude . . . (CIA 2002: 34).

The code then continues to state that a professional is one who "acts reliably and dependably," and adds nine pages of material on the dress code, which mandates that students "must be clean-shaven, with sideburns not exceeding the middle of the ear for men. Beards are not permitted." Mustaches "must be neatly trimmed and may not extend below the corner of the lips." Facial jewelry, "including jewelry in eyebrows, eyelids, lips, tongue, upper ear, or nose, is not permitted" (CIA 2002: 35). It goes on to insist that "Plain white undergarments are required for both men and women. Colored or logo tee shirts are not permitted." "Leather clothing is not permitted" and "No hair colors such as green, blue, pink, etc. will be permitted" (CIA 2002: 37).

These are not just obscure rules that no one implements. Enforcement is lively. Let me quote just one e-mail from a faculty member urging others to implement the dress code: "This morning I had to ask Ms. [X] if there was any possible way that she could wear her shirt so that her breasts were actually inside it. I would appreciate your support, so to speak, in keeping Ms. [X's] chest in check:)."[12] Part of the interest in the dress code is titillation. Some of it is to find opportunities to reprimand young people for violating sartorial modes of propriety that older cohorts often complain about, which might be a universal phenomenon. Yet much of it is seriously disciplining too, and it is the serious part that is most intriguing.

It is today as justifiable in the CIA as the actions of the Chief of Surgery who, in the 1890s, did not allow his surgeons "to be seen around the hospital eating, drinking, or even carrying soda or coffee" (Cassell 1998: 101–2). As at West Point, the Military Academy down the road from the CIA, the Culinary has a demerits system, akin to what Bledstein considered characteristic of "old-time colleges" such as Harvard until the end of the antebellum period, when "the official atmosphere approached that of a military school" (1976: 235). In 1830, when a student entered Harvard he received a copy of Orders and Regulations, with a complex system of merits and demerits where eight points were lost for being late at prayers, two points for missing it altogether, sixteen for lying on the grass or shouting from a window (Bledstein 1976: 235–6). The section on professionalism in the *Student Handbook* (2002) of the CIA notes: "While you are going to class, in class, leaving class, or in student dining rooms, the uniform and dress code must be adhered to, and will be enforced." It ends on the ominous note that "Of your final grade, 10% will be for Professionalism, Uniform, and Hygiene. The professor will assess each violation of the policy while you are in class . . . You can avoid these penalties by demonstrating professionalism in all that you do" (CIA 2002: 41). The 2014/2015 *Student Handbook & Planner* has a similarly substantial section called "Professionalism, Uniform and Hygiene Policy," which opens with "As professionals at The Culinary Institute of America, we are constantly working to enhance the status of the hospitality industry. Students, faculty, staff and alumni all share a common pride in their work, workplace, and appearance" (CIA 2014), and goes on to note that "professionals refrain from abusive and foul language," and that "mustaches must be neatly trimmed," etc. These are issues that have dropped out of the handbooks of most colleges with a more class-assured clientele.

It is apparent why both in medical colleges of the past and in cooking schools today so much stress is put on dress code. "Like many people whose position in society is somewhat precarious, physicians were much concerned to maintain a front of propriety and respectability" (Starr 1982: 85). Tracey L. Adams's work on dentistry as a profession confirms such a hypothesis. She writes, "Dentistry gained professional legislation [in Canada] in 1868. However, like other professionals, dentists did not at first have an easy time enforcing this legislation. The main difficulty, in dentists' eyes, was that the public did not recognize their claim to professional status—they had no social legitimacy" (Adams 2000: 6). To convince the public that they were deserving of public respect, they "drew on a number of social ideologies and institutions, but gender, in combination with class and race, was central to their efforts" (Adams 2000: 6–7). Part of the argument by self-conscious dentists was that everything about a dentist, "his appearance, demeanour, conduct in practice and interactions with others," should convey his status as "a *middle-class, white gentleman.* Dental leaders believed that if all dentists behaved like middle-class professional gentlemen, then the public would come to respect them" (italics in original; Adams 2000: 6–7).

In fact the whole idea of a *profession* has served the purposes of middle-class men (a) to distinguish themselves from the propertied classes above them and the working-class below them; and (b) in establishing a masculine public sphere of salaried work separate from the unpaid domestic work of middle-class women. Nothing makes that clearer than an apocryphal story published in the *Hartford Daily Times* by the attorney Charles Moore in 1886, titled "The Woman Lawyer." It is a story that was said to be the tale of a young woman, Mary Padelford, who wished to practice law. "She arrives in Moore's hometown, Old Litchfield, Connecticut, on a stagecoach. Upon seeing her 'slender figure' and the determined look on her face, attorney Walter Perry, 'a *man* vigorous in mind and body,' declares that if Padelford 'possesses enough physical strength' she might succeed." But things predictably fall apart when it is discovered that she is no match for the rigors of the courtroom during a stormy trial that pits her against two tough, unscrupulous adversaries, when:

> Padelford falls from her chair in a swoon. "Oh take me away, take me away," she whispers. A physician later diagnoses her condition as "brain fever." Constant study of the law had taxed her constitution "to the utmost" and long trials have brought her "mental and physical exhaustion." She announces that, although loath to give up her profession, she must on the advice of her physician cease trying cases. Padelford forsakes the courtroom, marries Perry, and spends the rest of her life helping him in a law partnership (Grossberg 1990: 133).

With attitudes like that it is no surprise that women constituted only 1 percent of the bar by 1910 (compared to 6 percent of the medical profession) (Epstein 1993: 4; Walsh 1976: 107–8). Barbara Harris contends that "practicing law was even more incompatible with nineteenth-century ideas about women than was practicing medicine" (Harris 1978: 110). Lawyers could not claim that their practice was an extension of women's nurturant work, or occupy feminine corners of the profession such as pediatrics and gynecology. Woman lawyers were clearly intruding into the public domain and they were made to pay the price for such intrusions (Harris 1978: 110).

Beyond gossip about the few women in the profession, the question, of course, is: How exactly did middle-class men contain women's participation in the labor force? Victorian ideological separation of women's sphere and the public, paid, male's sphere played some role in the gendered allocation of labor and the moral exclusion of women. Father's and husband's material, cultural, and emotional power over women in the household was used to exclude and discourage women from paid work, from colleges, and hence automatically from professions. Beyond the ideological rewards of modesty, men reaped the benefits of free household labor, so that in part men could pursue careers in the various professions. That still works today. But that was only one of the strategies of exclusion.

Middle-class professional men, akin to their working-class brothers, created organizations of civil society such as craft unions and professional associations that explicitly agitated for the exclusion of women and for a "family wage." Most professional organizations built a culture of masculinity within the profession. Furthermore, when middle-class men failed to exclude women, sometimes due to the pressures of the labor market where employers sought to sidestep labor and professional organizations (because women were considered cheaper and more malleable), these men and their organizations responded by segregating certain inferior grades of work within the profession as women's work, such as book-binding and print-finishing in the printing trades, nursing in medicine, and school teaching as opposed to university teaching in education. In the sphere of cooking, Antonin Carême was setting the template at the end of the eighteenth-century by distinguishing professional practice from *cuisine bourgeoise* and *cuisine de femmes* (Roosth 2013: 7). These confinements and concessions are never settled forever. They are trials of strength with temporary crystallizations. For instance, men cornered the market for school teaching through much of the nineteenth century, but were pushed back so far that today, school teaching is a feminized profession, and college teaching at the assistant professor level is already primarily feminine today, while full professorship is still more masculine. That is changing too, first in the feminized liberal arts and the humanities, then in social work and public policy, perhaps eventually in business, surgery, and corporate law.

Men also sought to back up their organizations in civil society with legislation at the level of the state where women were excluded by law from certain trades or professions, or certain kinds of jobs such as combat positions in the military, presumably for their own good, which also closed their professional opportunities. Most American medical colleges, for instance, did not allow women until the last quarter of the nineteenth century; many retained maximum quotas of about 5 percent into the first few decades of the twentieth century; today the female population reaches about 45 percent of medical school students, although surgical specialties still have single-digit female representation.

Statutory barriers to women entering the bar stayed in place until the first decades of the twentieth century. The Supreme Court had ruled in *In re Lockwood* in 1894 that the state of Virginia could refuse to license Belva A. Lockwood as an attorney because she was a woman. The argument followed those of the Wisconsin chief justice Edward Ryan, who, when he denied R. Lavinia Goodell the right to practice law, said that "persons" in the licensing statute cannot be read in a gender-neutral way because if we follow that logic we would "emasculate the constitution itself and include females in the constitutional right of male suffrage and male qualification" (cited in Grossberg 1990: 146). But women were not just passive victims of state- and civil society-based strategies of exclusion and segregation. Sometimes borrowing the discourse of feminine work and sensibility, sometimes contesting such essentialist constructions, women also developed certain projects of professionalism, as in the case of nursing and school teaching, where women were active albeit subordinate participants in claiming certain spheres of skilled work for themselves.

Women need not apply

The CIA has had a handful of female students since its inception, ranging from 1 to 3 percent of the graduating class until the end of the 1970s. There were periods, such as 1948–52 and 1968–71, when there were no graduating females. Systematic, longitudinal data is missing from the CIA archives, but by 1983 about 20 percent of the graduating class was female, by 2003 it was 33 percent female, and in 2012 it was 64 percent male, 36 percent female (Moskin 2014: D6).

The first increase from single digits to 20 percent around 1980 is real, but the jump from 20 percent to 36 percent is a little misleading, because through the 1990s the Baking and Pastry program, which has always been more feminized, expanded. The gender ratios are inverted between the Culinary and the Baking and Pastry Programs. In 2002, when I was teaching at the CIA, 74 percent of the AOS culinary students were male (N=1,209), while 71 percent of the AOS Baking and Pastry students were female (N=435). If we exclude the Baking and Pastry program, only about a quarter of the student body is female.[13] The small body of students in the Bachelor's program exhibits gender ratios similar to the culinary program.

In 1946, under the heading "Who May Enroll," the New Haven Restaurant Institute (precursor to the CIA) stated that they would admit "Any young man or woman who has completed a high school course or its equivalent."[14] By 1950, the prerequisite was slightly altered to read, "Any man or woman who has completed a high school course *or its equivalent in experience in the hotel or restaurant industry*," in an obvious attempt to expand the pool of applicants (italics mine). By 1954, an age criteria was added to the requirement: "Any man or *woman between the ages of 17 and 39* who has graduated from a high school or trade school," perhaps echoing the age-grading that was becoming dominant in American high schools (italics mine). Most interestingly for our purposes here, suddenly, by 1966–7, the criteria for admission were changed to *exclude* women, complicating the typical Whig interpretation of history. It read: "Any *man* between the ages of 17 and 35 who has graduated from high school may enroll" (italics mine). By 1969–70 we get an explanation for this intriguing development: "Girls are not accepted for the regular course—but are welcome in the special summer courses. The reason is that with so few girls applying it is uneconomical for the Institute to provide the special facilities, washrooms, etc. required." By the next year a special section is added to the brochure under the title "Admission of Women":

> It is a matter of regret to all concerned at the Culinary Institute that existing facilities do not permit admission of women. However, the admission of women is under consideration by the Board, and the final decision will depend on the number of women who apply. Women who are interested in attending the Culinary Institute are asked to write for an application form and if the number is sufficient, it is possible that the Institute Board may be able to work out early admission plans.

By 1971–2, when the CIA was expanding its facilities, women were once again allowed to apply along with men, while the age limitation of seventeen to thirty-five was continued. The age criteria was removed in 1974–5 and in the following year it is stated that "Admission is open to anyone who is a high school graduate or can furnish a high school equivalency certificate, *regardless of age, sex, race, religion, or, national origin*" (italics mine). That continues to be the effective criteria today. It appears, at least from an interrogation of the archival material at the CIA, that the Institute did not exclude women for ideological reasons, unlike many other colleges at the time, but that women did not apply to be a part of the profession for reasons outside the ambit of the institution.[15]

So the secular trend appears to be a dramatic increase of the female population from single digits until the late 1970s, to almost 20 percent by the 1980s, and then a steady upward trend towards 25 percent by the year 2001, with about the same percent by 2010 (if we adjust for the gender distribution of the Baking and Pastry program). The 1980s appear to be the hinge of a substantial transformation. That is when the second-wave, post-feminist generation reached college age. It appears that the perseverance of the feminist struggle, from the 1950s to the 1970s, to break into the preserve of professional employment finally bore fruit in the 1980s, by which time fewer women were burdened with the exclusive responsibility of cooking and cleaning at home. As women could do other things than cook, clean, and raise children at home, they were willing to opt for baking, if not cooking, as a career.

Out of thirty female students, alumni, and faculty members that I interviewed systematically on the issue of gender at the CIA, few were critical of the institution, although a number provided instances of biased behavior (also see Harris and Giuffre 2010). Three found the whole experience abusive. Most women provided individualized examples such as the following: "I had a chef instructor (thankfully only one!) who tried to knock me down a peg simply because I was a female." Another female alumnus—Elizabeth Beals—provided a long and subtle response to my probing about doing gender at the CIA that conveys the complexity both of her perspective and the character of the institution she was characterizing. Her statements were exceptional in their eloquence, but the sense she so successfully communicates was common to many of my female interview subjects.

> CIA masculine? Hmmm . . . Yes and no. Although, historically, CIA was started by two women, it was a school for men taking advantage of the GI bill. Obviously there weren't as many women going to the school previously, but I really think that's changing. I think the CIA is making an effort to de-masculinize itself.[16]

Beals talked about how the photographers for the school were encouraged to get photos of women in the classes to show prospective students that there were women at the CIA, even though there were five women out of twenty-five in her cohort. She thought that her male classmates, by and large, didn't care if they were women or not, as long as they worked hard. Yet, in the final year when the student group-leader was putting the teams together and assigning stations, he wouldn't put any women on the hot line simply because they were women. But she also had a remarkably gratifying experience in the same year when Chef Griffith said that she was the best student that he had ever had, hands down. She was speechless. He followed that up with:

> But because you're THAT good, I have to warn you, that there will be people out there, particularly some men that will try to cut you down, simply because you are a woman. But don't be shaken by them. Don't pay attention to them; and succeed any way because that's what you are going to do!

She said she was really touched by the chef's concern for her.

Then she changed the track of her critique, talking about the uniform, which surprised me: "Their uniforms are definitely still masculine." She noted how much she relished finding chef coats that fit a female shoulder-width and arm-length, and have what are called "darts" in the back of the coat that provide shaping in the overall structure that men's coats do not offer. "Nothing major, but it's been nice not looking like a slob lost in my clothing!! And the pants at CIA!! Good grief, I've never seen any woman actually fit the CIA pants at all!" I was surprised by the turn in the conversation because I wasn't thinking in that direction at all.

A student and a chef, Marissa Sertich Velie (2015), added depth to that consideration by underlining the greater importance of women's clothing in masculine professions and the related work that goes into striking just the right balance of professionalism and attractiveness, without being too sexy, or vulnerable, or masculine. Depending on the location and trajectory of the individual in the field, and the shape of the field, sartorial transgressions can indicate "lack of cultural capital and unprofessionalism, or it can demonstrate a conscious, active, rejection of the career's constructed norms" (Sertich Velie 2015: 3). Sertich Velie illustrated that potential by taking the case of Rochelle Huppin, the founder and President of Chefwear Inc., addressing a 2010 graduating class at the Culinary Institute of America wearing a pink chef coat, with pink and green camouflage chef pants. Sertich Velie re-interrogated her own antipathy and sense of betrayal, provoked by Huppin in pink at that graduation. Congruent with the conclusions of a handful of researchers, Sertich Velie noted,

> While challenging or embracing social norms through fashion may seem trivial, it is a personal act and embodiment of individual and group identity (woman, chef). Additionally, refusing to assimilate can be a powerful tool to spark controversy among a professional group and disrupt previously assumed power roles. Fashion offers physical evidence for how women perform gender in the professional kitchen, changes in kitchen culture, and subtle forms of subversion (Sertich Velie 2015: 4. See also Furst 1997; Costello 2004; Hansen 2004; Druckman 2012).

Elizabeth Beals also drew attention to the physical setting, the height of stoves and kitchen counters, and the length of chef's knives that presume a bigger male body.

> The kitchens are, physically, set for a more manly height. I say this only because I now know that kitchen setting heights don't have to be ridiculously high! I now work for a woman (which I had never done before) and she has

> all of her commercial stove's legs cut down so that she can reach all the way to the back burner safely (she's my height).

She also has all the counters set much at a lower height. It has been a dream working at those heights, Beals says. She didn't have to push a milk crate around as her stool to step up and reach the counter to work at it. She also didn't have to worry about scorching underneath her arm when she reached towards the back of the stove.

> The length of the standard kitchen knife is still very masculine. I can tell you that almost all of us females went out and bought a much smaller chef knife to do most kitchen work. The standard chef knife is just a little bit unwieldy for women in ratio to the rest of their body. Men, overall, don't have that issue.

Beals offers a remarkable perspective that combines particular instances of bias within her own profession, and the very specific material world of professional chefs—knives and counters and sinks. Even more importantly she points to the silent embodiment of assumptions about the gender of the typical subject from the shape of the uniform, to the size and heft of knives, to the height of sinks and worktables. Gendered assumptions are built into the physical environment, sometimes against our best intentions. But then, on the other side, as the early history of CIA's recruitment of women shows, it is not always a matter of explicitly *mala fide* intentions of institutions.

In a conversation at the CIA, chef Eve Felder insisted that to learn cooking you have to have passion and work hard. From that demand for hard work and physical strength, Michael Ruhlman, one of the leading chroniclers of chefhood in the United States, concludes, "The difficulty of work, I sensed, partly contributed to a macho ethic in the kitchen. And it tended to produce, as far as I could see, a fair share of lunatics" (Ruhlman 1997: 174). The causation, I think, could run the other way. Everyday cooking has mostly been women's work, which, when extricated from the household, institutionalized, and upscaled, demands a kind of performative masculinity to generate protective boundaries of exclusion around it. Amy Trubek, a trained chef and an anthropologist, notes:

> The desire to be a professional, an artist, was part of a larger inclination to not be other things and to avoid any suggestion that the practice of chefs had links to activities lower in the social division of labor. The practice of chefs was cooking, so they were particularly concerned with disengaging themselves from the association of cooking with women's work, work that occurred solely in the domestic sphere (Trubek 2000: 126).

Boundaries are based on salient social categories, primarily gender but also race and ethnicity, because the other categorical locus of low-prestige cooking, in addition to the home, is the cheap ethnic eatery.

Wages of Whiteness

For American men, professionalization has been a compelling way of separating themselves from any burdens of race or ethnicity. The influx of "ethnic" immigrants—Irish, Italian, and Eastern European Jews—and freed blacks into the labor force, precisely at the moment of origin of many new professions such as doctors and dentists between 1860 and 1920, challenged elite professional standards that mixed prejudice with Progressive-era visions of competence. Patrician attorney George Templeton Strong, writing in his diary in 1874, praised Columbia Law School's institution of admission tests and requirement of a college diploma, which would "keep out the little scrubs (German Jew boys mostly) whom the School now promotes from the grocery-counters . . . to be gentlemen of the Bar" (cited in Grossberg 1990: 145). The assumption has been that professional men had to be racially neutral, which always meant white, with all its changing historical resonances (meaning that Germans, Irish, and Eastern European Jews have been included or excluded from the category of "white" depending on the context and the ongoing contestations between classes, ethnicities, and races). But there is something more to why cooking schools, even today, are so white.

African-Americans are only about 2 percent of the student body at the CIA in 2010 (whites 59 percent; Asian/Pacific islander 3 percent; Hispanic 5 percent; international 7 percent; unknown 24 percent—in all probability white) and even fewer faculty members are black, although the early history of public cooking in the US is replete with black men, especially on the railroads, which was the pre-eminent locus of the profession of cooking in the nineteenth century.[17] It must be noted parenthetically that there was one African-American student—Jefferson Evans—in the first graduating class at the the New Haven Restaurant Institute on January 28, 1947, who was eventually hired as a faculty member, and the CIA continued to graduate a handful of African-American students (based on the evidence from surviving photographs of graduating classes), perhaps reflecting the racial integration of the military, prior to the integration of civilian society.

Nevertheless, the conflation of whiteness and professionalism may be why cooking schools are not so good at recruiting African-American students in general. An important additional reason for the low density of African-Americans at the CIA is the community's active and immediate historical memory of servitude. People with recent memories of servitude are not good at playing at the theater of service because it is too historically close for comfort. Until very recently, non-whites with any choice about their careers have in general stayed away from the culinary profession, much like women. The larger point here is that professionalism may be a way of insinuating colorlessness, middleness, and masculinity that white men have used quite successfully to their advantage, especially between 1860 and the First World War, when many modern professions were born (Witz 1992; Davidoff and Hall 1987; Ryan 1981; Morgan 1996; Tosh 1999).

Cultures of schools: From boys to men

Returning to our specific comparison with First-Wave Biomedicine, there appears to be a compelling parallel between the institutional culture of medical schools at the turn of the nineteenth century and cooking schools today, which can be described as solemn and judgmental, allowing little room for ambiguity, ambivalence, or skepticism. Students in colleges of yore and cooking schools today are urged to be industrious, independent, positive, courteous, and ambitious, where "happiness is congenital," in William James's scathing description of the medical college he attended (cited in Bledstein 1976: 148; for a later analogy see Becker, Geer, Hughes, and Strauss 1961). Above all, training is as much in morals and manners, where technical skills are seen as a medium to inculcate professional values.

"Unlike many educational institutions these days," Michael Ruhlman writes in *The Making of a Chef*, the CIA deals "not only in knowledge and skill but also in value judgments. It [teaches] a system of values that [is] almost religious in scope and beautifully concrete, physical, immediate" (1997: 142). Hand-in-hand with such a posture goes a certain infatuation with masculinity—a physical toughness, with moral consequences for things such as tardiness and other sources of misbehavior. It exudes an asceticism that builds virtue on the basis of rejection of minor vices associated with alcohol, tobacco, and sloth. That posture complements a long tradition of teaching by humiliation. "Brutal jokes, aphorisms, adages, and indignities are passed from generation to surgical generation," writes Joan Cassell (1998), as they are by chefs in teaching the next generation. It is quite impressive to see how solicitous students are of their chefs. A non-chef faculty member at CIA wrote the following e-mail with the obvious intention of upbraiding his chef colleagues (which backfired):

> In my IPC [Interpersonal Communication] class, one assignment is to answer the following question. "When emotions are involved, the emotions become the message." Do you agree? Give examples to back up your answer. How does emotion block communication on the job?[18]

He then goes on to provide a critique of chefs teaching through fear and intimidation, in the words of the student: "Hostile chefs create a lack of interest in the student, a desire to stop listening, to emotionally shutdown and close their mind to learning new things—the exact opposite of what the chef instructor is supposedly trying to achieve." A chef quickly responded, to much electronic applause from others, with, "Could you keep a record of this statement and send it back to this student after they have been in the industry for 5 to 10 years and let us see how their thoughts on this subject have changed." The chef then moved to juxtapose the moral world of practicing chefs against the wielders of words:

> When reality hits, your dishwasher just called out; your saucier just gave notice; you currently are putting in about 80 hours a week; you need a new dishwashing machine because the old one is on its last legs; your business has been down the last couple of weeks because of high gas prices, and it's absolutely crucial that the local newspaper's review of you is a good one; and so on and so on! Now that's intimidation. And yes chefs do yell sometimes!

Another chef wrote back, "I'm not buying into this and neither are our better students. If 'Preparation is Everything' is our motto then it should mean something or be changed to 'We'll hold your hand until you feel good about yourself.'" The chef continued that he had just had dinner with six students and the author Michael Ruhlman, and Ruhlman had asked: "I'm hearing from some students that the school is getting soft, that instructors aren't as hard as they used to be, true or false?" Unanimously, the students agreed with the statement, the chef noted. They named names of his colleagues who the students described as "Great guys, but too easy going." Maybe it was because he was there and they wanted to please him, he conceded, but they described him as a "hard-ass: not a hand holder." Letting "the whiners make us feel guilty for demanding high standards only sets the bar at the lowest common denominator." Anger, especially in the form of chef's temper, in fact plays an organizing role in the flow of kitchen time.

> Anger permits time to be controlled: permitting workers to "go on to the rest of the night." By expressing anger, one closes a frustrating event and reestablishes rhythm. Whether this catharsis is effective is less significant than that it is believed to be. Anger is seen as a means of achieving temporal stability and coping with the behavioral reality of the kitchen (Fine 1996: 69).

Humor, especially bawdy humor, is the other side of the same coin, which compensates for the angry outburst, cements the imagined community of bad taste, and makes men out of those who can stand it. Nothing unites people more than their self-conscious bad taste, which, through being vulgar, creates a distance between "us" and "them out there," with their repressive pretensions. Humor can be equalizing where anger is hierarchical—both necessary for an imagined community. Hence, in spite of its best efforts, the CIA has been unable to legislate away either the chef's angry outburst or his bawdy jokes. Instead, the Institute classifies them as unprofessional behavior, which makes them both rarer but also so much more tempting to use, and more powerful as subversive anti-corporate speech.

Diatribes on proper comportment and posture, vocabulary and attire, seek to separate the "disciplined middle class from the dissipated lower classes" (Bledstein 1976: 154). Such indicators of the fears of falling are a clear sign of the anxieties of social climbing that is emblematic of the process of professionalization (Ehrenreich 1989). Because the virtuous professional class is imagined as nothing but working men with character, even apparent iconoclasts such as Anthony Bourdain in *Kitchen Confidential* (2000) continue to harp on character over class, something I have elaborated on elsewhere (Ray 2007a). Michael Herzfeld's work among artisans in Rethemnos on the island of Crete in Greece proposes that such masculine idioms of work are quite widespread and may even be the substratum on which more generalized modern notions of selves are crafted. Herzfeld found that it was "meaningless here to separate the aesthetic or the technical from the moral: all are fused in a claim to value pure and simple. Pride in technical reliability is indistinguishable from what we might regard as the separate issue of the aesthetic qualities of the objects produced," and the sense of self (Herzfeld 2004: 124).

The military plays a central role in the history of the cooking profession in the United States, and some of the masculinity of cooking schools is a carry-over from such a homosocial institution. One could argue that some of the hyper-masculinity of the professional chef is a residue from the days when military men were central to the institutional culture of the CIA. The CIA was set up after the Second World War by two upper-class women, Francis Roth (a lawyer) and Katharine Angell (wife of a Yale University President), to retrain working-class military men for civilian careers. The preliminary brochure from 1946 (which announces that the school will be opening) says "Military training and service will be given credit towards admission" and "Approved by the Veterans Administration," and subsequent brochures and catalogs repeat such statements. The 1947 catalog identifies the institution as "a non-profit trade school, to train personnel for the industry and to give the returning veteran an opportunity to receive practical instruction in the preparation of foods and the management of restaurants." The catalogs from ca. 1949–51 say, "organized at the suggestion of the New Haven Restaurant Association in May 1946 to help returning veterans build permanent careers in the food trade."[19]

In 1951, the House of Representatives held hearings "investigating GI schools" that were established to take advantage of the GI Bill but were cheating the government out of money without really training people. Frances Roth was invited to testify on behalf of the New Haven Restaurant Institute. In her testimony she says that veterans were given preference by the school, as were wives and widows of veterans. For the first five years almost 100 percent of the recruits at the CIA were ex-military men. For a long time after that they remained the backbone of the Institute. Carroll F. Dooley, the first Director of the Division of Food Preparation at the New Haven Restaurant Institute, was a former United States Naval Reserve officer in charge of commissioned officers' messes at Pearl Harbor. Even today, almost all of the older male chefs at the CIA have some connection to the military—still one of the central institutions of upward mobility for working-class boys in the United States.

The CIA, from its very beginnings, has carried the hopes and troubles of young military men cooking. Richard Allen Burns, a folklorist and an ex-cook in the United States Marine Corps, points to the ambivalence of being a cook in the military. He writes, "Avoiding combat entirely, I took up a spatula and spoon. My only consolation to retaining my dignity was that all Marines during boot camp were and still are trained as riflemen, and I still periodically was required to qualify at the rifle range" (Burns 2002: 2–3). Admittedly, he developed ambivalent feelings about being a warrior with an "effeminate job . . . of a cook" (2002: 4). As a result, most Marines dread mess duty, and it is often considered a form of punishment. Without getting too speculative about it, here one can see how the aggressive male swagger of the profession can be read as compensation for that very ambiguity—a few good men doing women's work.

Ruhlman's *The Making of Chef* is an adumbration of the same theme—masculine "character" in the face of adversity. His narrative snaps into place with a blizzard that hit the mid-Hudson Valley when he was enrolled as a student at the CIA. I was there too. Everything was shut down. Next day, as it continued to snow, Ruhlman called the main switchboard at the CIA with some hope. "Yes, we're open," the voice told him with some bemusement. When he called his Skills Development teacher, Chef Pardus, to apologize for not showing up, he got an earful. He was told, "Part of what we're training students to be here is chefs—and when chefs have to be somewhere, they get there" (Ruhlman 1997: 68–9). He didn't stop there. Chef Pardus berated Ruhlman. "You're cut from a different cloth," he told Ruhlman. "College boy. White collar. Smooth. *Writer*." He was a cook through and through. "'We're different,' he said. 'We *get* there. It's part of what makes us a chef . . . We *like* it that way. That's why this place never shuts down. And we're teaching the student this'" (1997: 68–9). That ethos is common to the history of surgeons. It is echoed in what Cassell sees as a stoic posture prevalent among surgeons:

> Surgical training is so rigorous, so time-devouring, so stressful, that whether or not the chief rules by fear, candidates invariably absorb some aspects of the iron-surgeon mystique. By the time they have finished their training, surgeons have incorporated a stoic ethos that defies physical weakness and sets them off from the quotidian world. This ethos has been *learned by the body*. It is not subject to discussion, analysis, negotiation. It is not something that the surgeon *has*, like knowledge that can be brandished; it is something that the surgeon *is* (italics in original; Cassell 1998: 103).

Embodied, unarticulated, austerity of action and function idealizes a particular kind of subject—masculine and proficient—produced in the crucible of a valorized labor process, consecrated as a ritual. The precise sequencing of process, project, and self was also discovered by Gary Alan Fine among the restaurant workers he observed for *Kitchens: The Culture of Restaurant Work* (1994). It is paradoxical that the pursuit of sensory pleasure in haute cuisine can only be produced by the austere suffering and unrelenting labor of the working body that are often imagined as masculine traits. The culture includes an orientation towards active intervention, a propensity toward definitive decision making, an unwillingness to admit doubts, and an inclination to perpetuate the mystique of the confident, lone, heroic male. They inculcate thinking styles that are more categorical than probabilistic and tend toward certainty (Katz 1999: 203). As I read the published journals of physicians at the turn of the nineteenth century I was increasingly persuaded about how much of that posture works to describe the culture of chefs that I had experienced at close quarters at the CIA. "Sometimes in error, never in doubt," is the motto a chief of surgery ascribed to surgeons, cited in Cassell's work *The Woman in the Surgeon's Body* (1998: 18). She continues, "male-identified occupations such as surgeon, test pilot, soldier, firefighter, and race car driver focus on one pole of a set of cultural oppositions: practitioners describe themselves and their comrades as active, strong, decisive, brave, aggressive" (Cassell 1998: 18). She contends,

> In each of these vocations, we find ritualized ordeals for initiates, active male bonding, and profound distrust and exclusion of females as participants. And in each, we find the threat of death. What is it about the "ancient, primordial, irresistible" challenge that women would pollute, destroy, negate? What is it about the association Tom Wolfe notes between "the right stuff" and death—about heroism, in short—that makes it something men do *to* and *for*, not *with*, women? (Cassell 1998: 18).

Such an action-oriented attitude sits very well with chefs. Such a focus on "grit" and "character" is also typical of an emergent profession—as was the case with physicians about a hundred years ago, and surgeons over the last half-century. Things like resilience, punctuality, and the dress code become external manifestations of the soul that is the character of a real professional. Character inevitably leads to charisma.

Dr Robinson exclaimed, "I don't like offices. I can't sit in an office to see patients. I am a surgeon!" (Katz 1999: 35). Similarly, a cook condemning his chef boss confided to Gary Alan Fine, "One day I think he even put it that he likes brains over brawn, which means he would rather sit and do his paperwork than sit and get his fingers dirty" (Fine 1996: 92). The last straw for the cook was that "[He'd] rather sit in his office." The active posture, so central to the image of the surgeon and the chef, is also the reason they show such disdain towards their offices and desks. Chefs so recoil from their desks at the CIA that often three or more chefs are assigned to the same desk and office space, which they rarely use. Most use their desks in the kitchen, which appears to be an intermediate zone between the doer and the thinker (the latter is often read as the procrastinator).

Subterranean tension between those who sit at their desks and chefs erupted predictably on a hot summer day when a supervisor complained about the fire hazard associated with chefs propping their kitchen doors open. One chef noted in response, "When confined in a space where the temperature commonly exceeds 90 degrees on a comfortable day (as it is in K1 at the moment) for 6-and-a-1/2 hours a day (or 13 hours as those of us on doubles frequently do) these goals become very difficult to achieve." With statements riddled with barbs against the "suits," the chef continued:

> A person sitting in an air conditioned office is much higher up on Maslow's hierarchy than someone in a 100 degree kitchen breathing grease fumes and sweating into their eyes. As such, the person in the office has the luxury of noticing a squeaky hinge or worrying about "convenience" while the person in the kitchen has all they can do to keep from cursing at anything within ear-shot.
>
> C'mon down to any production kitchen any day this summer. Spend a shift with one of us. We'll put you in whites, give you a knife and a sauté pan, stand you in front of a grill or range top for 6 hours. Walk a mile in our slip resistant shoes before you make the assumption that we are merely reacting to minor annoyances and inconvenience.

The link of chefs at the CIA to modern professions and professionalism is refracted through particularly American prisms of class, craft, and masculinity. Dorine Kondo's work among Japanese confectioners, Susan Terrio's ethnography among French chocolatiers, and Michael Herzfeld's work among Greek artisans show different but congruent routes of making oneself (Kondo 1990; Terrio 2000; Herzfeld 2004). In these varied national contexts the relationship between the artisanal body and the body politic is differently constituted because craftsmanship is valued differently than in the American context.

In closing

The making of a perfect consommé is evidence of expertise in a particular kind of Bocusian (after Paul Bocuse, the most influential founder of the current iteration of nouvelle French restaurant cuisine) cooking, a mode of doing that is shared by the evaluators. Such skills have to be demarcated, cut off, from the common world of everyday experience, contained in small "worlds" with internal evaluative judgments, about product, character, and comportment (Becker 1984; Fine 1996; Davis 2013). In this case, cooking haute cuisine in an expensive American restaurant at the turn of the twentieth and twenty-first centuries is what is being accessed and assessed. Lasater-Wille (2015) shows how that model is spreading to places such as cooking schools in Lima, Peru.

The CIA and its alumni claim that first and foremost the institution produces professionals. The professional chef is the mirror-image of the foreign-born, untrained, ethnic cook. The former occupies the heights of the culinary field in the USA today, just as the latter inhabits the bottom rungs of the hierarchy. To the degree that the foreign-born depends on experience, in terms of both taste and skill, the native-born chef is trained in schools and restaurants not only to acquire new skills and habits, but also to transform his habits so that he can be promoted in the class hierarchy. That is partly about remaking his relationship to gender, ethnicity, and everyday work. His palate and hands have to be remade, as his body, posture, and gesture have to be made to fit middle-class aspiration and upper-class consumption. I have shown in this chapter how the modern, American, professional chef has to be wrought from the deformed clay of a differently-classed body, which, through years of grueling training in expert esoteric knowledge and common everyday postures, is remade in the mirror-image of the ethnic cook so that he can occupy one end of an unbridgeable culinary field. If cooking schools want to make an upwardly mobile career out of cooking, they must, by structural necessity, distance their domain of activity from unpaid or poorly paid everyday cookery and increase the cost of entry into the field. Haute cuisine will always be gendered, classed, and racialized, but not in the same way, as we see in the changing profile of the chef at the CIA with all the new pressures of cooking by the book and proper behavior. Professions have histories. They also have life cycles. Chefs have just begun their journey towards professionalization in the USA. There are no completely open and democratic professions. All professions are ranked, gendered, and racialized in one way or the other, as superior or inferior. Every profession has to elbow others next to it, and pour disdain into the work of others whose work is akin to theirs, especially if that subordinate other is not a closed labor market. Here, chefs' attitudes towards housewives are the same as university scholars' posture towards autodidacts. That is the only way to build a profession. Professions produce new, more sharply defined forms of expert knowledge, and their own future. Every profession does that.

Ethnic cooks do not have the right skills to play in the field of haute cuisine. Formal training in schools becomes crucial to the making of a profession, which marries individual aspirations to class scripts, and eventually has to be consecrated by the state by way of naming, counting,[20] approving student loans, encouraging tourism, propagandizing culture, and approving rules of licensure. Actors here range from individuals, small groups, networks, to states embedded in the interstate system. Cooking schools are one of the productive intersections in the making of a chef.

Personally, I was transformed by my decade-long sojourn at the CIA and not only learned to appreciate a good consommé, and the uses of a sharp and heavy chef's knife, or the power of a raging flame with very high BTUs, but was also trained to read and comprehend the wine-list and menu at elite restaurants. I realized I was not a chef. I did not have the right skills. That put me in my place. Yet, what had previously made me nervous—approaching expensive restaurants, with their rituals and language of description and the scripted but fluent dialogue with sommeliers and servers—came naturally to me by the end of the sojourn. I began to feel comfortable in expensive restaurants and relish the rituals of ordering and enjoying the food, the ambience, and the company of chefs and connoisseurs. As a non-chef, I was trained in making a few things, tasting many others, and acquiring the social graces of an elite restaurant. I became a camp-follower of chefs and critics. That was my bodily, moral, and aesthetic transformation.

The CIA is an exemplary institutional incubator, imparting bodies of knowledge that simultaneously effectuate material, moral, and aesthetic reconfiguration of palates and class profiles. Hence the insistence on professionalism and uniformity. It is an institution that teaches its residents the art of making a great consommé, and to develop rules of evaluating it, while producing the professional who does not swear, smoke, use racist epithets, or ethnic slurs, so that he can ideally become the measured, soft-spoken, manager of people, emotions and bodies, as much as well-cooked proteins, carbohydrates, and fats. Bourdieu famously noted that class habitus is acquired at home and school. The CIA is an extraordinary school because it hopes not only to teach explicitly what was often taught implicitly at home and under apprenticeship as a craftsman, but also to explicate what is implicated in class cultures of consumption of wine, cheese, French sauces, and haute cuisine. The CIA, then, is home, school, and apprenticeship for the social production of culinary professionals. The social field of professional cooking, and institutions such as the CIA and haute restaurants, produce chefs as social subjects that exceed the bounds of individual intentions. There were no American chefs for most of America's history, and immigrant cooks were everywhere covered under the category of servants. That has changed drastically in the last few decades.

Understandably, the *Time* cover of November 2013 provoked a firestorm of criticism from female chefs, with Amanda Cohen of Dirt Candy raising the claims of Barbara Lynch, Dione Lucas, Madeleine Kamman, Josefina Velazquez de Leon, and Julia Child, among others (Cohen 2013a).[21] *Time* editor Howard Chua-Eoan unhelpfully clarified in an interview that he had considered adding Alice Waters but did not, because he wanted to go only with "reputation and influence" in the field rather than tokenism (see Branch 2012; Dixler 2013). The *Los Angeles Times* pointed out that

> this male-centric view of cooking is not something that originated with [*Time*] magazine's article. After all, of San Pellegrino's list of the 50 Best Restaurants in the World, only two are run by women—both of whom are one half of a male–female team. And the last seven James Beard Foundation chefs of the year have been men (Parsons 2013; See also Kohn 2013).

Marnie Hanel noted in *The New York Times* that only 12 percent of the winners of the James Beard award for Outstanding Chef and 16 percent of *Food & Wine*'s Best New Chefs have been women (Hanel 2014: 44).

In quick retaliatory response to the *Time* magazine cover, perhaps too quick, Grub Street produced a list of "Goddesses of Food," which listed Alice Waters, Elena Arzak, April Bloomfield, Anne Sophie-Pic, Dominique Crenn, Christina Tossi, etc. (Tishgart 2013). In the online comments, a reader sharply countered, "It's hypocritical to claim this list as a triumph for recognizing a diverse group of talented chefs where there are no people of color included, and no one outside of Europe and North America" (Tishgart 2013). Even ideological opponents of the masculinization of professional chefs are trapped within the social confines of the field, which cannot account for ethnic cooks. Notwithstanding good intentions of individuals and institutions, the field of haute cuisine still demands a chasm between the professional chef, the ethnic cook, and the housewife. That holds true even when the edges of the field are fraying and the center is shifting, as we will see in the next chapter.

Notes

1 That cover was distributed in Europe, Africa, and Asia, while the US cover profiled the recently re-elected New Jersey Governor Chris Christie.

2 Almost fifty years earlier, on November 25, 1966, Julia Child was on the cover of *Time* magazine under the title "Everyone's in the Kitchen." The issue included photographs of Vice President Hubert Humphrey, and August Busch III of Anheuser-Busch fame, cooking in their respective kitchens.

3 http://www.theworlds50best.com/list/1-50-winners/#t11-20 [accessed on December 4, 2013].

4 As Casanova notes with literature in mind, "those most distant from its great centres or most deprived of its resources, who can see more clearly than others the forms of violence and domination that operate within it" (2005a: 72).

5 An illustrative example is the CIA's recent (Feb 16, 2015) *ProChef Smart Brief* observation: "Singapore has transformed into a foodie destination, thanks in part to the CIA's first international branch, which teaches students European cooking techniques that can be applied to the nation's unique cuisine. 'Part of our being here is to professionalize and teach the whys of cooking, so it's not haphazard,' said CIA Managing Director Eve Felder. 'The whys are all the same. The difference is in the flavor profiles.'" (Zimmer 2015). Not only is the presumption astounding that Singapore could only become a foodie destination because of CIA's intermediation, but it is equally interesting to see how the deeper division between universal (haute French) techniques and vernacular flavors holds in this construction.

6 In responding to an early draft of this chapter, a colleague, a chef, and the current Vice-President of the James Beard Foundation, Mitchell Davis, noted "Part of your battle with this piece will be that the field of medicine is so revered here in America and doctors are such gods that lay readers will find it insulting (conversely, chefs will probably think someone finally understands how important their work is!)." In response I must reiterate that the intent of this chapter is not to assert that chefs' work is equal in importance to the physician's profession; instead it is to point to the similarities in culture that the process of first-wave professionalization engenders. No matter how great a chef, it is unlikely that his or her achievement will be favorably compared to innovations in surgical technique, epidemiology, biochemistry, or genetics, especially within the medical field, and even among the general public. That hierarchy of expertise and social acknowledgment remains intact even if celebrity chefs and surgeons make enormous amounts of money, which is our society's only way of acknowledging objective value. What we easily forget is that (a) early modern medicine was very close to cooking, and both were recorded in recipe books, which is etymologically related to the instruction to take, to prescribe = ℞; and (b) culinary knowledge as well as medical knowledge has always been produced collaboratively but professionalization in both, divergent fields now, entailed an illegitimate privatization of intellectual property (see Leong 2013, Claflin 2014).

7 For instance, most doctors in India attend medical school after high school without pedagogical burdens. In fact many of those trained in the Indian system do quite well when they migrate to the United States.

8 Thanks to my physician friend, Dr. Atul Limaye, for drawing my attention to this passage.

9 In 2000 the basic text was changed to the *Best Food Writing*, which is a collection of journalistic writing by Americans on American food.

10 For leading cooking schools, such as the CIA, the two-year AOS program cost about $35,000 in tuition and $45,000 including room and board, while the four-year BPS program cost about $60,000 in tuition and $80,000 in total, ca. 2001.

11 Thanks to Craig Goldstein for drawing my attention to this.

12 Names have been withheld for privacy.

13 The male baker, especially in pastry arts, is so exceptional that casting agencies specifically look for male bakers, as the following e-mail suggests: "Okay men, this is the opportunity that you have been waiting for. I just received a call from Barbara Bersell Casting Agency in Los Angeles. They are looking for male chocolatiers and bakers between the ages of 18 and 45. They will need 2 sets of photos with a head shot and a full shot for each set. They can be photos that you already have of yourself. If chosen, you will attend a one day photo shot in Manhattan for Levis jean and be paid $10,000. (They wanted actual professionals wearing the jeans in their ads.) Deadline is July 6th." Internal CIA e-mail.

14 This and subsequent quotations: CIA Archive, Boxes 1–2.

15 Interestingly, "Between 1900 and 1920 approximately 10 percent of all Ph.D.s awarded in the United States were granted to women. In the next two decades that figure rose to 15 percent before beginning a *thirty-year decline*" (italics mine; Glazer and Slater 1987: 25).

16 Interview notes.

17 Unfortunately there is no systematic historical data on race at the CIA, but interviews with numerous "old-timers" confirm a continuous low count of non-whites.

18 This and subsequent quotations from e-mail exchanges at the CIA are taken from field notes.

19 CIA Archives, Boxes 1–2.

20 Chefs were counted as skilled professionals by the 1980 Census for the first time in the United States as a result of lobbying by the American Culinary Federation and numerous leading cooking schools; cooks, on the other hand, were counted since the 1910 Census but until 1940 subsumed under servants.

21 Cohen points out that Diane Forley should have been included under Alain Passard, which would have then included Amanda Freitag and Suzanne Goin. A reader listed the following in the same spirit: Barbara Tropp, Cecilia Chang, Alice Waters, Marion Cunningham, Madeleine Kamman, Marcella Hazan, Lidia Bastianich, Judy Rogers, Dominque Crenn, Traci des Jardins, Nancy Oakes, Susan Spicer, Michelle Bernstein, Elizabeth Faulkner, Niki Nakayama, Suzanne Goin, Susan Feniger, Nancy Silverton, etc.

5

Ethnicity and Expertise: Immigrant Cooks with Haute Aspirations

An immigrant chef noted: "I could not get a job at a decent restaurant in New York City. I was told, 'You are Indian. I cannot hire you for anything else.'" I pressed the chef: "What was your response to that?" He retorted,

> There is a chip in my shoulder, where I have to prove myself as a chef. That is why I opened this place, to show them that I can cook. But I refuse to do what is done by other Indian restaurateurs. I don't want that red paint on my tandoori chicken. I don't want my restaurant to be a dark, incense-laden, god-riven place with waiters who cannot speak English.

The immigrant chef here is touching the social limits of the field of haute cuisine in New York City in the twenty-first century.

It is more than a decade since Chef Cardoz first became a celebrity, running a restaurant that in 2010 grossed $8 million, yet it rankles him, this dismissal of his acquired expertise in favor of the ascribed one. The presumption that his ethnicity was a sign of lack of expertise in haute restaurant cookery in New York City is something that "ethnic" chefs with haute aspirations struggle with (see Ferguson 2004; Trubek 2004; Janer 2006). So they become particularly self-conscious in avoiding their ethnic ghetto. Roy Choi long refused to cook Asian food, until he realized that was his forte, and fusion Asian acquired a new prestige (due to the rise of East Asia). He could embrace Asian cookery only after he had acquired self-confidence in the field, and after successfully sending out signals that he could cook, because he had cooked with Eric Ripert at Le Bernardin. Similarly, Cecilia Chiang set out to design the first haute cuisine Chinese restaurant in San Francisco with a million dollars and four "No"s. "No gold. No red. No dragons. No lanterns. I didn't want my Chinese restaurant to be like any other" (Chiang with Weiss 2007: 21). Boundaries between the two worlds had to be marked. There is a clear tension here between the embodied experience of the ethnic and the professional proficiency of the expert chef with his designer restaurant, which encapsulates the incongruence between two kinds of identities.

Identities have to be wrested in dialogue with others, in conflict between contending domains of the self, and are shaped by the properties of the field one is assigned to (ethnic) or hopes to play in (haute cuisine). Common sense conceptions of consumer culture as the domain of free, identity-affirming activity, in alliance with academic focus on consumption, have tended to elide work-based identities in the United States. With the decline of class-based politics and class analysis, it may appear, inaccurately, that work has been drained of all identity. As a result we have an immense amount of work on the food-related identities of consumers (Bourdieu 1984; Warde and Martens 2000; Bennett *et al.* 2009; Johnston and Bauman 2010, to name only a handful) but very little on the identity of those who do all the material work of making such symbolic claims available to consumers. In the consumer-oriented scholarship, all the work of producing food-related identity is done by the consumers and the commentators, and none whatsoever by the producer of food.[1] I argue that such a picture is empirically incomplete and theoretically inadequate. This chapter challenges that consensus and shows how, in one instance, identity work is done through public, food-related labor. Based on extensive interviews with foreign-born American chefs, analysis of cookbooks they have written, and restaurant reviews on the web and in print, I show how work-related food identities are crucial to an understanding of the social division of labor inherent in the production of professions. The field of New American haute cuisine still subjugates "many while celebrating a chosen few," as was the case in eighteenth-century France, studied from the cook's point of view by Jennifer Davis (2013: 11).

A number of high-profile Indian chefs in New York City, such as Floyd Cardoz, Hemant Mathur, Maneet Chauhan, Jehangir Mehta, and Vikas Khanna, to name a few, often in spite of their current popularity, find themselves struggling to bridge two irreconcilable identities. Irreconcilable in so far as they acquire their legitimacy from modes of being-in-the-world that occupy two contradictory poles in the field of gastronomy: the chef and the ethnic cook. Julia Moskin writes "In the food world, chefs are the 1 percent, and the rest of us are the 99 percent. At this time every year [Christmas season], we dream of catching crumbs from their tables: shiny new cookbooks, stuffed with recipes so brilliantly simplified as to lift us to their level" (2011: D1). Although only a handful of individuals, these chefs and restaurateurs illuminate the shape of the field by lighting up its limits. In this chapter I mine those interviews to make a larger point about the world of ethnic chefs that is the counterpoint to the preceding chapter on the CIA.

The shape of the field of gastronomy has been most sharply delineated by Zilkia Janer, who writes, "In spite of the celebration of multi-culturalism, most professional cooking schools in the world still teach using a French technical framework." She continues, "there is no neatly packaged way to become an expert on Indian cuisines," thus, by extension, "[c]uisines that have not codified their culinary knowledge in a way that makes it easy for outsiders to learn and [be] efficient for a restaurant kitchen are at a disadvantage" (Janer 2006: 7). She contends:

> We can understand what French cuisine is all about after reading a few books, but understanding the cuisine of Rajasthan or Nagaland, among many others, implies travel, meeting people, and challenging the very categories on which Eurocentric culinary knowledge is based. The proliferation of so-called ethnic cookbooks does not necessarily solve this problem since the genre itself imposes the categories and structures of European cooking, failing to grasp the epistemologies that shape different culinary systems (2006: 6).

That is crucial, that difference in the culinary systems and the difference it makes to Western understandings of taste and skill. Her argument is promising even if we pick out some of the rhetorical barbs (for instance, it is probable that it takes a little more than reading cookbooks to be able to adequately cook French haute cuisine), and after we have acknowledged, as I have done in Chapter 3, that Japanese and other European cuisines, such as Italian, Spanish, Greek, and, currently, Nordic cooking have joined the pantheon of venerated culinary cultures in the global hierarchy of restaurant cuisines (Ray 2007b, 2010). Just as the French body, with its acquired artisanal and aesthetic skills and embodied everyday accent—the accent is the perfect marker of a habituated body that is never fully self-conscious—was the dominant player in the institutionalization of the chef in major global cities of the nineteenth and twentieth centuries, a few extra-European bodies (especially Japanese) have joined the fray in the early decades of the twenty-first century (see Chapter 4 and Trubek 2004; Spang 2000; Ferguson 2004; Davis 2013). In the following sections I show how Indian, Thai, Filipino, and other ethnic chefs navigate a tenuous trajectory in those networked hierarchies, with the resultant production of a distinctive rhetoric of middleness between profession and ethnicity.

Native and foreign: Body and skill

There is a rich sociology of the acquisition of expertise, especially its rhetorics and status claims. Drawing on that literature, I have shown in the previous chapter how chefs develop the tasting skills, the cooking skills, and the postures and gestures of professionalism, at similar stages of their life cycle to physicians more than a hundred years ago, and how they are trained to do so at a leading institution that produces chefs such as the Culinary Institute of America.

In contrast to the rhetorics, status, and pure politics of relational professional turf battles, Harry Collins and Robert Evans propose a realist approach that begins with the assumption that "expertise is the real and substantive possession of groups of experts and that individuals acquire real and substantive expertise through their membership of those groups" (Collins and Evans 2007: 3). Where I want to inflect their frame is in the understanding that those groups can be ascribed and aspired ones, such as ethnicity and profession. For Collins and Evans, acquiring expertise is a process of socialization into the practices of an expert group, and expertise can be lost if time is spent away from the group. "Acquiring expertise is, however, more than attribution by a social group . . . In the case of relational theories, on the other hand, all the work is done by the attributors. Under our treatment, then, individuals may or may not possess expertise independently of whether others think they possess expertise" (Collins and Evans 2007: 3). In my view the relational/rhetorical and the substantivist theory of expertise are not mutually exclusive. Expertise is real, produced by different degrees of instruction and immersion, and returns to the expert (professional) depend on the value put on certification, boundary-work, and the social organization of advantages, between various grades of neighboring experts and their political relationship to other experts and non-experts. The rhetoric can be learned, embodied, and internalized as a natural fit between body, posture, skill, and profession. Here schooling and the social world that professions produce play a crucial role in producing expertise and exclusions from it.

Collins and Evans go on to give an example that works very well for cooking, because cooking, like speaking, can be an everyday skill:

> To give a simple example, in France everyone can speak French, "even the little children," and it is not thought of as an expertise. On the other hand, in Britain a person who is fluent in French is thought of as an expert and can, for example, command a salary as a translator or teacher. It's the opposite way round in France, where it is speaking English that counts as the useful expertise (Collins and Evans 2007: 3).

Within this substantivist frame, the ethnic cook is analogous to the native speaker and the chef is the acknowledged foreign-language expert with skills that do not come naturally through regular everyday socialization. So it is a question both of a skill set and the context of its valuation.

That is why, as I have shown in Chapter 2, it is understandable that until 1960 an authoritative native informant is always invoked in discussions of Indian food by *The New York Times*. Craig Claiborne's first major piece on Indian cooking on February 25, 1960 relied on Manorama Phillips (Claiborne 1960). As I noted earlier, the article was accompanied by a photograph of Miss Phillips in her apartment, clad in a sari, and framed by exquisite Indian handcrafted textiles, as crucial visual props of authenticity. As the genre of restaurant criticism was established, the critic acquired expertise in tasting and writing about Indian food, and developed a regular public that was willing to take him seriously. It took some time to naturally include Indian cuisine in the repertoire of the American critic. Only after enough Indian restaurateurs emerged who were willing (with capital investments) to play in the gastronomic field of haute cuisine in Manhattan, and new consumers became available, could a novel posture be developed towards Indian food. By March 29, 2011, Sam Sifton, the *New York Times* restaurant reviewer, could write:

> Hemant Mathur is the force behind Tulsi. He was an owner and a chef at Devi, where he often could be seen fussing nervously at the edges of the dining room before retreating to the kitchen to cook with rare brilliance. At Tulsi he does the same dance and, if the setting is less attractive, louder and less special, it places his cooking in sharper relief.
>
> No one in New York makes lamb chops like he does—heavy, ugly things caked in yogurt but tasting of gamy perfection. His magical Manchurian cauliflower has made the transition as well (spoiler: its secret ingredient is ketchup, well caramelized).
>
> He serves a wickedly fine duck moilee—a delicate curry softened by coconut milk—and a deeply flavorful curried monkfish with pomegranate sauce. And there are very good tandoori prawns. Tulsi's vegetable dishes do not disappoint either, most notably the house dal (Sifton 2011).

Minimally, you have to know what a "dal" is to play in this field in Manhattan today. You have to learn to play along with the manufactured taste for Manchurian cauliflower, sweet, sticky, and oily, neither Manchurian nor particularly Indian by any stretch of imagination, other than as an ersatz product of Indian restaurants. To recoil from it is to miss the joke. To miss the joke is to reveal your hand—a novice. And as Sifton suggests, Hemant Mathur does fuss, nervously. That is the authenticating touch. You know the chef; the details in terms of the lineage and trajectory of the chef, the strengths and weaknesses of his cooking, the revealed secret, are normal for write-ups on all kinds of celebrity chefs today. It is a small and well-informed world of the chef, the critic, the connoisseur, and the informed consumer.

In association with the expert with the byline, electronic mediation has allowed the possibilities of numerous forums for other potential experts to expound on their expertise. When there is disagreement about judgments of taste about food in an Indian restaurant in New York City, contemporary commentators take recourse to the opinions of expatriated natives. In evaluating Tulsi, the same upscale, midtown, Indian restaurant that Sifton reviews above, reviewers on yelp.com (one of the more ubiquitous sites among restaurant reviewers) deployed the typical rhetoric of the native speaker:

> I'm Indian and I've eaten at some of the best Indian restaurants in India and elsewhere. Tulsi is right up there with them. I ate at Bukhara, the iconic Indian restaurant at the Sheraton in Delhi last month and I have to say Hemant Mathur's lamb chops (burra kebab) is just as good if not better! (Yelp.com n.d.)

In contrast, another self-proclaimed native noted:

> Being an Indian, [I] can vouch for the fact that there are much better Indian restaurants in the area—the food is much below average (never order their Spicy Chicken Curry—that's not spicy at all). This is probably a brave attempt to cater to the Indian as well as the American palate, but fails miserably. Very expensive and tasteless at that. Poor service too—go at your own risk. (Yelp.com n.d.)

In *India Abroad* (the most widely circulated diasporic Indian newspaper in the United States), the journalist and restaurant reviewer Arthur J. Pais notes that Chef Mathur opened Tulsi after he left Devi, "the only Indian restaurant in New York to get a Michelin star" (Pais 2011b: M5). We quickly find Pais (the journalist) and Mathur (the chef) in alliance, distinguishing themselves from two directions, the excessively upscale, fancy, Western restaurant without much flavor, and the overly down-market curry house. Mathur is quoted as saying, "I believe a dish should not only look appetizing but should taste good as well," which appears to be a dig at high-concept haute cuisine, to which the authentic ethnic is always the imagined ameliorative other. Then on the other hand, the curry house is contained by Pais's assertion that "He is not a fan of heavy cream that is often the basis of many dishes in standard Indian restaurants" (2011b: M8). By now Pais is so in agreement with Mathur that the quotation is dispensed with. The article goes on to mark the trajectory of

Chef Mathur through five-star, super-luxury Indian hotels such as the Rambaugh Palace Taj Hotel in Jaipur, the private kitchen of curry-eating British tycoon Sir James Goldsmith, and finally the New York trajectory of Diwan Grill, Tamarind, Amma and Devi (of which Sifton had mentioned only the final step). Pais commends:

> More than 16 years ago, when most Indian chefs—with the exception of Floyd Cardoz at Tabla—were afraid to go beyond chicken and lamb, Mathur was offering succulent boar chops at Diwan. At Devi, he courageously offered calf brain, venison chops and rabbit dishes. While only a handful of Indian chefs offered quail, Mathur would go farther and serve duck with a coconut and curry leaf sauce (2011b: M8).

Here, "going further" into the cosmopolitan omnivores' territory is *de rigueur* for any rising New York City chef. Furthermore, by the rules of the gastronomic field the authentic chef has to be original, in contrast to the authenticity of the ethnic cook who is urged to reproduce the unaltered original. These are two very different modes of fabricating culinary value. It is worth digging a little deeper into the contrasting language of these domains, and to do that I enter the inscribed world of cookbooks because their durability allows me the opportunity to hold the discourse still for sustained analysis.

Cookbooks and the chefs they produce

Michael Batterberry, the founding editor of the highly reputable Manhattan food magazines *Food Arts* and *Food and Wine*, compliments Suvir Saran's cookbook *Indian Home Cooking* as a "redolent book on the simple home cooking of his native India" that brings "Indian cooking into twenty-first century American kitchens" (Saran and Lyness 2004: viii–ix; preface by Batterberry). Simple, native, and twenty-first century American kitchens are doing a lot of work here in terms of translating and transcribing between different groups of practitioners. Saran makes the classic move of chefs who want to distinguish themselves from the down-market curry houses. Echoing Cardoz's "incense-laden, god-riven places" (that I cited at the opening of this chapter), Saran notes:

> The food that most Indian restaurants in America serve is northern Indian cuisine, the meat cuisine of the Moghuls—Muslim Turks who invaded India in the sixteenth century and built the great Moghul empire. But I, a Hindu and a vegetarian, also teach a lot of meatless Indian cuisine, dishes that I have adapted from the largely vegetarian communities of northern and

> southern India. Some of these dishes are spiced quite differently from Moghul food and are unfamiliar to many Americans (Saran and Lyness 2004: 1).

He then collates a remarkable collection of southern Indian rasams, manufactured institutional dishes such as cauliflower Manchurian, whole-spiced baby potatoes, "my grand-uncle's khitcheree," etc., framing them within the requisite gestures of authenticity, nativity, familiarity, such as the acknowledgment to his two grandmothers and the praise for the domestic servant "Panditji's" cooking in Delhi. That genuflection towards authentic expatriate domesticity is essential for the ethnic cook, and quite different from the rhetoric of the chef, especially a chef's chef, such as many have come to identify Thomas Keller, as we will see below (Keller 1999, 2009). Suvir Saran's *Indian Home Cooking* is bristling with crimsons, emerald greens, and turquoise, like a bride decked out to seduce by her demure domesticity: the exact opposite of the demeanor and design of Keller cookbooks (or for that matter the El Bulli and NOMA cookbooks).

The dust jacket of *The French Laundry Cookbook* (1999) is minimalist and modern, with whites, beiges, browns, clear lines, and stringent folds. Clearly this is no ethnic thing. No loud color, no ancestral sentimentalism, no deep collective authenticity, only individual originality. Austere, yes, understated surely, yet with a certain confident, even arrogant, presumption of perfection. The name of the restaurant and the cookbook is clever, quirky, misleading, especially compared to the obvious referent *Indian Home Cooking*. French, yes, but a laundry? Well, the building was once a French steam laundry built in Yountville, Napa Valley, California, circa 1900. It was a saloon, a brothel, and a residence too. But the avant-garde self-consciousness and homage to France would work well with the name *The French Laundry*. It would become one of a brand with the artisan's signature in the form of Per Se and Ad Hoc, two other referents in the Keller empire of the quirky Francophilic genre leading into New American haute cuisine. Sam Sifton, the same *New York Times* restaurant critic who reviewed Tulsi above, opens his assessment of Per Se on October 12, 2011, with: "So this is the best restaurant in New York City: Per Se, in the Time Warner Center, just up the escalator from the mall, a jewel amid the zirconia" (Sifton 2011: D1). He concludes, "It represents the ideal of an American high-culture luxury restaurant," where a dinner for two with wine could set you back a thousand dollars. Sifton bestows the ultimate reward of four stars on Per Se.

The introduction of *The French Laundry Cookbook* frames the issue as the pursuit of "pleasure and perfection." Addressed to the home cook, the co-author Michael Ruhlman notes, "This is not fast food, nor is it four-star cooking simplified for home kitchens. It is four-star cooking, period" (Keller 1999: 9).

Quickly it plunges into a *barigoule* (a stew of artichoke hearts braised with carrots and onions, fresh herbs, oil, and wine) and salmon tartare with sweet red onion crème fraîche served in a *tuile*. The pictures are rarely of composed dishes, mostly of stemware, kitchen utensils, two bright yellow squash blossoms, tousled sprigs of mustard, the chef, his hands, and the purveyor. Artisan and artifact. Produce, purveyor, tool, craftsman—a whole realm of possibilities, open in various directions, limited only by quality and skill. "I take pleasure in precision," writes Keller (2009: 4). Perfect food by the best chef: that's his reputation in the culinary field. There is some sentiment about "dad" and the categorical imperative to "Take care of your parents" (2009: 3). Here the chef's directive is expected to be followed to the letter. "An hour before you want to eat, preheat the oven to 325°F. If you're grilling over coals, start the fire then too; if you're grilling over propane, know that you'll begin the chicken about a half hour after you start cooking, and preheat the grill . . . so it is hot when you're ready to put your chicken on. Put the bacon in a heavy Dutch oven" (Keller 2009: 2). Followed by beautiful abstract equations: spring onions + parmesan cheese + persimmon + pine nuts + prosciutto = fall salad. This is the distillate of the rhetoric, the posture, the confidence, and the skill, embodied in a star New American restaurant chef. Keller's is the quintessential signature of the professional, where colleagues and family are acknowledged but never the customer. That would be too crass. That is the difference between a professional and a quack—a quack panders to his customers. There is no hedging, either, in terms of the reach towards universal and abstract proficiency, timeless and placeless, different from the rhetorical style, say, of Michael Psilakis, a rising American chef playing in the medium of Greek food, with its distinct location in the hierarchy between New American and Indian restaurant cuisine.

In the case of *How to Roast a Lamb* (Psilakis 2009) the inviting title is familiar, and the subtitle "New Greek Classic" tries to make room between the old ethnic Greek diner and the New American fancy food. The acknowledgment is overwrought, the cover classic Mediterranean, which is olive oil in a traditionally stoppered bottle, a lemon cut in half, garlic bulb, bunch of thyme, and olives on a plate with a stereotypically Greek key-patterned border. This is going to be about "recipes and reminiscences" and, in Barbara Kafka's foreword, is identified as a book about "contemporary Greek cooking" which "deserves to join the pantheon of other great foods of the world" (Psilakis 2009: ix). Clearly this is a cuisine that needs updating and promoting, a little like the native cuisine of India brought into the twenty-first century American home that we encountered earlier, yet in this case we do not have to travel that far.

The first visual offering, after the cover, is an old fashioned spoon with a dab of Greek yogurt on a traditional oval plate. Nothing designer here. No

Bauhaus. Deep essence and authenticity, underlined by old, torn, black and white photographs of family and friends in difficulty, but with the possibility of joy. The story is about families in hardship, their intensity polished by adversity, until they get to America and the next generation, the author's, comes along. It is a story about Cretan men, the patriarch, and the father figure, strong, stoic, and self-sacrificing, "men among men" (Psilakis 2009: 2). Here is the future chef as the immigrant kid "dressed for school as if he were going to church. They were eating hot dogs and hamburgers for lunch. I was eating *souvlaki* and *spanakopita*" (2009: 3). The classic bundle of youthful anxieties and grown-up "pride of culture, cuisine, and heritage" leads eventually to an unhappy life as an accountant. He accidentally falls into Café Angelica, which almost closes, but is then saved by a review in *The New York Times*. The rest is history. More sepia-toned pictures, memories, and gorgeous recipes for salads with wild bitter greens, grilled onions, dried tomatoes and Kefalotiri; artichoke and potato salad; roasted whole fish; cod *skordalia* with pickled beets; hanger steak with braised dandelion, lemon and oil; and shellfish *youvetsi*.

> When I decided to close my restaurant on Long Island and take my chances opening a restaurant in New York City, I had one very specific goal in mind: to shatter the confines, boundaries, and expectations that had been imposed on Greek cuisine. I aimed to elevate the way in which Greek cuisine—the cuisine of my heritage—is perceived by critics and diners alike (Psilakis 2009: 224).

The storyline that Chef Psilakis is after ends with a soaring claim: "Greece is the birthplace of democracy and Western civilization as we know it today. It is also the birthplace of cuisine" (2009: 225). Of course we ought to be familiar with the first contention, but the second one? A typical product of ethnocentric exuberance? Recompense for the long history of the one-dimensional Francophilia of American taste-makers? He is going to show how Greek cuisine is the best in the world. That is one-half Psilakis's swagger, the other half insider ambition for outsider approval. That is the dream of every upwardly mobile ethnic, expatriate chef forced to play on a field where he does not fully belong.

From the evidence among various evaluators of cuisine, such as Zagat, Chef Psilakis is not alone among Greeks in his hopes. Greek cuisine has been climbing rapidly in the estimation of critics, as shown in Chapter 3. As a result, the average price of a meal at a Greek haute cuisine restaurant in New York City has been climbing, ranked twelfth in 1985, to the seventh rank in the same list in 2014, with an average price of a meal at $45.50, after French, Japanese, Continental, New American, Italian, etc. (see Figure 3.9 on page 86 of Chapter 3). Indian haute cuisine in the USA is also coming into view among critics and connoisseurs, but occupies the tenth spot in that ranking in 2014, at the average price of $37, surrounded by Mexican, Southern, Chinese, Vietnamese, and Thai. Indian haute cuisine is some distance from Japanese, French, and New American at the top of the heap, and closer to Greek at the seventh position in the Zagat hierarchy, but not there yet.

In this estimation, like Michael Psilakis's Greek cuisine, Indian cuisine needs updating. Then there is something more: Suvir Saran had to be found by the cognoscenti, unlike Psilakis, who can announce himself, here marking the slightly more exotic and down-market characteristic of the Indian find, hidden in the subcultural heap. "We," Batterberry notes, "first caught wind of Suvir in the mid-1990s when an Indian travel consultant . . . told us of a young caterer catching fire along New York's food-centric party circuits" (Batterberry in Saran and Lyness 2004: viii). That is a distinguishing feature of an "ethnic" chef—he has to be found. Amy Lasater-Wille (2015) notes a similar process at play in the discovery and celebration of Peruvian cuisine by metropolitan taste-makers from Spain and the United States. In contrast, Psilakis's ability to announce his own arrival is another sign of the up-scaling of Greek cuisine, out of the ethnic category, that isn't afforded to Indian yet. Psilakis is the Anglophone son of an immigrant, while Saran is the immigrant who looks and sounds different (and is not up to speed with American youth cultural artifacts such as music, clothing, and hairstyle). But to play in the upscale field, both Psilakis and Saran have to distinguish their food from the run-of-mill cheap joint, be it the Greek diner or the Indian curry house. Thus Saran launches into that distinction from the first line, while also appropriating a second posture: the guru instructing an Anglo initiate: "I was once asked by a student why my food tasted so different from other Indian food he'd eaten in America" (2004: 1). Saran explains that he also finds generic Mughlai cuisine of Indian curry houses "heavy and one-dimensional" and that instead he will create a pan-Indian collation with attention to the *rasams* from the south of India, and home cooking. Nevertheless, he goes on to instruct us how to make a spicy and oily "Kwality's chickpeas made famous by the restaurant of that name" (Saran 2004: 36). The point here is not that Saran has *mala fide* intentions but that the discursive field shapes him as a native interlocutor. Domestic authenticity, although important, can only take us so far. It needs the heat and grease of publicity to become a value worth transacting across zesty ethnic boundaries.

Floyd Cardoz, the celebrity Indian chef at the recently closed Tabla at Madison Square in Manhattan,[2] noted too: "The Indian food I'd eaten in the United States was another matter entirely—too oily, too hot, and full of mushy, mysterious ingredients that were not remotely seasonal. No wonder Americans, who had dived joyfully into the vibrant flavors of Mexico and Southeast Asia, resisted it" (Cardoz 2006: xv). While starting at the same point, in contrast to Saran, Cardoz fully embraces the technique and network of the professional cook in *One Spice, Two Spice* (2006), partly because he is professionally trained while Saran isn't. Named after Floyd Patterson, the famous African-American boxer, through enticingly delicate cosmopolitan tracings of an imagined world of longing and ambition, Chef Cardoz did end up in the world his name was intended for. It would take the intermediation of another famous personality, the restaurateur Danny Meyer, whose Italian chef Michael Romano, having fallen in love with an Indian woman, had traveled to India in 1994 picking up all the excitement brewing in the sub-continent. At Union Square Café, Romano introduced what Danny Meyer calls "sort of Indian food under the radar," which turned out to be some of the most popular dishes (Cardoz 2006: xi). As a result, Meyer suggested to Chef Romano that "we consider creating a *new* restaurant to be rooted in authentic Indian tradition and spices and use Western culinary techniques and local, seasonal ingredients as well" (2006: xi).

Here is the other formula by which excluded cuisines are drawn into haute cuisine, which is as spice, added to Western culinary technique, because in this tradition of cooking (and discourse) non-Western techniques are either invisible as techniques or considered inappropriate for the genre rules of that kind of food. Analogously, Lasater-Wille notes that:

> the fact that most "fusion" cuisine (including Peru's haute cuisine) requires that indigenous ingredients be subjected to French preparation techniques in order to be internationally recognized is itself a troubling analogue to the still-common notion that indigenous Peruvians need to adopt European mannerisms and dress in order to qualify as "civilized" (2015: 31).

Meyer would take the metaphor of flavoring American food with Indian spices further in naming his restaurant Tabla (an Indian drum and a homonym for the Latin table) after listening to Indian drumming at the Metropolitan Museum of Art as an accompaniment to the clarinetist Richard Soltzman's jazz riffs, where he noted the "fascinating synchronicity of the Western and Indian music forms" (Cardoz 2006: xii). Yet, in keeping with the importance of the ethnic genre, you need native translators (Floyd as "U.S. ambassador to the state of New Indian cooking"), who can make each "recipe sing" and narrate "deeply felt stories" (2006: xii). These, by the way, are the rules of the discourse that cannot be ignored by anyone playing with Indian food in upscale Indian restaurants and in the media today, including my own work. Discourses produce subjects in particular ways, subjecting them to bigger storylines that no one in particular really controls. Subjectivity is produced in subjection, as both Foucault (1978: 38) and Bourdieu (1977) have shown in their own inimitable ways.

Then there are the usual distinctions made in this discursive domain of haute cuisine: for instance, the insistence that this is not your usual curry house. "Certainly, in a city where so many people associated Indian cuisine with predictable menus of raita and dal, vindaloos, keemas, curries, and chutneys, we thought there was a great opportunity to showcase the glories and range of Indian flavors in a fresh way" (Cardoz 2006: xi). Meyer, along with the Swiss-born American restaurateur Gray Kunz, were at the leading edge of the transformation of Indian cuisine into a legitimate haute category that is today occupied by others in Manhattan such as Devi, Tamarind, Vermillion, Junoon, Tulsi, etc. That trajectory has also provided routes *out* of identifiably Indian food, such as by Chef Jahangir Mehta at his miniature restaurants Graffiti and Mehtaphor, the latter by name and posture trending more towards Keller, where he serves delicious pork dumplings with crushed *sev* (a spicy dried deep-fried lentil paste) on top. Even on the way out, there are echoes of the old palate and habits of taste, as in the *sev* for Mehta or in the burger at North End Grill for Cardoz:

> I did a burger at North End Grill that was a short rib burger with onion chutney, mustard, and pepper with onion rings that were spiced. That's the way I'd do a burger. I don't think a plain patty with salt and pepper does it for me. There's got to be flavor in there (Guff 2014).

Here is ethnic flavor and Oriental body creatively posited against Occidental technique.

Cardoz's food is plucked straight from the world of Amitav Ghosh's novels, global networks before and aside from European hegemony. It is a cuisine that looks outward from the peninsular subcontinent—or subcondiment, as Rushdie (1997: 4) remarks!—rather than towards the heartland. It is cooking from the world of Abraham Ben Yiju, the twelfth-century Tunisian Jewish merchant from Cairo, and Bomma, the Indian servant and business agent in the Malabar, commemorated in Ghosh's *In an Antique Land* (1994). It is the palatal memory of networks traversing the Arabian Sea that predate European colonialism, and were inflected by the transient Portuguese dominance that made Goa a part of the Lusaphone, Catholic empire. Rightly, Cardoz asserts, "What's known in the West as fusion food—different cultures together on a plate—started for me in the cradle, because fusion was, quite simply, a way of life for our family" (2006: xiii). While making a chicken curry for his father, at the age of twenty, he

> recklessly added . . . rosemary from the farmer's market and part of a bottle of Reisling. The fragrance and heat of the rosemary connected with that of ginger in the sauce and turned into something marvelous. The wine

> smoothed and rounded out the flavors in a way I hadn't imagined. And my father declared it the best thing he'd ever eaten (Cardoz 2006: xiv).

From that bastard-but-delectable chicken curry a segue was inevitable to hotel school in Bombay (now called Mumbai) and Switzerland. He notes, parenthetically, "(This sort of thing wasn't really done in middle-class circles in Bombay. You can imagine what my parents thought of this move). I persevered, and a few years later I came to America and found an entry-level job in Gray Kunz's legendary kitchen at Lespinasse, in New York City" (2006: xiv). Identities are claimed and maintained in very specific haute cuisine networks: hence the details of who did what with whom are crucial, as in this case and in the following cases. The proper prestige and career that could not be accomplished through medical or engineering school was suddenly opened up again for Cardoz with the rise of the chef in the American pantheon and the intermediation of Danny Meyer (for whom he worked for seventeen years). From Gray Kunz's Swiss–Singapore trajectory that produced a slice of black sea bass in a bowl of Thai-inspired kaffir lime leaf emulsion, Cardoz's long-suppressed repertoire of the mixed cuisines of the Arabian Sea acquired a second life and gave him a subsequent opportunity. His first dish at Lespinasse was the Hydrebadi lamb chops with squash, lentils, carrots, and cracked wheat. But the cardamom was too strong and the chilis too hot. He had to cool it down. He came to a very postcolonial conclusion, mixing biomedicine and Ayurveda, for a Catholic man from Goa: "I wasn't back in India, where chilies are needed to aid digestion and circulation, cooling the body down by perspiration" (Cardoz 2006: xv). From there he quickly moved to green mango-marinated fluke with pickled daikon and beetroot (with the feisty vim of ginger and the verve of fenugreek), tuna tartare with apples (with a pinch of *chaat masala* and mustard oil), roast lamb with mint-black pepper sauce, veal chops stuffed with hominy and lemon chutney, Goan spiced crab cakes with avocado salad, and the spiced shellfish *nage*. This is where the cuisine of the Arabian Sea pierces the Mediterranean, and might have produced the Mogor dell'Amore, the Florentine Mughal of Love, the forsaken child of Qara Köz, Lady Black Eyes. Qara Köz was the youngest sister of Babur, the founder of the Mughal dynasty in Delhi, and Argalia a Florentine soldier of fortune, exquisitely fabricated by Rushdie in *The Enchantress of Florence* (2009).

The immigrant Cardoz's food, restaurant (Tabla, White Street), cookbook, and personality, are a quieter, more conservative, cautious, South Asian incarnation of the radical new mixing of haute and not-so-haute that David Chang, a second-generation Korean-American, has mastered in the Manhattan fine-dining marketplace. Chang's widely acclaimed Momofuku empire—Noodle Bar, Ssäm Bar, Ko, Milk Bar and so on—all located within a few blocks in the East Village (and now replicated in Toronto and Sydney), styles itself as the quintessential network of anti-restaurants. No tablecloth, no wine glass, no elegant silverware (plain wooden chopsticks), shared tables, no chairs (backless stools), kinetic, young, inter-racial clientele with a yen for miscegenated food. The *Momofuku Cookbook* (2009) written by David Chang with Peter Meehan, exhibits all the loud, avant-garde, celebrity-focused, exquisitely delicious, "bad pseudo-fusion cuisine" that is at the leading edge of American restaurant food today, where "labne and ssämjang and Sichuan peppercorns and poached rhubarb" all end up on the same plate (2009: 8). Chang writes, "We were going to serve good food regardless of the environment, regardless of the paper napkins, the shitty silverware, the fast food-style condiment island in the middle of the dining room" (Chang 2009: 122).

Chang brings us the possibility of ethnic haute for the first time, quite different from the properly somber, elite, institutional, Continental, French, Swiss, or even Japanese cuisines we have seen so far play in the gastronomic field of Manhattan. This is radical, this alternative route to American haute cuisine.[3] The *Momofuku Cookbook*, in style, design, and content, lands right between *How to Roast a Lamb* and *The French Laundry Cookbook*. It is a classic Clarkson Potter book with its clean lines, few colors, close-ups of ingredients, dynamic and hazy pictures of chefs caught mid-activity, yet attentive enough to hire a "male hand model" for all those crafty hand-of-the-chef-as-artisan shots. In substance, what is radical here is that the inspiration is no longer a restaurant in the French model but the great *ramenayas* of Tokyo. "I liked the periphery," Chang writes, "of the culinary world: fast food, ramen, subs, pizza. Simple and delicious food people could afford" (2009: 117). Chang comes from the edge, much like another Korean-American chef, Roy Choi, who revolutionized notions of the restaurant in Los Angeles by marrying Korean and Mexican fare with the hipster food truck movement, calling them "loncheros," building a following on tweets and blogs. Choi, with a number of Kogi Korean BBQ taco trucks, is one among a number of radical re-visioners of the urban foodscape that includes Chef Ludo Lefebvre with his "pop up" restaurants in other peoples' kitchens, which he characterizes as a "touring restaurant" or a "travelling circus," part performance art, part restaurant (Baertlein 2011). Choi is the master of the new genre of gangster Asian food, the inverse of the model minority. This is bad-ass, bad-mouthed, wicked and loud food. Garrulous. Strident.

The traditional restaurant in the Parisian model invented in the eighteenth century, that so dominated all notions of Western culinarity, is dying right in front of our eyes, and David Chang and Roy Choi have helped that along in LA and Manhattan. Through that crack in the edifice a whole lot of ethnic-inflected food is pouring into the domain of Manhattan haute cuisine, muddying the turgid classificatory schemas of high and low, erudite and silent cooking.

But is Chang's career trajectory and culinary product that different from what we have come to expect in a fast-moving field? Is his insurrection that revolutionary? To find out, we have to attend to his precise pathway. He came to Momofuku via a liberal arts degree (which he says he did not find any use for, which of course can be attested to only by those who have it), through training at the French Culinary Institute in New York City, and cooking at Café Boulud, property of New York's eponymous legendary French chef Daniel Boulud, who had himself come through the French *stagiaire* system working with the likes of Roger Vergé, Georges Blanc, and Michel Guérard. Then Chang travelled, lived, and ate through Japanese cities such as Osaka and Tokyo, the new culinary co-hegemon with France and Italy since the days of the nouvelle French cuisine of Chef Paul Bocuse (by the late 1970s). This is analogous to Roy Choi's trajectory through the Culinary Institute of America, staging at Eric Ripert's Le Bernardin, wrestling with Jacques Pepin's La Technique and the imprimatur of Japanese Iron Chef Rokusaburo Michiba. What David Chang (or Roy Choi) has done with East Asian-inflected American cuisine, borrowing from sources in Japanese and Korean noodle shops, is extraordinarily original, but his career path has been the standard route of the new American chef since the late 1980s.[4] He received all the help from the right restaurant reviewers just at the right time, as he willingly acknowledges, such as Frank Bruni of *The New York Times*, Joe Dziemianowicz of *The Daily News*, and Robin Raisfeld and Rob Patronite of *New York* magazine. As Laura Shapiro noted on Gourmet's website in 2008:

> When Gabrielle Hamilton opened a tiny, uncomfortable place called Prune in 1999, her idiosyncratic menu caught on, the restaurant became successful, and today she's a much-admired figure on the scene. When David Chang opened a tiny, uncomfortable place called Momofuku Noodle Bar in 2004, his idiosyncratic menu caught on, the restaurant became successful, and today he's a much-admired figure on the scene—with numerous awards, scads of magazine profiles, two more restaurants and a public that worships him. However you account for the difference between these two career trajectories, it's got to include something besides the food (Shapiro 2008).

Chang was consecrated quite early by the right set of institutions, such as the James Beard Foundation (2006 Rising Star Chef of the Year), and *Food & Wine* magazine (Best new chefs in 2006). They even gave him room to trip up at Ssäm Bar, at first producing soggy Asian-Mexican wraps that did not work, after which he quickly transitioned back to the more sure-fire Asian noodle-shop theme. He was aided by a small group of powerful Manhattan chefs such as Tom Colicchio at Craft, Jonathan Benno at Per Se, Andrew Carmellini at Café Boulud. That makes it difficult to classify Chang (or for that matter Choi) as an outsider in any sense. Chang is perhaps more an imaginative insider who has rattled the canon of Manhattan haute cuisine, with wide reverberations in the field. It is important to pay attention both to the specificity of the culinary idiom and the external sociological critique. Of course, the nature of such an overheated field is that by the time this is written down and goes to print we would have moved on to the next iconoclast. Nevertheless, the dynamic remains the same, although the personality changes. That is what makes chefing so close today to the world of fashion, the grueling competition, riffs, and resonant antipathy. Chefs are all talking and eavesdropping and arguing with each other, just as, say, cultural sociologists are, to remain within the field.

To map the scope of the David Chang intervention, the scholar Chi-Hoon Kim, who is working on a dissertation on Korean cuisine at Indiana University, writes to me that a small number of Korean-American chefs have become visible in the last five to seven years (looking back from 2015) who can be regionally grouped in the following way:

East: David Chang (Momofuku empire), Hooni Kim (Danji and Hanjan), and Jungsik Yim (Jungsik Restaurant)

South: Edward Lee (610 Magnolia and Milkwood)

Midwest: Beverly Kim (Parachute) and Bill Kim (BellyQ and Belly Shack)

West: Roy Choi (Kogi, A Frame, and Pot) (Chi-Hoon Kim 2015: personal communication).

She notes that there is a strong, pronounced divide between East and West coast chefs. The chefs in the South and Midwest are more fluid and flexible, she avers. The East coast chefs (New York) all have Michelin stars and operate upscale restaurants. There are some differences as well. David Chang is Korean-American and defines his cuisine as New American. Hooni Kim was born in Korea but immigrated to the US when he was ten years old, and cooks modern Korean food. Jungsik Yim is the most recent transplant from Korea, cooking New Korean with French influences. The West coast (Los Angeles) is dominated by Roy Choi, the celebrated food truck legend, who was born in Korea and immigrated to the US at the age of two. His cooking philosophy is to bring Korean food to the people in a casual and approachable way. His style is heavily influenced by Latino and hip-hop culture and he represents a segment of Korean-American men who are now termed "Bad Koreans." The image of Korean-American chefs as "Bad Koreans," Chi-Hoon Kim notes, was popularized by Anthony Bourdain in his show "Parts Unknown".

Bourdain points to male Korean-American chefs as driving American cuisine (Lee 2014). The differing tactics could reflect differences in the socioeconomic and political context of Korean immigration in these two cities. For example, Kim notes, LA has the largest Korean population outside of Korea, where poorer and middle-class Koreans settled. Korean immigrants to NYC are mainly upper middle-class businessmen, medical professionals, and students studying abroad, who are more attuned to upper-class culture and self-conscious about it.

Inter-Asian competition has also heightened. Outsiders like Eddie Huang, trying to break in, often target Chang in their construction of more authentic, ethnic selfhoods. One way of doing that is to play up the race angle and the lack of culinary training. Eddie Huang screams,

> Americans. Americans. AMERICANS. They've called me chink. They've treated me like the Other. They laughed at my food, they laughed at my family, they laughed at my culture, they wouldn't give me a proper interview because of my *face*. Americans. They did that. When 9/11 happened, I was an observer. I mourned for the victims and felt for the people as individuals, but this wasn't my fight (Huang 2013: 223).

He continues:

> I always felt as if America took half the good traits of a person and impressed them on Asians and the other half on black people, since clearly, no person of color could be a well-rounded, intelligent, confident individual that served himself or herself. Asian men must be emasculated, Asian women must be exotic, black men must be dick-slinging thugs, and black women must be single moms (2013: 235).

These are fighting words, too strident even for the counter-cultural David Chang. Huang identifies strongly with the subversive, masculine, no-holds-barred hip-hop scene (before Puffy, Master P, and Eminem), and clothing that is "transgressive, satirical, do-it-yourself democratic street culture" (2013: 229). Attire and music: two things young (and, following them, old) Americans are invested in heavily in terms of their identity. He says he gives credit where it is due, even gets sentimental about New York City, "despite the misfires, overhyped openings, and super-restaurants that mar the landscape, New York is the best eating city not Tokyo or Taipei, and we owe it to the people Fresh off the Boat" (2013: 245). And he is scathing and impolite when he insists that

> When foreigners cook our food, they want to infuse their identity into the dish, they have a need to be part of the story and take it over. For some

> reason, Americans simply can't understand why this bothers us. 'I just want to tell my story?!? I loved my vacation to Burma! What's wrong with that?' It's imperialism at work in a sauté pan. You already have everything, do you really, really, really need a Burmese hood pass, too? Can we live? (2013: 247–8).

He says he wanted Baohaus to be a youth culture restaurant (2013: 258) and he finds New York full of restaurants with good food, but few with an independent mind, and the dining section of the *Times* a mere stepchild of the style section.

Then he takes on Chang. "David Chang is the chef who unwittingly popularized a bastardized version of Taiwanese gua bao. He tells the story of how he created the Momofuku pork bun in his book *Momofuku*" (2013: 260). Huang finds the whole story "ludicrous on a number of levels": first, in the authentic eatery the pork belly is served in a pancake, not a bao; second, you typically eat the skin in the pancake and the body separately by itself.

> To this day publications like *New York* magazine still credit Chang for introducing New York to the gua bao. I was mad, but I respected the hustle. The only way to get even was to set up shop myself. I thank David. Just like he came up on gua bao, I jumped off his success and brought the title home. A Taiwanese kid makes the best gua bao in New York just like it should be (2013: 261).

He both acknowledges David Chang and defeats him (at least in his show). Everyone was comparing Baohaus to Momofuku. "The difference was that we braised our pork. Although Chang is Korean-American, his technique is French. Even *bo ssam*, a Korean pork belly dish, used steamed pork belly. Asians don't use the oven for anything" (2013: 264). Huang exposes Chang, for roasting his pork belly, as just not Asian enough.

Huang tells people he is not a chef. Food isn't his thing. Baohaus is not a restaurant, but an idea. "An idea that couldn't be understood with the language and vocabulary of traditional restaurants . . . Nothing was inspired by famous chefs, farms, or trends in food. It was the manifestation of my friends, family, and memories" (2013: 261). No trained chefs, no restaurant skills, no skilled staff. Staff, in fact, were picked on the basis of their taste in music and open-mindedness. A typical advertisement went: "Baohaus Hiring Multi-Tasking Nice People Who Listen to Ghostface" (2013: 264). And he considered the Baohaus style of service as the Anti-Danny Meyer. He says that they almost never hired experienced cooks, "because the goal was to create a team of artists who just happened to work at Baohaus while pursuing other dreams" (2013: 268). Yet these quarrels of distinction make it possible to develop the imagination, make self-reference, and even acquire a certain degree of autonomy that outlines a separate field of gastronomy in the current urban popular cultural terrain. This is how gastronomy fares in regions far from eighteenth century France that do not replicate the social conditions it was born in and yet, in some sense, presume.

Ethnic haute cuisine: A category problem

Huang is no haute cuisine buff. He is playing at the frayed edges of the celebrity market. Ethnic haute is an impossible category to fit into. What is true about the usual Indian cook in Manhattan can also be extended to a number of neighboring ethnic sub-fields, such as Thai and Filipino. Chef Martin and his business-partner wife Julie noted, in a long and revealing discussion, much about the relationship between ethnicity, authenticity, and haute cuisine. I present a productive extract below to further that distinction and show its slow hesitant genealogy.

I: When did all this begin, Martin?

Martin: We moved to New York City in 1979. I was really disappointed by the food here.

I: Did you work in restaurants in NYC?

Martin: Yes. It was Continental-style, whatever that was. It was called Ambrosia.

I: When did you get your own restaurant?

Julie: That did not happen until 1995. I was in Merrill Lynch and he was working in different restaurants. I enjoyed my ten years there. The boom and bust of the 1980s disillusioned me. We were afraid that we were getting older and we wanted to live the life we wanted to. We had to be our own boss if we wanted to be happy.

I: And that meant owning a restaurant for you?

Julie: Yes.

I: What restaurant did you envision? [Directed to her chef husband].

Martin: I imagined it around my cooking with an Asian base.

I: Did you develop your own identity with your cooking?

Martin: Yes, I developed my own style. I developed my own sensibility.

I: Did you cook at home when you were growing up? Did you cook in the Philippines?

Martin: No. I did not cook at home. I never cooked at home. [Here is a faint link to Muhammad Rasool's disavowal of domestic cooking.]

I: Is it because men of your class do not cook?

Martin: No, there are some exceptions. But most did not cook. I did not cook. Me, I had never cooked before.

I: Not until Philadelphia?

Martin: I started as a dishwasher. One day the chef left with all his cooks. The owner asked me to help the cook. I had never cooked before. *I started reading cookbooks, the very cookbooks read by people like Alice Waters.*

I: So you learned to cook from cookbooks?

Martin: Yes, to imagine what French restaurant cooking was about. To develop the same vocabulary; know the language of cooking.

[At this point Julie took over the interview as she was intrigued by her husband's thinking about cooking. The following questions were asked by her to her husband].

Julie: Where did that sense come from?

Martin: Food was really not a part of my world. We did a lot of cooking in the family. We had a large family. I knew how to dress a chicken. But I never thought I would cook. Until I cooked in Philadelphia.

Julie: So why did they ask you to cook in the restaurant? Why not anyone else?

Martin: The staff was Thai. The chef was Thai. They asked me perhaps because I was the only guy available and willing.

Julie: So because you were the only one available! [Both laugh.]

Martin: I would read cookbooks. I was getting interested. I would try it out and then serve the food to the wait-staff. They liked it because it was done with some effort and good intent even when the food wasn't particularly good. This was food made with care instead of throwaway dishes at the restaurant.

I: What was your relationship with Filipino food then?

Martin: Nothing. My only encounter with Filipino cooking was with potlucks. But I never cooked it.

I: So how did your own taste and technique develop?

Martin: Later on, I started East–West fusion. Putting ginger here, putting lemongrass there, and wrapping things in banana leaf. But that was a little later when I became a chef already, when I had some authority.

I: Why did you start adding those things?

Martin: There was this New American cuisine restaurant called Hubert's in New York. It was committed to making New American cooking in general. They were interested in encouraging and experimenting with new American things. They would do Colonial American cooking. Then immigrant iterations such as Irish and Italian. Finally, new immigrants who were not already established, like me, elements that were not part of the American cuisine yet, were encouraged. He encouraged me to dig into my background. But I did not know anything at all about Asian cooking or Filipino cooking! Then I started reading. Going to Chinatown, scavenging weird stuff.

I: Did you start reading Asian or Filipino cookbooks?

Martin: Not so much. Most of the Asian cookbooks were Chinese and I was not interested in Chinese cooking. I was interested in Southeast Asian cooking and there were hardly any cookbooks.

I: So it was your own practical exploration?

Martin: Yes, with the aid of my taste memory. At that time I was still more French or what used to be called Continental. But I was beginning to dabble a little into this or that Southeast Asian ingredient.

Julie interjected: This was in the early 1980s, right? You would get gingko nuts and use them. Fish in banana leaves. At that time it was mind-blowing for a lot of people.

I: Did you miss Filipino cooking?

Martin: Kind of . . . [drifting away. Julie picked up the thread.]

Julie: Well, the first thing I did was to start cooking. I did not know how to cook Filipino food. I cooked it here in the US for the first time. Actually, I learned to cook Filipino food here. [This echoes the experience of upper class immigrant women such as Cecilia Chiang and Madhur Jaffrey.]

Julie: We wanted to do a few Filipino dishes. We did not want it to be a Filipino restaurant. We wanted to do French dishes. We knew we would be in trouble if we called our food Filipino. There is a traditional Filipino home-cooking and then there are basically diners we call by the generic name

Turo-Turo, which is "point, point," where we point at stuff on the board and they give it to us. We did not want to do that.

Julie: Filipinos were not used to upscale restaurant cooking. There was no consensus about what upscale Filipino cooking should be, because it was just conceptual, ideological, not practical. No one was doing it. That is why we called ourselves a Pan-Asian restaurant.

At this point Martin interjected: "And also because I did not know anything about Filipino cooking," which made Julie impatient. She continued:

Julie: I knew some basic Filipino dishes. I bought this old, beaten up, Filipino cookbook. I would take a look and see how it was done. The stuff I was missing. Then I would do it. Approximate it. But when food writers came to our restaurant I realized that if you are a food writer you cannot say they are neither this nor that and because we were from Philippines they started calling us Filipino. And we had Filipinos showing up and giving us a lot of trouble. They started quarrelling with us and telling us that this is fake Filipino food. It was a war. They gave us very bad reviews. The Filipinos. Not the non-Filipinos. The non-Filipinos were happy. We did not like aspects of Filipino cuisine. It is fatty and soupy. We couldn't do that in an upscale restaurant. Home cooking and restaurant cooking are completely different animals. We did not want to do that.

Julie: But they would like to bring white people, especially white husbands, to our upscale restaurant because it was stylish and clean, especially because we had clean restrooms. That is what we were told. One customer said, "you know, I first came and checked your restroom, before I invited my husband, because he is white, you know."

Julie: You will not understand if you were not colonized. What it is to grow up colonized. What it is to grow up in a poor country, filled with brown people, and your concept of beauty is a white person. Haute cuisine is white people's cuisine. "What are you trying to do? You are getting out there and trying to be one of them." That was the allegation. That was the implication. The more exposure we got the more virulent the Filipinos got. I was talking to a Vietnamese woman and she was saying the same thing about Vietnamese.

Julie: But at some point we realized we had to be more Filipino.

I: Why?

Julie: I think we hit a glass ceiling. We could not go any further without the aid of Filipino authenticity.

Martin [Disagreed quite strongly]: I think we were trying to get back to our heritage. Before I was coming from a Western point of view. Now my point of view had changed. I am going to uplift Filipino food to a restaurant standard. Now I am coming from that direction, asking, "so what are the flavors of the Philippines?"

I: Was the Filipino audience important?

Julie: About 30 to 40 percent of our audience was Filipino. We could depend on them. [Here in contradiction to what they had said earlier.] Food is about sharing, community, and culture. That is why I do not like excessively stylish and elitist restaurants.

Martin: We are still within the same movement as local, regional, and sustainable, just like the new American cuisine. We consider ourselves a part of that. We are trying to use Filipino food. May be a sense of elitism. ["No," Julie disagreed again, "we are not elitist, but we use organic because we want to avoid the chemicals."]

I: What is the average price-range of a meal at your restaurant?

Julie: $30–35.

Chef Martin eventually acquired a substantial reputation playing in the very small field of Filipino haute cuisine in Manhattan, after he was granted a role first in the domain of haute cuisine and then in a version of Filipino cooking. In 2014 there were only four Filipino restaurants in Manhattan. Chef Martin echoes (without necessarily endorsing) Janer's claim cited earlier that standardized French restaurant cooking is not that difficult to learn as a skill and that "We can understand what French cuisine is all about after reading a few books . . ." (Janer 2006: 6). Chef Martin's immersion in nouvelle cuisine networks allowed him to pick up the new techniques along with the mandatory new language of sustainability, locality, and organic, by "reading cookbooks, the very cookbooks read by people like Alice Waters." Yet, once he mastered that domain of the chef he felt the pressures of appropriating the skills and markers of ethnic authenticity, to distinguish his place in the field (as did Roy Choi in LA with Korean-Mexican tacos). Julie's rich commentary on color, colonialism, and taste is insightful. They—this husband–wife team—were early in breaking into the field of haute cuisine in spite of their Filipino heritage because of their networks in New American cuisine restaurants such as Hubert's. They wedged their way into the field on the back of New American Cuisine and accidents of biographical proximity, with undoubtedly enormous effort and imagination. We also have class as a countervailing force to nationality here. They came with graduate degrees from American universities and globally networked families of physicians. Fields have structure and relative stability, but they also provide openings to exceptionally networked and talented individuals. A few exotic others can be, and historically have been accommodated. Yet, I would say, they never reached the heights they deserved because of their ethnicity.

Networks, immersion and doing: Concluding comments

Martin's and Chang's career paths and networks are usually unavailable to cooks confined to the "ethnic" corner of the field, who have to trade more in the domain of authenticity than the realm of innovation in haute cuisine. For instance, cooks in most of the Indian restaurants in Manhattan have never cooked Indian food, not on the subcontinent, not at home, nor in a restaurant, until they get in the galley of a ship or a restaurant kitchen in Europe or North America. About one half of Indian restaurant cooks in Manhattan are Sylheti (after the province of Sylhet in Bangladesh; according to my survey), many of them were (or their ancestors were) lascars who worked the galley onboard merchant marine ships. Some eventually cooked in curry houses and acquired the skills in that genre of cooking. They do not belong to the other network of cooking-school-trained or European-apprenticed chefs and commentators. They do not read about them. They do not know about them. They have never been trained in institutions of haute cuisine (in schools or restaurants) to acquire the skills and rhetoric of the new American chef.

The mirror-image of the foreign-born, untrained, ethnic cook is the native, white (and increasingly Asian), Anglophone (and Francophile) chef, trained at the Culinary Institute of America (CIA) or the French Culinary Institute (recently renamed International Culinary Center). The chef occupies the heights of the culinary field in the USA today, just as the ethnic cook inhabits the bottom rungs of the hierarchy. To the degree that the foreign-born depends on everyday experience in both taste and toil, the native-born chef is trained in schools and restaurants not only to acquire new skills and habits, but also to be promoted in the class hierarchy. He has to be remade not only with a subtle palate and hands, but also with a body, posture, and gestures fit for upper-class consumption, even when he belongs to the iconoclastic avant garde.

The question hinges on expertise, the pathways in which it circulates, modes of acquiring it, and its associated rhetoric and valuation. It is about learning the tricks of the trade, maintaining skills, learning from each other, pressing on each other to acquire more skills, and arguing for one's position in a crowded hierarchy of already established professions. There are real differences between a native/naïve cook and a professional/ideological chef. They are produced by two ways of acquiring expertise, one primarily via explicit instruction, and the other mostly by absorbing implicit knowledge. The latter route is what Jean Lave and Etienne Wenger (1991) have famously called "situated learning" and "legitimate peripheral participation," which is learning by watching, trying out, repeating on one's own. As a result of activities of learning and doing in a particular social world, the person is correspondingly "transformed into a practitioner, a newcomer becoming an old-timer, whose changing knowledge, skill, and discourse are part of a developing identity—in short, a member of a community of practice" (Lave and Wenger 1991: 122). But this is also where achieved, acquired, embodied skill looks a lot like the ascribed skills of gendered, racialized, and ethnic ways of being-in-the-world.

At first glance, ethnics and experts appear to be quite different things in incongruent classificatory systems. In the case of ethnicity, subjects are born into the category, while professions are made. In the case of professions, formal training is essential, usually outside the household, and increasingly certified. Yet, current work on both ethnicity and professions shows that a subject has to be produced in both instances, with implicit and explicit systems of training the body to be so. Coming from vastly different research traditions, Judith Butler (1990) (from postmodern theorizations), and Harry Collins and Robert Evans (2007) (from realist hypothesis-building agendas), have concluded that you are mostly what you do, and do well. Others have elaborated further that the training to be something happens in the triple register of performance: to do something, to do it right, and to do it for show (Kirshenblatt-Gimblett 1999). Gender, race, and ethnicity (often already visible to the audience and hence already assigned), are never without their performative possibilities, most dramatically coming into view when the act fails. The process of ethnicity- and race-making is similar, but the outcomes are different, based on current hierarchies of value. In Bourdieu's terms, the ethnic cook is produced at home and in unexplicated communities, and the new American chef is produced in explicated pedagogical settings such as schools, restaurants, and self-conscious networks. Most importantly, one kind of skill is valued more, much more, than the other.

To take one example, the "Indian," for instance in the case of Cardoz and Mathur, is produced not only by the injunctions of a nation-state and its governing claims which are registered in authorized documents such as passports and birth certificates, but also through tacit practices of long duration in language, religion, bodily posture, gesture, volubility, taste, morals, and aesthetics. Some of that training has to be explicated, especially when immersed in conflictual contexts, with exhortations such as, "As Indians we don't do that," "Indians do this," "that is what makes us Indians." Nevertheless, the most important instruction happens at home, at school, and in the playground, where the insipient and pervasive ways of being-in-the-world are as completely naturalized as the mother tongue is inscribed on the body as durable, unconscious habit.

The reverse is the case with professions, where it is assumed that much of what is learned is taught explicitly in an institution separated from the home, such as a medical or culinary school, a hospital or a restaurant kitchen. These specialized institutions teach the requisite skills, usually in much shorter duration than it takes, say, to teach the mother tongue or chopstick etiquette at home. Yet professions also train us in ways of being-in-the-world, especially in the early stage of professionalization (as we saw in the previous chapter). The instructive title of a highly popular advice book for physicians, written by a physician, was *Aequanimitas* (Osler 1906), arguing that "good natured equanimity" in the face of medical challenges is central to the body-language of a physician. You are how you act—preferably calmly under pressure.

At the turn of the nineteenth and twentieth centuries, when Max Weber (ca. 1900) was analyzing identities as ascribed or achieved, the fracture-line between body and profession was the leading edge of the contention around modes of identification. In that frame of analysis, ascription was the group assignment, such as race, gender, ethnicity, which was typically based on visible markers to outsiders, and the achieved or aspirational status referenced identities such as physician, pastor, lawyer, professor, poet or worker, based on the social division of labor. Proliferation of professions and semi-professions, and new biomedical identities, are reconfiguring the relationship between ascription and aspiration. For instance, biomedicine since the early 1980s has made it possible to claim gay identities as genetically determined, socially ascribed, and politically aspired, simultaneously. It has provided new groundings for tethering the body. Biosocialities are social claims wagered on the basis of certain kinds of bodies. An ethnic is a bearer of a body marked as neither fully foreign, nor wholly native, which is evident from looks, accents, carriage, volubility, and networks of proximity to similar others. A chef also entails certain kinds of bodily skills, membership in some networks, and notions of self, based on assertions and quarrels among a relatively small group of professional chefs, critics, and camp followers in global cities in the Western world. The difference is that the ethnic cannot avoid being seen, while the chef can barely restrain himself from claiming the privileges of the profession he chooses.

In the preceding pages I have illustrated some convergences and tensions between these two ways of being-in-the-world. Experts on expertise see the matter less and less as something abstract and conceptual. Instead they see expertise as something practical and competence based. Something that you can do rather than something you can learn in abstract. So mastering a field is a lot like mastering a natural language, or cooking like a native. Yet, the genre rules and returns on native home cooking and haute restaurant cooking are different, which makes all the difference.

With the rise of the modern professional chef at a number of urban, cosmopolitan, consecrated restaurants, we witness a brutal rhetorical elbowing out of cooks and housewives because there are no empty social spaces waiting to be filled by a rising profession. In other words, chefs do not become chefs by moving into a slot waiting and open for them with the right skills. They have to dislodge or demean other occupations to make room for themselves. That explains the professionalism and the masculinity of the professional chef. Any ascending group has to produce new forms of knowing and doing, and develop stringent modes of mutual evaluation (as in peer review) that accentuate knowledge formation and bound the world of the professed chef, in this case. And that has to be done always at the expense of others, usually people not already constituted in a bounded, policed, and networked "world." Unorganized and unconsecrated cooks and housewives are easy to bully and displace. That is the nature of professions. For instance, the physician, nurse, pharmacist, and orderly, with their domains of expertise were mutually constituted via conflict and alignment. They had to push the midwife and other experienced practitioners into the abject domain of old wives' tales. In the case of the professional chef, the necessary others are those who have always done all the cooking, always with very low costs of entry, and without a self-conscious profession and guild-like articulation; in particular, they are housewives and immigrant cooks, as I have shown here.

All new professions are born by demeaning and destroying old divisions of labor. It is a process of alignment with some social actors and positions, and an abjection of other social positions. Chefs are as guilty of it today as disciplined scholars. They must of necessity express disdain towards unconstituted social others (cooks and autodidacts in these cases), or preferably ignore them once their own professional status is consolidated, as evidenced in the current authoritative calmness of the physician when confronted with the midwife. Insecure, emergent, and unstable professions (such as chefs and non-scientific scholars) are typically more virulent towards their unbounded, unconsecrated others. Stabilized professionals, such as gynecologists and psychiatrists, can afford to open up again to midwives and talk therapists.

Questions of professional certitude are never permanently settled. The politics of professions, and the certainty with which their knowledge claims are made, ebb and flow over time and across national and transnational spaces. For instance, in the Japanese context, the sushi chef and the Ramen cook are much better lodged in the hierarchy of Japanese professions than, say, the Indian or Turkish chef, who must loudly assert his difference in professionalism from those who do about the same thing under different conditions. It is analogous to the role of the traditional scholar, the Brahmin, the Imam, and the Vaid, who have paid the price for the rise of the Western-trained university professor and physician in India. That is the virulent politics of knowledge production that lends its tempo and character to the social production of more or less useful knowledge. All professions are made by unmaking other occupations.

New and old professions produce useful knowledge—useful for many in society at large and useful for their own careers. The tempo of knowledge generation is accelerated by competition within new professions. But such professionalizing moves are also self-aggrandizing moves by those included within them, and a severe loss to those excluded. The process always produces losers in the fight to form professions and the losers are usually the poorer and more disenfranchised segments of the sectors where the new professions emerge—around cooking in this context. That is a social cost some people pay for the price of other peoples' professionalism.

A narrative of dramatic improvement was necessary to First-Wave Biomedicine as a field, with antibiotics, anesthetics, surgery, antisepsis, and immunization, which had different degrees of continuity and discontinuity with older forms of knowing and acting in the world at the end of the nineteenth century, when modern biomedicine began to emerge, unevenly, as a profession separate from the everyday care-giving which was within the ambit of women's work. We see professional cooking undergoing similar transformations—from Escoffier's and Bocuse's haute cuisines to Adrià's techno-emotional cuisine—in some parts of the world, with losers and winners distributed differently between genders, races, and ethnicities. The Gods of Food have a particular gender and ethnicity, and that is shaped by global hierarchies of taste, and professions of paid skill. There is nothing natural about it. It has to be acquired in virulent contestation with others. There are losers and there are winners. And it is always skewed in terms of gender, race, class, and ethnicity.

In this chapter I have used a handful of detailed empirical instances of food-related ethnic and professional identities, visible in the written record and sounded in interviews, to argue that it is theoretically and methodologically productive to illuminate the boundary between the two separate worlds of ethnicity and expertise that both academic and popular constructions of identity have safely assumed. This chapter also reveals how the production of ascribed and aspirational boundaries and notions of self are mutually constitutive. Finally, I suggest that this improbable twinning of ethnicity and expertise is central to the fabrication of contemporary identities in urban settings such as in Manhattan. Almost all the actors that I have touched on here are ethnics now aspiring to be professionals, or, if already there as professionals, bending back to catch their own tail so that they can live with deep authenticity. Martin, our Filipino chef, had to turn back to Filipino cooking because no one would take him seriously as a chef without his heritage. He was tethered to his past, notwithstanding his skill. David Chang might be able to do it, that is cross over, because he is not an immigrant, unfamiliar with the habits of being an Anglophone American, with deeply embodied aesthetic knowledge that includes rich referents to music and youth culture. That is why Eddie Huang can do it too, especially after he writes a book and has a television show. Eric Ripert can do it because he is already ensconced in the world of the French chef, where foreignness is an asset in signaling the profession. That is what the field of culinary capital now demands of its subjects within newly consecrated modes of sensory urbanism.

Notes

1 Some of the exceptions are Fine's work on small-group interaction, workplace dynamics, and aesthetics of work (Fine 1996), in a field where other related directions of research have focused on organization theory (Rao *et al.* 2003, 2005), and field theory (Ferguson and Zukin 1998; Ferguson 2004).

2 Since 2012, Floyd Cardoz was the chef at restaurateur Danny Meyer's North End Grill. In 2014 he broke away to open his own White Street with funding from the producers of the movie *The Hundred-Foot Journey*. See Guff 2014.

3 In that spirit, see Ivan Orkin (2015) recommending five must-eat *ramenayas* in Tokyo.

4 For a recent discussion of *ramenayas* see Peter Meehan and Jonathan Gold (2015).

6

In Closing

New York City and sensory urbanism

Sharon Zukin, a long-time resident of New York City and one of its pre-eminent sociologists, has consistently written about the changing shape of the culture of the city. She has written about it lovingly, sometimes with rage about its transformation, often with nostalgia about its gentrification, but she was one of the few to consistently look at the street-level culture of restaurants and parks, and make room for them in her work over the last four decades beginning with *Loft Living* (1982), through *The Cultures of Cities* (1995), to *Naked City. The Death and Life of Authentic Urban Places* (2010).

I, on the other hand, am an upstart, a new immigrant to the City, on the margins of sociology, barely here for a handful of years, yet full of opinions about it. My New York City is different from Zukin's. Or more accurately, it looks different to my eyes, as it has done to the third of New York City's residents who have been foreign-born (more than 50 percent if you include their children) since its very beginnings as a major American city. For one, I am less nostalgic about it, for I haven't had time to develop nostalgia. But I am also less sure about Zukin's comments on short-term temporal patterns, while more attuned to longer relationships of the rise and fall of nations and cities (because of my training with World-Systems theorists). I am surer of what I can read from the archive—census reports, urban plans, and artifacts—but less sanguine about what escapes such authorized accumulations as trivia and ephemera in the near past (such as Zagat surveys). But like every new immigrant I bring threads of other histories to this site and weave them into the tapestry of lives on the street, in subway cars, on sidewalks, in homes, and in restaurants. I also bring longer social memories of colonialism and post-colonialism that allow me to put things in a different perspective.

Zukin was early to the study of the city's art galleries, restaurants, and theme parks, assuming their importance at the same ontological level without apology or special pleading. She proposed and conducted, with nine graduate students, an "interesting preliminary study" in the form of the chapter "Artists and Immigrants in New York City Restaurants" in her book *The Cultures of Cities* (1995), where she quickly sketched important themes that needed filling out. She underlined restaurants as important cultural sites, but only because they were meeting places "for corporate patrons, culture industry executives, and artists" (Zukin 1995: 155). She couldn't yet take a mere site of cultural consumption seriously without some outsize corporate players playing in the pool. She was also a harbinger (with Ferguson) of the rise of the high-status American chef, an observation which is both prescient, but also thinly sketched. She noticed how restaurants "synthesize global and local cultures," receiving culinary styles, entrepreneurs, and skilled workers from the world to reproduce a cultural artifact on the menu for a local clientele, in a sense re-territorializing the global. She commented on the cross-fertilization of matter and sign, culture and commerce, to create both a neighborhood culture and a sense of the city at large. She noted how a local neighborhood restaurant could become the focus of "transnational economic and cultural flows" (1995: 159). She noticed that hotels, restaurants, finance groups, and media and entertainment companies were where the new jobs were accumulating as the old manufacturing sectors entered a phase of terminal decline. She is obviously distressed by these developments, and she ought to be, for they are disruptive and destructive of many working-class lives. But in being an American and a New Yorker, her horizon only extends across the American century, and she looks with fondness to its solid post-war years as something deep and authentic, while all this play with the symbolic economy is figured as somewhat fake and unsustainable. She writes with a real sense of loss about how "The metamorphosis of American-made products into Mexican blue jeans, Japanese autos, and East Asian computers emptied the factories where those goods had been made" (1995: 8). That is, of course, only the perspective from the *belle époque* which is also the twilight of the American century. At the end of *The Cultures of Cities* she poses the putatively urgent question "whether New York City can be maintained as a cultural capital" and what needs to be done to keep it so (1995: 293). That is both very New Yorker in its presumption—the claim that it *is* the cultural capital—and very American in its insistence that it should remain so. Referencing Disney, Sony, Seagram's, and MCA in the closing paragraph of the book, she fears that the public culture of the city may just be a "residual memory of tolerance and freedom" (1995: 294). Looking back at her prognosis from about twenty years later, Zukin's fears look overwrought and overstated. New York City survived, although transformed, in spite of the unforeseeable brutal punch and counterpunch of terrorism and the security state. But it did so well partly because the city did not have a transcendental common culture, separate from the immanent everyday culture that she continuously laments in her books about the city.

Furthermore, a forty-year time horizon is too short to pass judgment on the fate of cities. The United States was not the first nation to lose its manufacturing core to others and peddle in signs and symbols. Great Britain did so more than a century ago when it lost its most profitable manufacturing sectors to the United States. The British, of course, had replaced others before them (Wallerstein 2003; Arrighi 1994). They had destroyed Indian manufacturing, especially in calicoes in the eighteenth century, to allow Manchester to nudge Lucknow out of the reckoning, setting the *chikan* sellers on their outward journey to the West. Such post-colonial narratives do not soften the blows of the current transition on the American poor, but they do cast a new light on the sense of loss of its middle-class. Eventually,

> No longer did the city's dream world of commercial culture relate to the bourgeois culture of the old downtown or the patrician culture of art museums and public buildings. Instead, urban commercial culture became "entertainment," aimed at attracting a mobile public of cultural consumers. This altered the public culture of the city (Zukin 1995: 19).

It surely did. Today, in 2015, that process has gone even further: street fairs and promenades such as Highline have become common, mixing culture and commerce in vulgar, democratic, and lively ways. Restaurants have become even more important to the culture of a city, both in the soft power domain of haute cuisine, but also as the place for vendors and trucks to compete for meager commerce and cultural cachet. Zukin hints at it in the *Naked City* but she cannot brush off the nostalgic lament of "The City That Lost Its Soul" with which she begins this, her most recent of volumes (2010: 1–31).

My criticism is not about nostalgia *per se*, which has generated too much misplaced attention in critical theorizing. I have always considered some elements of nostalgia to be productive (as in my first book, *The Migrant's Table*; Ray 2004). At the level of the individual, nostalgia has been misdiagnosed as a disease, from which we get the word, coined by Swiss doctor Johannes Hoffer in 1688 to analyze Swiss mercenaries abroad. Recent psychological research is showing that nostalgia gives our lives roots and a sense of continuity. As another doctor recently asserted, "It made me feel good about myself and my relationships. It provided a texture to my life and gave me strength to move forward" (Tierney 2013). Yet nostalgia can be unproductive at the social level if we seek to imprison the present in the past and misrepresent another time and place. Nostalgia can be exclusionary. This city belongs to those who have been here for a long time. But this city has always also belonged to people who have just moved in.

New York City retains its soul: it is just a different one, and it can be found in a different locale, if we are attuned to it. The loss is the loss of power of city and national governments, and communities, against the flow of capital and peoples. But if you come from a place where cities, governments, and communities never had that kind of power, you cannot fathom the loss. The sense of loss is also remitted if you look at the city from the bottom up as flesh and stone, bodies and edifices, building it up one step at a time in de Certeauian fashion from "an ubiquitous character, walking in countless thousands on the streets" whose murmuring voice comes before text (de Certeau 1984: v). Everyday food practice as stated earlier "is the place of a silent piling of an entire stratification of orders and counterorders," where Giard seeks to compensate Bourdieu's reticence on doing cooking, and other feminine activities which "are a place of silence or disinterest that his analysis does not trouble to take into account" (de Certeau *et al.* 1998: 183). This project is an attempt to understand culture as everyday practice, often beyond the reach of official valuation, focused on doing, talking, and writing by immigrant entrepreneurs, American chefs, and scholars listening and provoking them. This book is an attempt to recuperate the arts of doing against the totalizing claims of science (on the one hand) and critical thinking (on the other).

We are entering a post-liberal arts era and Food Studies is one of the symptoms of that transition. It has to reconfigure itself to the transition that is underway. Conceptually and ideologically, the liberal arts could not survive the de-legitimation of a Western civilizational project which was mostly about high-minded reflections of the white, male, high-culture literati. The Civil Rights and the Feminist Movements in the United States had undermined the academy's raison d'être, and the entry of women and colored men into the liberal arts academy, which those movements opened up, provided the coup de grâce for what had become an unsustainable project. Post-colonial, trans-national, migrant intellectuals, are accentuating the crisis of Western humanism.

The liberal arts are being undermined from the outside with increasing demands for technical specialization, which are replacing cultural habitus and social networks among elites as the currency of the realm of professionalism. Internally, the liberal arts are demanding a reconfiguration, with the decline of high-minded rationalism and armchair critical thinking. The necessity of doing, and the realization that both thinking and reason may have been overrated, are challenging the old-fashioned liberal arts. That realization is dawning at the heart of the humanities. Cathy Davidson, in her 2013 Presidential address to the Modern Languages Association, noted "we must redesign our institutions and modes of instruction not just for 'critical thinking' but for 'creative contribution.' We need to encourage not just a culture of critique but a culture of making and participating" (Davidson 2014: 5). I see Food Studies as going beyond the standard vision of the liberal arts to engage with work, and the science of how objectivity and subjectivity can be done.

Our current late-modern doubts can only be resolved via pragmatism and practice. What is different in this conjuncture is that old epistemological questions are being reconfigured as ontological assumptions, showing us how facts are fabricated (Mol 2003: x). In that sense, Food Studies represents a world that comes after the old-fashioned liberal arts, whatever name we choose to give it.

The ethnic and the making of American culture

There are two subsidiary theoretical transformations proposed in this book. The first develops Pierre Bourdieu's (1984) insight that the difference between palatal taste and aesthetic taste is a theoretical subterfuge that does not account for taste fully in either of those domains. The second confounds Post-Bourdieuian works, such as *Foodies* (Johnston and Baumann 2010), that dominate urban sociological analyses. Bourdieu was right in showing that highbrow taste is nothing more sophisticated than vulgar palatal preference. Nevertheless, many of his followers were waylaid into the assumption, which does not follow, that in every subcultural field, the taste of the dominant class is dominant, and the subaltern classes have no role in producing culture. The matter is more contested than that, and it changes over time. That is an empirical question that needs open-minded and imaginative data collection and analysis.

What I show in this book is that elite consumers do not control the modes of reproduction of cultural hierarchies in the culinary field. Professionalism in cooking and criticism have transformed the field. The aesthetic of the dominant classes is no longer the dominant aesthetic in urban food consumption. Just as popular music slipped out of the control of elites in the second half of the twentieth century, so did palatal taste at the end of the twentieth century. The habitus of chopsticks and aggressive hip-hop music is not something that well-bred, traditional, Western humanistic elites are trained in. Second, the conversion ratio of culinary capital to money capital is no longer one-to-one. The simplest evidence is that the most expensive restaurants are not necessarily the most acclaimed ones. It costs about $40 to eat at a David Chang restaurant. A wide range of classes and occupations can afford such a bill. In fact, it is the cultural elite that has to play catch-up, as much in the domain of the palate as they have had to do with music. Of course, the omnivorousness of elites can cover a lot of ground and money and degrees help in making cultural claims, but elites are in this case playing catch-up and they do not set the standard for culinary taste, which is a simple and clear measure of class hegemony. Chang and his restaurants have a lot more cachet than other restaurants where the typical cost of a meal for one person would run up to over $300. That does not mean it is all a level playing field. As I have shown previously, that is hardly the case. The chef reproduces the abjection of the ethnic cook and the housewife. Yet, public culinary culture in American cities is a domain of the social field where the old elites rarely call the shots. That is a symptom of the decline of cultural power of established classes.

The dramatic upward trend in talk about restaurants in the United States by the mid-1970s is symptomatic of something new and different. That is related to the fact that food has entered the fashion cycle for a substantial segment of an urban, bi-coastal, American public: the kind of public that would read *The New York Times*, or websites such as *Lucky Peach* and blogs such as *The Braiser* and *Eater National*, and imagine others reading and watching them; the kind of public that is constituted by a discussion of restaurants and cuisine, transforming its lifestyle into a stylization of life, and orchestrated by new kinds of cultural experts such as restaurant critics, bloggers, and photographers. Born of post-War affluence, it embodies a new way of looking at the world that aestheticizes elements of everyday life (Bourdieu 1984): a gaze that is prefigured in the nineteenth century flaneur, but with an important difference. While the flaneur was a decadent, upper-class, drop-out, the current analogue is the hipster foodie and the tourist from the metropole, who travel upwards socially and outwards (remote regions) and inwards (ethnic enclaves) geographically (MacCannell 1976). On his return, television cameras accompany him to faraway places and intimate nooks, such as the kitchen, in the process educating us all to appropriate his gaze (Ray 2007b). That is how food enters the fashion cycle.

Fernand Braudel noted that in the case of Europe, "one cannot really talk of fashion becoming all-powerful before about 1700" (1981: 316). Until then, in housing, furnishing, and attire, he notes the general rule of changelessness, not because there is no change at all, but because the rate of change is slow. We have the reign of custom and habit that eventually gives way to a faster rate of change, self-consciousness about changing style, and the willingness, nay the imperative, to change. What Urban (2001) has called the metaculture of newness achieves dominance. Somewhere between the fifteenth (Urban 2001) and the eighteenth century (according to Braudel 1981) the European world opens up to fashion, at a differential rate for different classes (aristocrats and peasants), in different places (Paris and the provinces), in different spheres (clothing and cuisine). What makes it possible to pursue fashion (and, for instance, discard perfectly usable but unfashionable clothes) is the level of productivity, which relates to Jack Goody's (1982) argument about the means of production. But what changes is also a cultural element that now values newness more than custom. In addition, there are changes in the pathways through which culture travels, broadcast through the media, along with narrow replication in the household. What have to be added now are more numerous players with the changing media ecology, to include innumerable commentators on *Yelp* and *Facebook* and *Eater.com*.

The world of cultural replication, a world, for instance, of face-to-face, household-to-household replication of process and product, is supplanted by a world of cultural dissemination that is broadcast and retorted back. In the inertial system of habit and custom, change happened but as entropy, or was explained away as such, while under the new dispensation of late-modernity, change is not only embraced but exaggerated. In societies built on custom, fashion does not exist. In the late-modern world everything is susceptible to fashion, although not always equally or everywhere at the same rate (see Lieberson 2000).

Fashion is not only behind the cultural impetus of restaurant-going and restaurant criticism; it also underpins the economic logic of independent restaurants, the very institutions that are venerated as sites where cuisine is cultivated. In an economy that has come to be dominated by large corporations over the last hundred years, small arenas are conceded to the independent restaurateur, which is the site of most of the cultural discussion about taste. As Michael Piore (1980) and Roger Waldinger (1986, 1993) have shown, the dual economy of large corporations and small firms is a characteristic of the American economy, divided between large, stable markets, and small, unstable bazaars driven by fickle changes in fashion. "The demand for small-business activities emanates from markets whose small size, heterogeneity, or susceptibility to flux and instability limit the potential for mass distribution and mass production" (Waldinger 1993: 420). In the case of cooked foods, the greatly fragmented New York City market and its erratic changes over time protect it from chains and corporations, providing opportunities to new immigrants and native entrepreneurs, but at the cost of excessive competition, narrow profit margins, and high risk of failure (especially with rising real-estate costs). That is where the commodity meets the cultural entrepreneur. It is the quotidian cultural entrepreneur—in the figure of the restaurateur, the restaurant critic and the journalist—who stands squarely in the middle of the discussion about American culture.

My broadest argument here is analogous to the one prefigured in Simon Gikandi's recovery of sullied blackness at the heart of eighteenth century aesthetic in *Slavery and the Culture of Taste* (2011). His study is instructive in a number of ways. First, his deliberate and detailed elaboration of how Western culture, even high culture, was never a white, Anglo, monologue is crucial. That is the central contention that scholars working in the field of palatal taste must account for, and have missed. Subordinated subjects such as natives, slaves, women, and ethnics could not be properly excluded, even from the second-order pleasure of art (in Gikandi's work), which was in itself a desperate attempt to return sensuousness to life in the first-order affective pleasures of food, sex, shelter, and everyday decoration (in my case). Second, we continue to find in the twentieth century what Gikandi shows in the eighteenth: the adamant "desire to quarantine one aspect of social life—the tasteful, the beautiful, and the civil—from a public domain saturated by diverse forms of commerce" (Gikandi 2011: 6–7). As I have shown, the ethnic entrepreneur of taste plays an essential and constitutive role in urban, American consumer culture, where commerce and culture meet; American cities cannot sustain one without the other, and they have never done so without immigrant entrepreneurs.

Nevertheless, Gikandi's reconstruction is incomplete because he never enters the domain of everyday cooking, where he could have recovered more of the depth of activities of the enslaved and the subordinated than he could ever find in oil on canvas. In the twentieth century, working-class ethnic males and females, in the cookshop and at home, could develop a counter-poetics of personhood outside the authorized idiom of taste. They would develop an allegory of a displaced culture, a forced poetics, as an original creation of the uprooted, faced with limited linguistic implements imposed on him. Just as the black body had to develop a double-consciousness of highest joy and deepest sadness in speech and song, bodily pleasure, and literal taste, the subordinate immigrant body had to find its place in a hierarchy of sensuousness and reason (often placing himself in virulent opposition to that very black body that had provided the openings for his emplacement). Ethnicity would be built around blackness because it came at a time and was deployed with the intention of superseding the functions of nineteenth-century racial identity. It was the carrier of a twentieth-century idea of manageable difference, aspirational equality with singularity, and democracy with distinction (here the authors of *Foodies* are right; Johnston and Baumann 2010).

By the 1960s, at the latest, immigrant entrepreneurs had turned their familiar foreignness into an object of taste. Their food could no longer be dismissed as trivial and secondary, for that is the site where cultural value was created and recalibrated, eventually to become the site from where disdain could be poured back on the dominant's everyday practices of good taste. The ethnic, hence subordinate, immigrant's notions of pleasure had to be radically different. His practice of pleasure had to acquire a different form and meaning. Food, language, and everyday decorative arts such as housekeeping practices, home-building, furniture-making, religious iconography, attire, pots, pans, and kitchen tools, those very things exiled from the universe of art in the temple of reason by dominant male Western philosophers, would come to not only represent beauty and pleasure, but also secure a measure of reflection, be connected to cosmologies and genealogies, and carry the mark of the ethnic as a modern, urban, subordinate, subject. These were concerted attempts to deploy the fragments of everyday life—chopsticks, the wok, the karai, the steamer, the idli maker, the rice cooker, the coconut grater, the boti, and un-interrogated motions of the body—for an affective possession of otherwise alien spaces such as the restaurant, the home, and the city. Everyday foods and goods came to express an aesthetic materiality in simple things, which were the only things that had the capacity to denote the doubleness of their own triviality in dominant eyes and yet register their durable bodily emplacement in the USA. Astonishingly, by the twenty-first century, by their durable resistance to measuring themselves in dominant academic eyes, ethnics had turned the tables on the everyday aesthetic of the governing classes and races, with their leading ideologies of mannered order, restraint, segregation, essential racial difference, and the fear of the sensual—elements that the culture of taste had tried to control.

The modern Western notion of art, is too circumscribed in its isolation from life and outside the framework of first-order enjoyment—in decoration, worship, touch, texture, and smell—to be of much value to anyone other than curators and philosophers. The containment of culture in cold and distant spaces of display, reflection, and cogitation—museums, classrooms, and libraries—could not match its real implication in the kitchen, in the home, and on the street corner. That is why the work of chefs, urgently trying to turn food into art, a second order of representation, presumably to reconcile technique and emotion, molecules and meaning, temperature and temperament, leaves me cold. Everyday cooking already contains those prolific polarities. Why isolate food from life and livelihood, self-care and care-giving? It is in everyday life, not in museums, where the mundane can become marvelous.

The Enlightenment culture of modernity was articulated in soaring rhetoric as liberation from tradition, religion and habit, which are all essential to the domain of food. Furthermore, comestibles could never be registered adequately in the narrative of migration, although food was one of the most important and immediate rewards of migration. Good food is what immigrants were after. Betraying the nation for good food (something which every historian of immigration and historian of labor has shown to have occurred) could not be accounted for in the high-mindedness of patriotism and freedom. The production of the rational subject unencumbered by immediate needs runs up against the shoals of schnitzel, smoked salmon, meatballs and gravy, and curried fish, as much as roast beef and apple pie. The modern project of freeing man from bodily and emotional dependence on others, where individuals were supposedly trapped in un-interrogated communities of faith, habit, and everyday practice, has failed dramatically, and the attractions of ethnic food are a monument to that hubris. The Enlightenment subject's ambition, and his modernist progeny's drive, was to construct a story of human life as the tale of a mindful subject, freed from the confinements of mere bodily needs of messy sensuality. Affluent, white, authoritative, thinking men could barely tolerate the unwashed hordes until they had been individualized, breached from their irrational communities of belonging, and cured of their smelly propensities of group practice in religion, and in forms of orality, taste, and talk. For Kant that ambition was to discover rules of conduct which are logically independent from experience and capable of rational contradiction. The analytic spirit was to "march triumphant" over local, contingent, everyday, experience (Gikandi 2011: 7). What made the divergent philosophers concur was that the qualities that distinguished the modern self were transcendental of the "array of cultural materials that actually constituted the modern self" (2011: 7). The ethnic insertion into urban culture is merely the late-modern acknowledgment, symptomatic in the failure to theorize the category, of the fundamental social importance of bodily difference, based on local and fleeting forms of classifications of skin, color, texture, hair, height, feature, and language in their relationships to race and nation. Ethnicity is not a thing. It is a relationship of domination and the very grounds on which the dominated have successfully pushed back.

In the eyes of its central theorists, the culture of modernity was premised on full and singular national belonging. Within that frame, emigration is a betrayal of the nation, and ethnicity a residue of un-meltable difference. That is why the rhetoric of choice and freedom had to be inflated, such that everyone trying to make a better living was turned into the poor and the huddled masses, fleeing oppression and tyranny. That was not true of most migrants, which is precisely why, as we have seen, the migrant had the resources to turn the table on the dominant culture of taste. Literal taste was subordinated to aesthetic taste, but the former has always carried the trace of the subordinate, which is precisely why it has been subordinated in the temples of high culture—museums, libraries, academies. That consensus is falling apart today and the air is rife with possibilities. Disputing taste has become a legitimate and popular activity, some of which is the doing of the ethnic restaurateur, playing with the presumed triviality of literal taste among various American publics. Foreigners have always fed Americans, and Americans have eaten it up, which is unaccounted for in the scholarly discussion of good taste. And that transaction in taste is central to the kinds of democratic openings we have in American culture that are tough to match almost anywhere else in the world, with their preference for roots.

Bibliography

Abarca, M. (2006). *Voices in the Kitchen: Views of Food and the World from Working-Class Mexican and Mexican American Women.* College Station, TX: Texas A&M University Press.

Abbott, A. (1988). *The System of Professions.* Chicago, IL: University of Chicago Press.

ACF (1957). Culinarian's Code. *American Culinary Federation* (website), 2014. Available at http://www.acfno.org/about/ [accessed June 17, 2015].

Achaya, K. T. (1994). *Indian Food: A Historical Companion.* New Delhi: Oxford University Press.

Adams, C. (1987). *Across Seven Seas and Thirteen Rivers. Life Stories of Pioneer Sylheti Settlers in Britain.* London: East Side Books.

Adams, T. L. (2000). *A Dentist and a Gentleman. Gender and the Rise of Dentistry in Ontario.* Toronto: University of Toronto Press.

Aldrich, H. E. and Waldinger, R. (1990). Ethnicity and Entrepreneurship. *Annual Review of Sociology* 16: 111–35.

Andrews, C. (2011). *Ferran: The Inside Story of El Bulli and the Man who Reinvented Food.* New York: Gotham Books.

Appadurai, A., ed. (1986). *The Social Life of Things: Commodities in Cultural Perspective.* Cambridge, UK: Cambridge University Press.

Appadurai, A. (1988). How to Make a National Cuisine: Cookbooks in Contemporary India. *Comparative Studies in Society and History* 30, 1: 3–24.

Appadurai, A. (1996). *Modernity at Large.* Minneapolis, MN: University of Minnesota Press.

Appleton, D. and Company. (1900). *Appleton's Dictionary of New York and Its Vicinity.* New York: D. Appleton and Company.

Arrighi, G. (1994). *The Long Twentieth Century: Money, Power, and the Origins of Our Times.* London: Verso.

Ashley, D. (1939). *Where to Dine in Thirty-Nine. 200 Recipes by Famous Chefs.* New York: Crown Publishers.

Baertlein, L. (2011). Reinvention Helps L.A.'s Foodie Status Soar. *Reuters* (website) August 4, 2011. Available at http://www.reuters.com/article/2011/08/04/uk-restaurants-losangeles-idUSLNE77301B20110804 [accessed August 4, 2011].

Bailey, T. (1985). A Case Study of Immigrants in the Restaurant Industry. *Industrial Relations* 24, 2: 205–21.

Bailey, T. (1987). *Immigrant and Native Workers. Contrasts and Competition.* Boulder, CO: Westview Press.

Bailey, T. and Waldinger, R. (1991). The Changing Ethnic/Racial Division of Labor. In M. Castells and J. H. Mollenkopf, eds. *Dual City: Restructuring New York* (43–78). New York: Russell Sage.

Bald, V. (2013). *Bengali Harlem and the Lost Histories of South Asian America*. Cambridge, Massachusetts: Harvard University Press.

Banville, J. (2003). Secret Geometry. Review of *Henri Cartier-Bresson: The Man, the Image and the World. The New York Review of Books* July 3, 2003: 17–19.

Barber, B. (1963). Some Problems in the Sociology of the Professions. *Daedalus* 92, 4: 669–86.

Baron, A. (1990). Acquiring Manly Competence: The Demise of Apprenticeship and the Remasculinization of Printers' Work. In M. C. Carnes and C. Griffen, eds. *Meanings for Manhood. Constructions of Masculinity in Victorian America* (152–63). Chicago: University of Chicago Press.

Batterberry, M. and Batterberry, A. (1999). *On the Town in New York: The Landmark History of Eating, Drinking, and Entertainments from the American Revolution to the Food Revolution*. New York: Routledge.

Battersby, C. (1989). *Gender and Genius: Towards a Feminist Aesthetics*. London: The Women's Press.

Beck, L. (1898). *New York's Chinatown*. New York: Bohemia Publishing Company.

Becker, H. (1984). *Art Worlds*. Berkeley, CA: University of California Press.

Becker, H. S., Geer, B., Hughes, E. C., and Strauss, A. (1961). *Boys in White: Student Culture in Medical School*. New York: Transaction.

Bégin, C. (2012). "The Slap Slap Motion of the Tortilla": Taste and Race in the American Southwest in the New Deal Era. Paper presented at the American Historical Association Meeting, January 2012.

Belasco, W. (2006). *Appetite for Change. How the Counterculture Took on the Food Industry, 1966–1988*. New York: Pantheon.

Benjamin, W. (1982). *Passengenwerk*. Suhrkamp Verlag: Auflage.

Benjamin, W. (2002). *The Arcades Project*. Cambridge, MA: Harvard University Press.

Bennett, J. (2010). *Vibrant Matter: A Political Ecology of Things*. Durham, NC: Duke University Press.

Bennett, T., Savage, M., Silva, E., Warde, A., Gayo-Cal, M., and Wright, D. (2009). *Culture, Class and Distinction*. New York: Routledge.

Bentley, A. (2004). From Culinary Other to Mainstream America. In L. Long, ed. *Culinary Tourism* (209–25). Lexington: The University Press of Kentucky.

Berg, M. (1997). *Rationalizing Medical Work: Decision-Support Techniques and Medical Practices*. Cambridge, MA: MIT Press.

Berger, S. and Piore, M. (1980). *Dualism and Discontinuity in Industrial Society*. New York: Cambridge University Press.

Berman, M. (1982). *All That Is Solid Melts Into Air*. New York: Penguin.

Bilken, S. K. (1995). *School Work. Gender and the Cultural Construction of Teaching*. New York: Teachers' College, Columbia University Press.

Bishop, E. C. (1911). *Twenty-First Biennial Report of the State Superintendent of Public Instruction to the Governor of the State of Nebraska*. Lincoln, NE: Department of Public Instruction.

Bledstein, B. J. (1976). *The Culture of Professionalism. The Middle Class and the Development of Higher Education in America*. New York: W. W. Norton.

Blumin, S. M. (1989). *The Emergence of the Middle Class: Social Experience in the American City, 1760–1900*. New York: Cambridge University Press.

Boisvert, R. (2013). Cooking up a New Philosophy. *The Philosophers' Magazine*. Available at http://philosophypress.co.uk/?p=1168 [accessed May 27, 2014].

Boisvert, R. (2014). *I Eat, Therefore I Think*. Madison, NJ: Fairleigh Dickinson University Press.

Borgman, C. L. (2015). *Big Data, Little Data, No Data: Scholarship in the Networked World*. Boston, MA: MIT Press.

Bosk, C. L. (1979). *Forgive and Remember: Managing Medical Failure*. Chicago: University of Chicago Press.

Bourdain, A. (2000). *Kitchen Confidential*. New York: HarperCollins.

Bourdieu, P. (1977). *Outline of a Theory of Practice*. Cambridge: Cambridge University Press.

Bourdieu, P. (1984). *Distinction: A Social Critique of the Judgment of Taste*. Cambridge, MA: Harvard University Press.

Bourdieu, P. (1993). *The Field of Cultural Production*. New York: Columbia University Press.

Branch, E. (2012). *Transforming Tastes: M. F. K. Fisher, Julia Child, Alice Waters and the Revision of American Food Rhetorics*. Doctoral dissertation, University of North Carolina at Chapel Hill.

Braudel, F. (1981). *The Structures of Everyday Life. The Limits of the Possible*. New York: Harper & Row.

Braudel, F. (1992). *Civilization and Capitalism. 15th–18th Century, Volume 1: The Structure of Everyday Life*. Berkeley, CA: University of California Press.

Bray, F. (1997). *Technology and Gender*. Berkeley: University of California Press.

Brenner, L. (1999). *American Appetite. The Coming of Age of a Cuisine*. New York: Avon Books.

Brieger, G. H., ed. (1972). *Medical America in the Nineteenth Century: Readings from the Literature*. Baltimore: The Johns Hopkins Press.

Brodkin, K. (1998). *How Jews Became White Folks*. New Brunswick, NJ: Rutgers University Press.

Browne, J. H. (1869). *The Great Metropolis*. Hartford: The American Publishing Company. Available at http://books.google.com/books?id=wotCAAAAIAAJ&pg=PA23&source=gbs_toc_r&cad=4#v=onepage&q&f=false [accessed November 14, 2012].

Bruni, F. (2005). The Contemporary Dining Scene, Estd. 1985. *The New York Times* October 12, 2005: Dining Out section, F1 & F4.

Buettner, E. (2012). "Going for an Indian": South Asian Restaurants and the Limits of Multiculturalism in Britain. In K. Ray and T. Srinivas, eds. *Curried Cultures. Globalization, Food, and South Asia* (143–74). Berkeley, CA: University of California Press.

Bugge, A. B. and Lavik, R. (2010). Eating Out. A Multifaceted Activity in Contemporary Norway. *Food, Culture & Society* 13, 2: 215–40.

Burnett, S. (2007). Selling Ethnicity. Ethnic Restaurants and the Marketing of Difference. Paper submitted at the Food Studies doctoral seminar, December 21, 2007, New York University.

Burns, R. A. (2002). Foodways in the Military. Paper presented at the Annual Meeting of the American Folklore Society, October 19, 2002, Rochester, New York.

Burton, A. (2003). *Dwelling in the Archive. Women Writing, House, Home, and History in Late Colonial India*. Oxford: Oxford University Press.

Butler, J. (1990). *Gender Trouble: Feminism and the Subversion of Identity*. London: Routledge.

Butler, J. (1993). *Bodies That Matter: On the Discursive Limits of Sex*. New York: Routledge.

Cairns, K., Johnston, J., and Bauman, S. (2010). Caring about Food: Doing Gender in the Foodie Kitchen. *Gender and Society* 24, 5: 591–615.

Calhoun, C. (2007). *Nations Matter: Culture, History and the Cosmopolitan Dream*. New York: Routledge.

Capatti, A. and Montanari, M. (2003). *Italian Cuisine. A Cultural History*. New York: Columbia University Press.

Caplow, T. (1978). *The Sociology of Work*. Greenwood Publishing Group.

Cardoz, F. (With Lear, J. D.) (2006). *One Spice, Two Spice. American Food, Indian Flavors*. New York: William Morrow.

Carnes, M. C. and Griffen. C., eds. (1990). *Meanings for Manhood. Constructions of Masculinity in Victorian America*. Chicago: University of Chicago Press.

Carter, J. (1925). Little Brown Men Carry Britain's Flag. *The New York Times* August 30, 1925: SM9.

Casanova, P. (2005a). Literature as a World. *New Left Review* 31, January–February 2005: 71–90.

Casanova, P. (2005b). *The World Republic of Letters*. Cambridge, MA: Harvard University Press.

Cassell, J. (1998). *The Woman in the Surgeon's Body*. Cambridge, MA: Harvard University Press.

Castells, M. (1996). *The Rise of the Network Society*. Oxford: Blackwell.

Cathell, D. W. (1890 [first ed. 1881]). *The Physician Himself and What He Should Add to His Scientific Acquirements*. Baltimore: Cushing & Bailey.

Çelimli, I. (2010). Cook v. Chef. The Production of Inequality in Two New York City Restaurants. Paper presented September 24, 2010 at *Feast/Famine*, Colloquia of the Department of Nutrition, Food Studies and Public Health, New York University.

Cellini, B. (1728). *The Autobiography of Benvenuto Cellini*. 1999 Edition. Penguin USA.

Center for Urban Pedagogy/Street Vendor Project. (2009). *Vendor Power. A Guide to Street Vending in New York City*. New York: Center for Urban Pedagogy.

Chang, D. (with Meehan, P.) (2009). *Momofuku Cookbook*. New York: Clarkson Potter.

Chao, T. (1985). Communicating Through Architecture: San Francisco Chinese Restaurants as Cultural Intersections, 1849–1984. Doctoral dissertation, University of California, Berkeley.

Chappell, G. S. (1925). *The Restaurants of New York*. New York: Greenberg Publishers.

Charles, N. and Kerr, M. (1988). *Women, Food and Families*. Manchester: Manchester University Press.

Chatterjee, P. (1993). *Nationalist Thought in the Colonial World*. Minneapolis, MN: University of Minnesota Press.

Chatterji, J. (2013). Dispositions and Destinations: Refugee Agency and "Mobility Capital" in the Bengal Diaspora, 1947–2007. *Comparative Studies in Society and History* 55, 2: 273–304.

Chatterji, M. (2010). *The Hierarchies of Help. South Asian Service Workers in New York City*. Doctoral dissertation, Department of Social and Cultural Analysis, New York University.

Chatterji, M. (2013). Putting "the Family" to Work. Managerial Discourses of Control in the Immigrant Service Sector. In V. Bald, M. Chatterji, S. Reddy, and M. Vimalassery, eds. *The Sun Never Sets. South Asian Migrants in an Age of U.S. Power* (127–55). New York: New York University Press.

Chiang, C. with Weiss, L. (2007). *The Seventh Daughter. My Culinary Journey from Beijing to San Francisco*. Berkeley, CA: Ten Speed Press.

Chisolm, J. and Bubb, R. (2015). The Greasy Spoon Code: What Legal Norms Among NYC Restaurateurs Teach Us About Ethnic Entrepreneurship. Manuscript. Personal communication.

Cho, L. (2010). *Eating Chinese. Culture on the Menu in Small Town Canada*. Toronto: University of Toronto Press.

Chong, P. (2013). Legitimate Judgment in Art, the Scientific World Reversed? *Social Studies of Science* March 1, 2013: 1–17.

Chow, J. (2014). World's 50 Best Restaurants: How Did Asia Do? *Wall Street Journal* April 29, 2014. Available at http://blogs.wsj.com/scene/2014/04/29/worlds-50-best-restaurants-how-did-asia-do/ [accessed June 17, 2015].

Chu, L. (1939). *The Chinese Restaurants in New York City*. Unpublished Master's thesis. New York University, NY.

Chung, L.T. (1990). *Ethnic Enterprise in the Kansas City Metropolitan Area: The Chinese Restaurant Business, Volumes I and II*. Doctoral dissertation, University of Kansas.

CIA (Culinary Institute of America), Linda Glick Conway, ed. (1991). *The New Professional Chef. Fifth Edition*. New York: Van Nostrand Rhinehold.

CIA (1992). *Proposal for Baccalaureate Degree*. April 20 version. Hyde Park, NY: Culinary Institute of America.

CIA (M. Danovan, ed.). (1995). *The New Professional Chef. Sixth Edition*. New York: Van Nostrand Rhinehold.

CIA. (2002). *Student Handbook & Planner 2002–2003*. Hyde Park, NY: Culinary Institute of America.

CIA (2003). *2002 Bachelor's Degree Alumni Survey*. Hyde Park, NY: Office of Planning, Research, and Accreditation.

CIA (2006). *The New Professional Chef. Eighth Edition*. New York: Van Nostrand Rhinehold.

CIA (2015). About the CIA: Welcome to the World's Premier Culinary College. *Culinary Institute of America* (website). Available at http://www.ciachef.edu/about-the-cia/ [accessed June 17, 2015].

CIA (2014). Student Handbook and Planner 2014/2015. Hyde Park, NY: Culinary Institute of America. Available at https://www.ciachef.edu/uploadedFiles/Pages/CIA_Policies/student-handbook-ny.pdf [accessed June 17, 2015].

Cinotto, S. (2012). *Soft Soil, Black Grapes. The Birth of Italian Winemaking in California*. New York: New York University Press.

Cinotto, S. (2013). *The Italian American Table: Food, Family and Community in New York City*. Urbana-Champagne, IL: University of Illinois Press.

City of New York. (1906). *Report of the Mayor's Pushcart Commission*. New York: City of New York. Available at http://ia600200.us.archive.org/10/items/

reportofmayorspu00newyrich/reportofmayorspu00newyrich.pdf [accessed December 10, 2012].

Cixous, H., Cohen, K., and Cohen, P. (1976). The Laugh of the Medusa. *Signs* 1, 4: 875–93.

Claflin, K. W. (2013). Representation of Food Production and Consumption: Cookbooks as Historical Sources. In A. Murcott, W. Belasco, and P. Jackson., eds. *The Handbook of Food Research* (109–27). London: Bloomsbury.

Claiborne, C. (1959). Use of Native Spices Adds Interest to Unusual Cuisine of Balinese. *The New York Times* October 8, 1959: 46.

Claiborne, C. (1960). Native of New Delhi Prepares Indian Dishes Here. *The New York Times* February 25, 1960: 22.

Claiborne, C. (1964). Variety of French Food Sampled on West Coast. *The New York Times* July 15, 1964: 30.

Clarke, A. E., Shim, J. K., Mamo, L., Fosket, J. R., and Fishman, J. R. (2003). Biomedicalization: Technoscientific Transformations of Health, Illness, and U.S. Biomedicine. *American Sociological Review* 68, 2: 161–94.

Clarkson, J. (2009). *Menus from History: Historical Menus and Recipes for Every Day of the Year*. 2 vols. Santa Barbara, CA: ABC-Clio.

Coe, A. (2009). *Chop Suey. A Cultural History of Chinese Food in the United States*. Oxford: Oxford University Press.

Cohen, A. (2013a). Amanda Cohen on Time Magazine and Female Chefs. *Eater* (website) November 8, 2013. Available at http://eater.com/archives/2013/11/08/amanda-cohen-time.php [accessed November 8, 2013].

Cohen, A. (2013b). Talented Women Are Invisible to the Media. *New York Times* November 11, 2013. Available at http://www.nytimes.com/roomfordebate/2013/11/11/why-do-female-chefs-get-overlooked/talented-female-chefs-are-invisible-to-the-media.

Cole, M. (1788). *The Lady's Complete Guide*. London: printed for G. Kearsley.

Collins, G. (2012). Culinary School's Dining Room to get Fresh Air. *The New York Times* July 2, 2012. Available at http://www.nytimes.com/2012/07/04/dining/culinary-institute-to-renovate-a-teaching-restaurant.html?_r=0&pagewanted=print.

Collins, H. and Evans, R. (2007). *Rethinking Expertise*. Chicago: University of Chicago Press.

Collins, R. (1979). *The Credential Society*. New York: Academic Press.

Conley, F. K. (1998). *Walking Out On The Boys*. New York: Farrar, Straus, and Giroux.

Connerton, P. (1989). *How Societies Remember*. Cambridge: Cambridge University Press.

Conzen, K. N., Gerber, D. A., Morawska, E., Pozetta, G. E., and Vecoli, R. J. (1992). The Invention of Ethnicity: A Perspective From the U.S.A. *Journal of American Ethnic History* 12, 1: 3–41.

Costello, C. (2004). Changing Clothes: Gender Inequality and Professional Socialization. *NWSA Journal* 16, 2: 138–55.

Counts, G. S. (1925). The Social Status of Occupations: A Problem in Vocational Guidance. *The School Review* 33, 1: 16–27.

Csikszentmihalyi, M. and Rochberg-Halton, E. (1981). *The Meaning of Things: Domestic Symbols and the Self*. Cambridge: Cambridge University Press.

Cummings, R. O. (1970). *The American and His Food*. New York: Ayer.

Curtis, E. M. (2013). Cambodian Doughnut Shops and the Negotiation of Identity in Los Angeles. In R. J.-S. Ku, M. Manalansan IV, and A. Mannur. *Eating Asian America* (13–29). New York: New York University Press.
Dalessio, W. R. (2012). *Are We What We Eat? Food and Identity in Late Twentieth-Century American Ethnic Literature*. Amherst, NY: Cambria Press.
Dana, R. W. (1948). *Where to Eat in New York*. New York: Current Books, Inc/A. Wyn Publishers.
Daniels, R. (2002). *Coming to America. A History of Immigration and Ethnicity in American Life*. New York: Perennial.
Das, V., Jackson, M., Kleinman, A., and Singh, B. (2014). *The Ground Between. Anthropologists Engage Philosophy*. Durham, North Carolina: Duke University Press.
Davidoff, L. and Hall, C. (1987). *Family Fortunes: Men and Women of the English Middle Class*. London: Hutchinson.
Davidson. A. and Jaine, T., eds (1999). *The Oxford Companion to Food*. New York: Oxford University Press.
Davidson, C. (2014). Why Higher Education Demands a Paradigm Shift. *Public Culture* 26, 1: 3–11.
Davila, A. (2001). *Latinos, Inc.: The Marketing and Making of a People*. Berkeley, CA: University of California Press.
Davis, J. J. (2013). *Defining Culinary Authority. The Transformation of Cooking in France, 1650–1830*. Baton Rouge, LA: Louisiana State University Press.
Davis, M. (1990). *City of Quartz: Excavating the Future in Los Angeles*. New York: Vintage.
Davis, M. (2003). Personal Communications.
Davis, N. (2002). To Serve the "Other": Chinese-American Immigrants in the Restaurant Business. *Journal for the Study of Food and Society* 6, 1: 70–81.
de Certeau, M. (1984). *The Practice of Everyday Life*. Berkeley, CA: University of California Press.
de Certeau, M., Giard, L., and Mayol, P. (1998). *The Practice of Everyday Life. Volume 2: Living & Cooking*. Minneapolis, MN: University of Minnesota Press.
de la Cruz, Sor Juana Iñes (2009). *La Respuesta (The Answer)*. Translated and edited by E. Arenal and A. Powell. New York: Feminist Press.
de Quattrociocchi, N. (1950). *Love and Dishes*. Indianapolis: Bobba-Merrill.
De Voe, T. F. (1862). *The Market Assistant*. New York: Hurd & Houghton. Available at http://digital.lib.msu.edu/projects/cookbooks/books/marketassistant/mara.pdf [accessed November 14, 2012].
DeLanda, M. (2002). *Intensive Science and Virtual Philosophy*. New York: Continuum.
DeLanda, M. (2006). *A New Philosophy of Society. Assemblage Theory and Social Complexity*. New York: Continuum.
Denker, J. (2003). *The World on a Plate. A Tour through the History of America's Ethnic Cuisines*. Boulder, CO: Westview Press.
Derrida, J. (1991). "Eating Well," or the Calculation of the Subject. In D. Cadava, J.-L. Nancy, and P. Connor, eds. *Who Comes After the Subject?* (96–119) New York: Routledge.
Derrida. J. (2006). *Spectres of Marx*. New York: Routledge.
DeVault, M. (1991). *Feeding the Family: The Social Organization of Caring as Gendered Work*. Chicago: Chicago University Press.

Dickie, G. (1996). *The Century of Taste: The Philosophical Odyssey of Taste in the Eighteenth* Century. New York: Oxford University Press.

DiMaggio, P. and Mukhtar, T. (2004). Arts Participation as Cultural Capital in the United States, 1982–2002: Signs of Decline? *Poetics: Journal of Empirical Research on Culture, the Media and the Arts* 32, 3: 169–94.

Dimock, E. (1995). Bhakti. In Pika Ghosh, ed. *Cooking for the Gods. The Art of Home Ritual in Bengal* (27–31). Exhibit Catalogue. Newark, NJ: The Newark Museum.

Diner, H. (2001). *Hungering for America*. Cambridge, MA: Harvard University Press.

Dixler, H. (2013). Time Editor Howard Chua-Eoan Explains Why No Female Chefs Are "Gods of Food". *Eater* (website) November 7, 2013. Available at http://eater.com/archives/2013/11/07/eater-q-a-time-magazine.php.

Donnison, J. (1977). *Midwives and Medical Men. A History of Inter-Professional Rivalries and Women's Rights*. New York: Schocken Books.

Dornenburg, A. and Page, K. (2003). *Becoming a Chef*. Revised edition. Hoboken, NJ: John Wiley & Sons, Inc.

Downey, G. L. and Dumit, J., eds. (1997). *Cyborgs and Citadels: Anthropological Interventions in Emerging Sciences, Technologies, and Medicines*. Santa Fe, NM: School of American Research.

Dreyfus, H. L. (1991). *Being-in-the-World. A Commentary on Heidegger's* Being and Time. Cambridge, MA: MIT Press.

Druckman, C. (2010). Why Are There No Great Women Chefs? *Gastronomica* 10, 1: 24–31.

Druckman, C. (2012). *Skirt Steak: Women Chefs on Standing the Heat and Staying in the Kitchen*. New York: Chronicle Books.

Duffy, R. (1909). New York at the Table. *Putnam's* 5, 5: 567.

Durkheim, E. (1957). *Professional Ethics and Civil Morals*. 1992 edition. London: Routledge.

Dyson, F. (2003). A New Newton. *The New York Review of Books* July 3, 2003: 4–6.

Eberstadt, F. (2014). Outsider Art. *The New York Times* March 30, 2014: 1, 20.

Edwards, J. C. (1982). *Patriots in Pinstripe: Men of the National Security League*. Washington, DC: University Press of America.

Edwards, S., ed. (1999). *Art and Its Histories. A Reader*. New Haven, CT: Yale University Press.

Ehrenreich, B. (1989). *The Fear of Falling. The Inner Life of the Middle Class*. New York: Harper Perennial.

Ehrenreich, B. and Ehrenreich, J. (1971). *The American Health Empire: Power, Profits, and Politics*. New York: Vintage.

Eisenstein, E. L. (1983). *The Printing Revolution in Early Modern Europe*. Cambridge: Cambridge University Press.

Elias, N. (1982). *The Civilizing Process*. London: Blackwell.

Epstein, C. F. (1993). *Women in Law*. Urbana-Champaign, IL: University of Illinois Press.

Erenberg, L. (1984). *Steppin' Out: New York Night Life and the Transformation of American Culture*. Chicago: University of Chicago Press.

Escoffier, A. (1989) *The Escoffier Cookbook. A Guide to the Fine Art of French Cuisine*. New York: Crown Publishers.

Etzioni, A., ed. (1969). *The Semi-Professions and Their Organization: Teachers, Nurses, Social Workers.* New York: Free Press.
Fabricant, F. (2004). La Caravelle, a French Legend, Is Closing After 43 Years. *New York Times* May 12, 2004: F5.
Falk, P. (1994). *The Consuming Body.* London: Sage.
Featherstone, M., Hepworth, M., and Turner, B. S., eds. (1991). *The Body: Social Process and Cultural Theory.* London: Sage.
Federal Writers Project. (1939/1995). *The WPA Guide to New York City.* New York: The New Press.
Ferguson, P. P. (1998). A Cultural Field in the Making: Gastronomy in 19th Century France. *American Journal of Sociology* 104, 3: 597–641.
Ferguson, P. P. (2004). *Accounting for Taste: The Triumph of French Cuisine.* Chicago, IL: University of Chicago Press.
Ferguson, P. P. and Zukin, S. (1995). What's Cooking? *Theory and Society* 24, 2: 193–9.
Ferguson, P. P. and Zukin, S. (1998). The Careers of Chefs. In R. Scapp and B. Seitz, eds. *Eating* Culture (91–111). Albany: State University of New York Press.
Filippini, A. (1889). *The Table.* New York: Charles Webster.
Fine, G. A. (1992). The Culture of Production: Aesthetic Choices and Constraints in Culinary Work. *The American Journal of Sociology* 97, 5: 1268–94.
Fine, G. A. (1995). Wittgenstein's Kitchen: Sharing Meaning in Restaurant Work. *Theory and Society* 24, 2: 245–69.
Fine, G. A. (1996). *Kitchens: The Culture of Restaurant Work.* Berkeley, CA: University of California Press.
Fischler, C. (1989). La cuisine selon Michelin. *Nourritures, Autrement* 108. Paris.
Fischler, C. (1993). *L'Homnivore.* Second edition. Paris: Odile Jacob.
Fisher, J. (1999). Performing Taste. In B. Fischer, ed. *Food Culture: Tasting Identities and Geographies in Art* (29–47). Toronto: YYZ Books.
Fisher, T. C. G. and Preece, S. B. (2003). Evolution, Extinction, or Status Quo: Canadian Performing Arts Audiences in the 1990s. *Poetics* 31, 2: 69–86.
Fishman, R. M. and Lizardo, O. (2013). How Macro-Historical Change Shapes Cultural Taste: Legacies of Democratization in Spain and Portugal. *American Sociological Review* 78, 2: 213–39.
Flexner, A. (1910). *Medical Education in the United States and Canada. Bulletin Number 4 (The Flexner Report).* New York: Carnegie Foundation for the Advancement of Teaching.
Foner, N., ed. (2013). *One Out of Three. Immigrant New York in the Twenty-First Century.* New York: Columbia University Press.
Foner, N., Rumbaut, R. G., and Gold, S. J. (2000). *Immigration Research for a New Century. Multidisciplinary Perspectives.* New York: Russell Sage Foundation.
Fotta, C. (2003). A review essay of *Kitchen Confidential.* Paper submitted for "Food and Cultures" class, January 2003, Culinary Institute of America.
Foucault, M. (1973). *The Birth of the Clinic. An Archaeology of Medical Perception.* New York: Vintage Books.
Foucault, M. (1978). *Archaeology of Knowledge.* Translated by A. M. Sheridan Smith. New York: Pantheon Books.
Foucault, M. (1980). *Power/Knowledge: Selected Interviews and Other Writings 1972–1977.* Edited by Colin Gordon. New York: Pantheon.

Foucault, M. (1985). Final Interview. *Raritan* (Summer): 8.

Franey, P. (2010). *A Chef's Tale. A Memoir of Food, France & America.* Lincoln, NE: University of Nebraska Press.

Freedman, P. (2011). American Restaurants and Cuisine in the Mid-nineteenth Century. *The New England Quarterly* 84, 1: 5–59.

Freidson, E. (1970). *Profession of Medicine: A Study in the Sociology of Applied Knowledge.* Chicago, IL: University of Chicago Press.

Friedman, M. and Kuznets, S. (1945). *Income from Independent Professional Practice.* New York: National Bureau of Economic Research.

Furst, E. Cooking and Femininity. (1997). *Women's Studies International Forum* 20, 3: 441–9.

Fussell, B. H. (1983). *Masters of American Cookery. M. F. K. Fisher, James Andrews Beard, Raymond Craig Claiborne, Julia McWilliams Child.* New York: Times Books.

Fynsk, C. (1993). *Heidegger. Thought and Historicity.* Expanded edition. Ithaca, NY: Cornell University Press.

Gabaccia, D. R. (1998). *We Are What We Eat. Ethnic Food and the Making of Americans.* Cambridge, Massachusetts: Harvard University Press.

Gambetta, K. and Bandyopadhyay. R. (2012). The Problem. *Seminar* 636, August 2012 (special issue: Streetscapes: A Symposium on the Future of the Street): 1–8. Available at http://www.india-seminar.com/2012/636.htm (accessed February 25, 2013).

Garcia, T. (2014). *Form and Object. A Treatise on Things.* Translated by M. A. Ohm and J. Cogburn. Edinburgh, Scotland: Edinburgh University Press.

Garcia Álvarez, E., Katz-Gerro, T., and Lopez Sintas, J. (2007). Deconstructing Cultural Omnivorousness 1982–2002: Heterology in Americans' Musical Preferences. *Social Forces* 86, 2: 417–43.

Geison, G., ed. (1984). *Professions and the French State, 1700–1900.* Philadelphia: University of Pennsylvania Press.

Gelfand, T. (1980). *Professionalizing Modern Medicine: Paris Surgeons and Medical Science and Institutions in the Eighteenth Century.* Westport, CT: Greenwood Publishing Group.

Ghosh, A. (1993) *In an Antique Land.* New York: Vintage.

Ghosh, R. K. (2003). Art as Dramatization and the Indian Tradition. *The Journal of Aesthetics and Art Criticism* 61, 3: 293–5.

Giard, L. (1998). Doing Cooking. In Michel de Certeau, Luce Giard, and Pierre Mayol, eds. *The Practice of Everyday Life. Volume 2: Living & Cooking* (151–247). Minneapolis, MN: University of Minnesota Press.

Gibson, C. and Jung, K. (2005). Historical Census Statistics on Population By Race, 1790 to 1990, and By Hispanic Origin, 1970 to 1990. *Working Paper 76,* February 2005. Washington, DC: Population Division, United States Census Bureau. Available at http://www.census.gov/population/www/documentation/twps0076/twps0076.html.

Giddens, A. (1991). *Modernity and Self-Identity.* Stanford, CA: Stanford University Press.

Gikandi, S. (2011). *Slavery and the Culture of Taste.* Princeton, NJ: Princeton University Press.

Glasse, H. (1747). *The Art of Cookery, Made Plain and Easy.* London: the author.

Glazer, N. and Moynihan, D. P. (1975). *Ethnicity: Theory and Experience*. Cambridge, MA: Harvard University Press.

Glazer, P. M. and Slater, M. (1987). *Unequal Colleagues. The Entrance of Women into the Professions, 1890–1940*. New Brunswick, NJ: Rutgers University Press.

Gleick, J. (2003). *Isaac Newton*. New York: Pantheon.

Goffman, E. (1959). *The Presentation of Self in Everyday Life*. New York: Anchor Books, Doubleday.

Goode, W. J. (1960). Encroachment, Charlatanism, and the Emerging Professions: Psychology, Sociology and Medicine. *American Sociological Review* 25: 902–14.

Goode, W. J. (1961). The Librarian: From Occupation to Profession? *Library Quarterly* 31: 306–20.

Goody, J. (1982). *Cooking, Cuisine and Class. A Study in Comparative Sociology*. Cambridge: Cambridge University Press.

Graham, R. (2011). Jazz Consumption Among African Americans from 1982 to 2008. *Journal of Black Studies* 42, 6: 993–1018.

Granovetter, M. S. (1985). Economic Action and Social Structure: The Problem of Embeddedness. *American Journal of Sociology* 91, 3: 481–510.

Granovetter, M. S. (1995). The Economic Sociology of Firms and Entrepreneurs. In A. Portes, ed. *Economic Sociology of Immigration* (128–65). New York: Russell Sage.

Grimes, W. (2009). *Appetite City: A Culinary History of New York*. New York: North Point Press.

Grossberg, M. (1990). Institutionalizing Masculinity: The Law as a Masculine Profession. In M. C. Carnes and C. Griffen, eds. *Meanings for Manhood. Constructions of Masculinity in Victorian America* (133–51). Chicago: University of Chicago Press.

Grosz, E. (1994). *Volatile Bodies*. Bloomington, IN: Indiana University Press.

Guardian (2006). If the World's Greatest Chef Cooked for a Living, He'd Starve. *Guardian*. Available at http://observer.guardian.co.uk/foodmonthly/futureoffood/story/0,,1969713,00.html [accessed November 22, 2011].

Guff, S. (2014). Floyd Cardoz on his New Restaurant, *The Hundred-Foot Journey*, and Moving Beyond Burgers. *Grub Street* (website) August 5, 2014. Available at http://www.grubstreet.com/2014/08/floyd-cardoz-white-street-shake-shack.html [accessed January 1, 2015].

Guglielmo, J. and Salemo, S., eds. (2003). *Are Italians White? How Race Is Made in America*. New York: Routledge.

Guibernau, M. and Rex, J., eds. (1999). *The Ethnicity Reader*. New York: Polity.

Guilfoyle, W. (2004). Personal Communication. Professor of Marketing, CIA.

Guyette, W. C. (1981) Executive Chef: Manager or Culinarian. *The Cornell HRA Quarterly* 22, 3: 71–8.

Habenstein, R. W. (1954). The American Funeral Director. Doctoral dissertation, University of Chicago.

Habermas, J. (1989). Work and Weltanschauung: The Heidegger Controversy from a German Perspective. *Critical Inquiry* 15, 2: 431–56.

Hage, G. (1997). At Home in the Entrails of the West: Multiculturalism, "Ethnic Food" and Migrant Home-building. In H. Grace, G. Hage, L. Johnson, J. Langsworth, and M. Symonds, eds. *Home/World. Space, Community and Marginality in Sydney's West* (99–153). Annandale, NSW: Pluto.

Haley, A. P. (2011). *Turning the Tables: Restaurants and the Rise of the American Middle Class, 1880–1920.* Chapel Hill, NC: University of North Carolina Press.

Haley, A. P. (2012). The Nation before Taste: The Challenges of American Culinary History. *Public Historian* 24, 2: 53–78.

Hall, S. (1989). New Ethnicities. In J. Donald and A. Rattansi, eds. *Race, Culture, Difference* (252–9). London: Sage.

Halter, M. (2000). *Shopping for Identity: The Marketing of Ethnicity.* New York: Schocken Books.

Handlin, O. (1951). *The Uprooted.* New York: Little Brown & Company.

Hanel, M. (2014). A Woman's Place is Running the Kitchen. *New York Times Magazine* March 30, 2014: 40–4.

Hansen, K. T. (2004). The World in Dress: Anthropological Perspectives on Clothing, Fashion and Culture. *Annual Review of Anthropology* 33: 369–92.

Harman, G. (2007). *Heidegger Explained: From Phenomenon to Thing.* Chicago: Open Court.

Harman, G. (2009). *Prince of Networks. Bruno Latour and Metaphysics.* Melbourne: re.press.

Harraway, D. (1991). *Simians, Cyborgs, and Women: The Reinvention of Nature.* New York: Routledge.

Harris, B. (1978). *Beyond Her Sphere: Women and the Professions in American History.* Westport, CT: Greenwood Publishing Group.

Harris, D. and Giuffre, P. (2010). Not One of the Guys: Women Chefs Redefining Gender in the Culinary Industry. *Research in the Sociology of Work* 20: 59–81.

Hart, H. H. (1964). *Hart's Guide to New York City.* New York: Hart Publishing Company.

Hartmann, G. W. (1934). The Prestige of Occupations. A Comparison of Educational Occupations and Others. *Personnel Journal* 12: 144–52.

Harvey, D. (2006). *Spaces of Global Capitalism.* London: Verso.

Hassoun, J.-P. (2010). Deux restaurants à New York: l'un franco-maghrébin, l'autre africain. Créations récentes d'exotismes bien tempérés. *Anthropology of Food* 7: 1–20.

Heidegger, M. (1962). *Being and Time.* Trans. J. Macguarrie and E. Robinson. Oxford: Blackwell.

Heidegger, M. (1970). *Poetry, Language, Thought.* Trans. A. Hofstadter. New York: Harper Row.

Heidegger, M. (1976). *What is Called Thinking?* New York: Harper Perennial.

Heidegger, M. (1977). The Question Concerning Technology and Other Essays. Trans. W. Lovitt. New York: Harper and Row—Torchbooks.

Heisler, B. S. (2008). The Sociology of Immigration. In C. B. Bertell and J. F. Hollifield, eds. *Migration Theory. Talking Across Disciplines* (83–111). New York: Routledge.

Heldke, L. (2003). *Exotic Appetites. Ruminations of a Food Adventurer.* New York: Routledge.

Herzfeld, M. (2004). *Body Impolitic.* Chicago: University of Chicago Press.

Hess, J. and Hess, K. (1977). *The Taste of America.* Harmondsworth, UK: Penguin.

Hewitt, J. (1965). Gefilte Fish Finds Place on an International Menu. *The New York Times* April 3 1965: 20.

Higgins, K. M. (2007). An Alchemy of Emotions: Rasa and Aesthetic Breakthroughs. *The Journal Of Aesthetics and Art Criticism* 65, 1 (Special Issue: Global Theories of the Arts and Aesthetics): 43–54.
Highmore, B. (2009). The Taj Mahal in the High Street. The Indian Restaurant as Diasporic Popular Culture. *Food, Culture & Society* 12, 2: 173–90.
Hilgers, L. (2014). The Kitchen Network. America's Underground Chinese Restaurant Workers. *The New Yorker* October 13, 2014. Available at http://www.newyorker.com/magazine/2014/10/13/cooka%C2%80%C2%99s-tale [accessed October 15, 2014].
Hochberg, M. (2007). The Doctor's White Coat: An Historical Perspective. *The Virtual Mentor* 9, 4: 310–14. Available at http://virtualmentor.ama-assn.org/2007/04/mhst1-0704.html [accessed June 7, 2014].
hooks, b. (1992). Eating the Other. In b. hooks. *Black Looks: Race and* Representation (21–39). Boston: South End Press.
Horowitz, R. (2005). *Putting Meat on the American Table: Taste, Technology, Transformation.* Baltimore, MD: Johns Hopkins University Press.
Horowitz, R. (2008). The Politics of Meat Shopping in Antebellum New York City. In P. Y. Lee, ed. *Meat, Modernity and the Rise of the Slaughterhouse* (167–97). Durham, NH: University of New Hampshire Press.
Howes, D. 2005. Architecture of the Senses. In M. Zardini, ed. *Sense of the City. An Alternate Approach to Urbanism* (322–33). Montréal, Canada: Lars Müller Publishers.
Hsia, L. (2003). Eating the Exotic: The Growing Acceptability of Chinese Cuisine in San Francisco, 1848–1915. *Clio Scroll* 5, 1: 5–30.
Huang. E. (2013). *Fresh Off the Boat.* New York: Spiegel & Grau.
Hughes. C. (1939). For Gourmets and Others: Curry comes to the Table. *The New York Times*, March 12, 1939: 53.
Hughes, E. (1958). *Men and Their Work.* Glencoe, IL: Free Press.
Hume, R. H., trans. (1921). *The Thirteen Principal Upanishads.* Oxford: Oxford University Press.
Ignatiev, N. (1995). *How The Irish Became White.* New York: Routledge.
Illich, I. (1976). *Medical Nemesis: The Expropriation of Health.* New York: Pantheon.
India Abroad. (1992). Restaurateur. XXIII (13): 44.
India Abroad. (2001–2013). Weekly Newspaper. New York: *India Abroad.*
India Tribune. (2001–2013). Weekly Newspaper. Chicago: *India Tribune.*
Inwood, M. (1999). *A Heidegger Dictionary.* New York: Whiley-Blackwell.
Jacobson, M. F. (1999). *Whiteness of a Different Color: European Immigrants and the Alchemy of Race.* Cambridge, MA: Harvard University Press.
Jaggar, A. and Bordo, S. (1989). *Gender/Body/Knowledge: Feminist Reconstructions of Being and Knowing.* New Brunswick, NJ: Rutgers University Press.
James, R. 1930. *Dining in New York.* 1st edition. New York: John Day Company.
James, R. 1934. *Dining in New York.* 2nd edition. New York: John Day Company.
James, R. 1938. *Dining in New York.* 3rd edition. New York: John Day Company.
Janeja, M. (2010). *Transactions in Taste.* London: Routledge.
Janer, Z. (2006). The Geopolitics of Culinary Knowledge. *Seminar* #566, October 2006: Culinary Crossings. A Symposium on the Globalization of Indian Cuisine. Available at http://www.india-seminar.com/2006/566.htm [accessed October 12, 2012].

Janer, Z. (2008). *Latino Food Culture.* Westport, CT: Greenwood Press.
Jayaraman, S. (2013). *Behind the Kitchen Door.* Ithaca, NY: Cornell University Press.
Jin, D. 1997. The Sojourners' Story: Philadelphia's Chinese Immigrants, 1900–1925. Doctoral dissertation, Temple University.
Jinich, P. (2014). Tex-Mex Cooking: It's Not Mexican, Maybe That's the Point. *Washington Post* January 28, 2014. Available at http://www.washingtonpost.com/lifestyle/food/tex-mex-cooking-its-not-mexican-and-maybe-thats-the-point/2014/01/27/577c515c-850a-11e3-9dd4-e7278db80d86_print.html [accessed January 29, 2014].
Johnson, T. J. (1972). *Professions and Power.* Cambridge: Macmillan.
Johnston, J. and Baumann, S. (2007). Democracy versus Distinction: A Study of Omnivorousness in Gourmet Food Writing. *American Journal of Sociology* 113, 1: 165–204.
Johnston, J. and Baumann, S. (2010). *Foodies. Democracy and Distinction in the Gourmet Foodscape.* New York: Routledge.
Jordi, N. (2004). "Our Apprenticeship at the Art of Graceful Living": American Distinction Through French Cooking, 1941–1980. Thesis submitted at Brown University, Department of Gender Studies.
Jou, C. (2014). Neither Welcomed, Nor Refused: Race and Restaurants in Postwar New York City. *Journal of Urban History* 40, 2: 232–51.
Kallick, D. D. (2013). Immigration and Economic Growth in New York City. In N. Foner, ed. *One Out of Three. Immigrant New York in the Twenty-First Century* (64–89). New York: Columbia University Press.
Katz, F. E. (1969). Nurses. In A. Etzioni, ed. *The Semi-Professions and Their Organization* (54–81). New York: Free Press.
Katz, P. (1999). *The Scalpel's Edge. The Culture of Surgeons.* Boston: Allyn and Bacon.
Katz-Rothman, B. (2016 prospective). *A Bun in the Oven. Artisanal Responses to Industralized Food and Birth.* Manuscript version. Personal communication.
Keller, T. (with Ruhlman, M.) (1999). *The French Laundry Cookbook.* New York: Artisan.
Keller, T. (with Cruz, D., Heller, S., Ruhlman, M., and Vogler, A.) (2009). *Ad Hoc. At Home. Family-Style Recipes.* New York: Artisan.
Khare, R. S. (1976a). *Culture and Reality: Essays on the Hindu System of Managing Foods.* Simla: Indian Institute of Advanced Studies.
Khare, R. S. (1976b). *The Hindu Hearth and Home.* Delhi: Vikas Publishing House.
Khare, R. S., ed. (1992). *The Eternal Food. Gastronomic Ideas and Experiences of Hindus and Buddhists.* Albany: SUNY Press.
Khare, R. S. and Rae, M. S. A., eds. (1986). *Food, Society and Culture: Aspects in Food Systems of South Asia.* Durham: Carolina Academic Press.
Kinnear, M. (1995). *In Subordination. Professional Women, 1870–1970.* Montreal: McGill-Queen's University Press.
Kirshenblatt-Gimblett, B. (1999). Playing to the Senses: Food as a Performance Medium. *Performance Research* 4, 1: 1—30.
Kohn, S. (2013). Where Are All the Female Chefs? *The Daily Beast* (website) November 14, 2013. Available at http://www.thedailybeast.com/witw/articles/2013/11/14/where-are-all-the-female-chefs-on-time-magazine-s-cover.html.

Kondo, D. K. (1990). *Crafting Selves. Power, Gender and Discourses of Identity in a Japanese Workplace.* Chicago: University of Chicago Press.

Korsmeyer, Carolyn. (1999). *Making Sense of Taste: Food and Philosophy.* Ithaca, NY: Cornell University Press.

Kosiak, A. (2011). Art and Celebrity: The Role of the Chef in the Modern Food Industry. Term paper written for Contemporary Issues in Food Studies class. New York: New York University.

Ku, R., Manalansan, M. F., and Mannur, A. (2013). *Eating Asian America: A Food Studies Reader.* New York: New York University Press.

Kuh, P. (2001). *The Last Days of Haute Cuisine.* New York: Viking.

Kuhn, T. S. (1962). *The Structure of Scientific Revolutions.* Chicago: University of Chicago Press.

Lamont, M. (2012). How Has Bourdieu Been Good to Think With? The Case of the United States. *Sociological Forum* 27, 1: 228–37.

Landa, J. (1981). A Theory of the Ethnically Homogenous Middleman Group: An Institutional Alternative to Contract Law. *Journal of Legal Studies* 10, 2: 349–62.

Lang, J. H., ed. (1988). *Larousse Gastronomique.* New York: Crown Publishers.

Larson, M. S. (1977). *The Rise of Professionalism. A Sociological Analysis.* Berkeley: University of California Press.

Lasater-Wille, A. (2015). *The Taste of Distinction: Culinary Education and the Production of Social Difference in Lima, Peru.* Doctoral dissertation, Department of Anthropology, New York University.

Latour, B. (1986). *Laboratory Life. The Construction of Scientific Facts.* 2nd edition. Princeton, NJ: Princeton University Press.

Latour, B. (2005). *Reassembling the Social. An Introduction to Actor-Network-Theory.* Oxford: Oxford University Press.

Lave, J. and Wenger, E. (1991). *Situated Learning.* Cambridge: Cambridge University Press.

Lawson, A. H. and Deutsch, J., eds. (2008). *Gastropolis: Food and New York City.* New York: Columbia University Press.

Leavis, F. R. (1962). *Two Cultures? The Significance of C. P. Snow.* New York: Pantheon Books.

Lee, C. B. T. (1965). *Chinatown, U. S. A.* Garden City, NY: Doubleday.

Lee, H. R. (2013). A Life Cooking for Others: The Work and Migration Experiences of a Chinese Restaurant Worker in New York City, 1920–1947. In R. Ku, M. F. Manalansan, and A. Mannur, eds. *Eating Asian America: A Food Studies Reader* (53–77). New York: New York University Press.

Lee, J. 8. (2009). *The Fortune Cookie Chronicles. Adventures in the World of Chinese Food.* New York: Ten Press.

Lee, P. Y. (2014). The Kimchi Revolution: How Korean-American Chefs Are Changing Food Culture. *Salon* (website) April 7, 2014. Available at http://www.salon.com/2014/04/07/the_kimchi_revolution_how_korean_american_chefs_are_changing_food_culture/ [accessed 11 January, 2015].

Lehmann, G. (2003). *The British Housewife: Cookery Books, Cooking and Society in Eighteenth-Century Britain.* Totnes, UK: Prospect Books.

Lehmann, T. (1992). *New Career Paths for Baccalaureate Graduates: Survey of Industry Leaders.* Hyde Park: CIA.

Leland, R. G. (1931). Income from Medical Practice. *JAMA* 96, 20: 1687–91.

Leong, E. (2013). Collecting Knowledge for the Family: Recipes, Gender and Practical Knowledge in the Early Modern English Household. *Centaurus* 55: 81–103.

Leschziner, V. (2012). Recipes for Success: Elite Chefs, Restaurateurs, and Culinary Styles in New York and San Francisco. Doctoral dissertation, University of Toronto.

Leschziner, V. and Green, A. I. (2013). Thinking about Food and Sex: Deliberate Cognition in the Routine Practices of a Field. *Sociological Theory* 31, 2: 116–44.

Levenstein, H. (1988/2003). *Revolution at the Table*. Berkeley, CA: University of California Press.

Levenstein, H. (1988). *Revolution at the Table. The Transformation of the American Diet*. New York: Oxford University Press.

Levenstein, H. (1989). Two Hundred Years of French Food in America. *The Journal of Gastronomy* 5, 1: 66–89.

Levenstein, H. (1993). *Paradox of Plenty: A Social History of Eating in Modern America*. New York: Oxford University Press.

Levenstein, H. (2003). The American Response to Italian Food, 1880–1930. In M. C. Counihan, ed. *Food in the USA* (75–90). New York: Routledge.

Levi-Strauss, C. (1976). *Structural Anthropology, Volume 2*. New York: Basic Books.

Lewis, Scribner & Co. (1903). *Where and How to Dine in New York*. New York: Lewis, Scribner & Co.

Liaw, A. (2013). Is the Michelin Guide Relevant in Asia? *The Wall Street Journal* January 28, 2013. Available at http://blogs.wsj.com/scene/2013/01/28/is-the-michelin-guide-relevant-in-asia/.

Light, I. (1972). *Ethnic Enterprise in America: Business and Welfare among Chinese, Japanese, and Blacks*. Berkeley, CA: University of California Press.

Light, I. and Bonacich, E. (1988). *Immigrant Entrepreneurs*. Berkeley, CA: University of California Press.

Lindblom, C. E. (1997). Political Science in the 1940s and 1950s. *Daedalus* 126, 1: 225–52.

Litt, J. S. (2000). *Medicalized Motherhood: Perspectives from the Lives of African-American and Jewish Women*. New Brunswick, NJ: Rutgers University Press.

Liu, H. (2009). Chop Suey as Imagined Authentic Chinese Food: The Culinary Identity of Chinese Restaurants in the United States. *Journal of Transnational American Studies* 1,1: 1–24.

Liu, H. and Lin, L. (2009). Food, Culinary Identity, and Transnational Culture: Chinese Restaurant Business in Southern California. *Journal of Asian American Studies* 12, 2: 135–62.

Lizardo, O. and Skiles, S. (2012). Reconceptualizing and Theorizing "Omnivorousness": Genetic and Relational Mechanism. *Sociological Theory* 30, 4: 263–82.

Lobel, C. R. (2014). *Urban Appetites. Food & Culture in Nineteenth-Century New York*. Chicago: University of Chicago Press.

Lock, M. M. (1993). *Encounters with Aging: Mythologies of Menopause in Japan and North America*. Berkeley, CA: University of California Press.

Lock, M. and Farquhar, J., eds. (2007). *Beyond the Body Proper: Reading the*

Anthropology of Material Life (Body, Commodity, Text). Durham, NC: Duke University Press.

Long, L. M., ed. (2004). *Culinary Tourism*. Lexington, KY: University Press of Kentucky.

Lopez Sintas, J. and Garcia Álvarez, E. (2004). Omnivore versus Univore Consumption and Its Symbolic Properties: Evidence from Spaniards' Performing Arts Attendance. *Poetics: Journal of Empirical Research on Culture, the Media and the Arts* 32, 6: 463–83.

Lowe, D. (1982). *History of Bourgeois Perception*. Chicago: University of Chicago Press.

Lubow, A. (2003). A Laboratory of Taste. *New York Times Magazine* August 10, 2003. Available at http://www.nytimes.com/2003/08/10/magazine/10SPAIN.html [accessed May 26, 2014].

Ludden, D. (2003). Investing in Nature around Sylhet: An Excursion into Geographical History. *Economic and Political Weekly* 38, 48: 5080–8.

Lu, S. and Fine, G. A. (1995). The Presentation of Ethnic Authenticity Chinese Food as a Social Accomplishment. *Sociological Quarterly* 36, 3: 535–53.

Lupton, D. (1996). *Food, the Body and the Self*. London, UK: Sage.

Lupton, D. (1999). *Risk*. London: Routledge.

Lynn, K. S., with the editors of *Daedalus*, eds. (1967). *The Professions in America*. Boston, MA: Beacon Press.

MacCannell, D. (1976). *The Tourist. A Theory of the Leisure Class*. New York: Schocken Books.

Maccioni, S. and Elliot, P. J. (2004). *Sirio: The Story of My Life and Le Cirque*. New Jersey: Wiley.

Mackall, L. (1948). *Knife and Fork in New York. Where to Eat. What to Order*. New York: Robert M. McBride & Co.

Malamoud, C. (1996). *Cooking the World: Ritual and Thought in Ancient India*. Oxford: Oxford University Press.

Manhattan Classified Telephone Directory (1906). New York.

Manhattan Classified Telephone Directory (1929–1930, Winter). New York.

Manhattan Classified Telephone Directory (1939, Spring–Summer). New York.

Manhattan Classified Telephone Directory (1949, May). New York.

Manhattan Telephone Directory. Yellow Pages (1959). New York.

Manhattan Yellow Pages. New York City Area Code 212 (1969). New York.

Manhattan Yellow Pages. New York City Area Code 212 (1978–1979). New York.

Manhattan Yellow Pages. Manhattan Area Code 212 (1988–1989). New York: NYNEX.

Manhattan Yellow Pages. Area Code 212/917 (May 1998–April 1999). New York: Bell Atlantic.

Manhattan Yellow Pages. Area Codes 212, 646, 917 (October 2007). New York: Verizon.

Manzo, J. T. (1998). From Pushcart to Modular Restaurant: The Diner on the Landscape. In Shortridge, B. G. and Shortridge, J. R. eds. *The Taste of American Place. A Reader on Regional and Ethnic Foods* (215–25). New York: Rowan & Littlefield.

Marcuse, H. (1964). *One-Dimensional Man: Studies in the Ideology of Advanced Industrial Society*. Boston: Beacon Press.

Markovits, C. (2008). *Merchants, Traders, Entrepreneurs: Indian Business in the Colonial Era*. Houndmills, UK: Palgrave Macmillan.

Maroney, S. (2011). "To Make a Curry the India Way": Tracking the Meaning of Curry Across Eighteenth-Century Communities. *Food & Foodways* 19, 1–2: 122–34.

Martin, E. (1994). *Flexible Bodies: The Role of Immunity in American Culture from the Days of Polio to AIDS*. Boston, MA: Beacon.

Mauss, M. (1935). Techniques of the Body. *Journal de psychologie normal et patholigique* XXXII: 271–93.

McAllister, W. (1890). *Society As I Have Found It*. New York: Cassell.

McClellan, A. (1994). *Inventing the Louvre. Art, Politics and the Origins of the Modern Museum in Eighteenth-Century Paris*. Berkeley, CA: University of California Press.

McGuirk, T. (2010). Heidegger's Rift: The Epistemological Significance of Drawing. *Studies in Material Thinking* 4. Available at http://www.materialthinking.org [accessed July 2, 2011].

McInerney, J. (2010). It Was Delicious while it Lasted. *Vanity Fair* October 2010. Available at http://www.vanityfair.com/culture/features/2010/10/el-bulli-201010 [accessed May 26, 2014].

McWilliams, J. (2005). *A Revolution in Eating*. New York: Columbia University Press.

Meehan, P. (2004). Positively Sixth Street. *The New York Times* September 1, 2004.

Meehan, P. and Gold, J. (2015). The State of Ramen. *Lucky Peach* (website) January 20, 2015. Available at http://luckypeach.com/the-state-of-ramen-jonathan-gold/?utm_source=newsletterJan202015&utm_medium=email&utm_campaign=GoldStateofRamen [accessed January 20, 2015].

Mennell, S. (1985). *All Manners of Food*. London: Basil Blackwell.

Menupages.com (2007). [Dacca] Indian Cuisine, User Reviews. *Menu Pages* (website) December 11, 2007.

Menupages.com (2009). New York City Restaurants: Indian. *Menu Pages* (website) July 31, 2009. Available at http://www.menupages.com/restaurants/all-areas/all-neighborhoods/indian/ [accessed July 31, 2009].

Menupages.com (2015). New York City Restaurants: Indian. Menu Pages (website) June 10, 2015. Available at http://www.menupages.com/restaurants/all-areas/all-neighborhoods/indian/ [accessed June 10, 2015].

Merchants' Association of New York (1906). *Pocket Guide to New York*. New York: The Merchants' Association of New York.

Merleau-Ponty, M. (1969). *The Prose of the World*. Evanston, IL: Northwestern University Press.

Merleau-Ponty, M. (2012). *Phenomenology of Perception*. New York: Routledge.

Michelin (2014). Michelin Guide: New York City 2014. *Michelin Travel* (website). Available at http://www.michelintravel.com/michelin-selection/new-york-city-2014/ [accessed January 2, 2014].

Miller, D. (1987). *Material Culture and Mass Consumption*. London: Basil Blackwell.

Mills, C. W. (1951). *White Collar: The American Middle Classes*. London: Oxford University Press.

Min, P. G. (2013). Koreans. Changes in New York in the Twenty-First Century. In N. Foner, ed. *One Out of Three. Immigrant New York in the Twenty-First Century* (148–75). New York: Columbia University Press.

Möhring, M. (2007). Foreign Cuisine in West Germany. *GHI Bulletin*, 41: 79–88.

Möhring. M. Harris, V., Könczöl, B., and Motadel, D. (2014). Food for Thought: Rethinking the History of Migration to West Germany through the Migrant Restaurant Business. *Journal of Contemporary History* 49, 1: 209–27.

Mol, A. (2003). *The Body Multiple*. Durham, NC: Duke University Press.

Molotch, H. (2003). *Where Stuff Comes From: How Toasters, Toilets, Cars, Computers and Many Other Things Come to Be as They Are*. New York: Routledge.

More, L. B. (1907). *Wage-earner's Budget*. New York: Holt.

Moreno, M. (1992). Pancamirtam: God's Washings as Food. In R. S. Khare, ed. *The Eternal Food. Gastronomic Ideas and Experiences of Hindus and Buddhists* (147–78). Albany: SUNY.

Moreno, S. M. (1903). *Guia de Nueva York*. New York: Union Square Hotel.

Moretti, F. (2013). *Distant Reading*. London: Verso Press.

Morgan, C. (1996). *Public Men and Virtuous Women: The Gendered Language of Religion and Politics in Upper Canada, 1791–1850*. Toronto: University of Toronto Press.

Morgan, H. (1935). Our Wide Taste in Food. *The New York Times* October 13, 1935: SM17.

Moscucci, O. (1990). *The Science of Woman, Gynaecology and Gender in England, 1800–1929*. Cambridge: Cambridge University Press.

Moskin, J. (2014). A Change in the Kitchen. *The New York Times* January 21, 2014: D1–D6.

Mukhopadhyay, B. (2004). Between Elite Hysteria and Subaltern Carnivalesque: The Politics of Street Food in the City of Calcutta. *South Asia Research* 24, 1: 37–50.

Murcott, A. (2000). Is It Still a Pleasure to Cook for Him? Social Changes in the Household and the Family. *Journal of Consumer Studies and Home Economics* 24, 2: 78–84.

Nagle, J. J. (1960). Tastes Widening for Kosher Food. *The New York Times* November 6, 1960: F10.

Nandy, A. (2003). Ethnic Cuisine: The Significant Other. In Geeti Sen., ed. *India. A National Culture?* (246–51) New Delhi: Sage Publications.

Narayan, U. (1995). Eating Cultures: Incorporation, Identity and Indian Food. *Social Identities* 1, 1: 63–86.

Narayan, U. (1997). *Dislocating Cultures. Identities, Traditions and Third World Feminism*. New York: Routledge.

National Restaurant Association (1985). *Restaurant Industry Operations Report 1984*. Washington, DC: NRA.

National Restaurant Association (1988). *Current Issues Report: Foodservice Manager 2000*. Washington DC: NRA.

National Restaurant Association (1992). *Restaurant Industry Operations Report 1993*. Washington, DC: NRA.

National Restaurant Association (1999). *Ethnic Food*. Washington, DC: NRA.

National Restaurant Association (2000). Ethnic Cuisine II. Washington, DC: NRA. Available at http://www.restaurant.org/pressroom/pressrelease/?id=125 [accessed July 25, 2011].

National Restaurant Association (2001). *Restaurant Industry Operations Report 2000.* Washington, DC: NRA.

National Restaurant Association (2004). *Restaurant Industry Operations Report 2003.* Washington, DC: NRA.

National Restaurant Association (2010). *Restaurant Industry Operations Report 2003.* Washington, DC: NRA.

Navarro, V. (1986). *Crisis, Health, and Medicine: A Social Critique.* New York: Tavistock.

New York City Department of City Planning (2010). *NYC 2020: Results from the 2010 American Community Survey. Socioeconomic Characteristics by Race/Hispanic Origin and Ancestry Group.* NY: NYC Department of City Planning. Available at http://www.nyc.gov/html/dcp/pdf/census/acs_socio_10_nyc.pdf.

New York Daily Tribune. (1845). Eating Houses in New York. New York Daily Tribune, October 7, 1845: 5.

New York Daily Tribune (1901). Increase in Chinese Restaurants. *New York Daily Tribune* May 27, 1901: 4.

New York Sun (1901). The Italian's Cookery. *New York Sun*, July 1901.

New York Times (1862). Delmonico's New Restaurant. *The New York Times* April 7, 1862: 5.

New York Times (1871). Cheap Restaurants: Something About the German, French, and Italian Dining-Saloons of New York. *The New York Times* August 6, 1871: 5.

New York Times (1872). Middle-Age Cookery. *The New York Times* October 25, 1872: 4.

New York Times (1873). German Restaurants. *The New York Times* January 19, 1873.

New York Times (1880). An Octopus Eaten by Chinamen. *The New York Times* December 6, 1880.

New York Times (1881). Men Who Live Down Town. *The New York Times* December 4, 1881: 3.

New York Times (1883). Found in Garbage-Boxes Stuff that is Utilized for Food by Some People. *The New York Times* July 15, 1883.

New York Times (1885). The Restaurant System: Choice Cuisine at Reasonable Figures; How Foreign Fashions Are Acclimatized in New-York. *The New York Times* May 24, 1885: 3.

New York Times (1898). Teutonic Cookery. *The New York Times* June 5, 1998: Lippincott's Magazine, 17.

New York Times (1900). Heard About Town. *The New York Times* January 29, 1900: 7.

New York Times (1903). Chop Suey Resorts. *The New York Times* November 15, 1903: 20.

New York Times (1920). Business Changes in Times Square. *The New York Times* December 26, 1920: 82.

New York Times (1948). News of Food: Restaurateur from Lahore Transplants Indian Dishes to New Dining Place Here. *The New York Times* February 21, 1948: 10.

Newark Museum. (1995). *Cooking for the Gods. The Art of Home Ritual in Bengal.* Philadelphia, PA: Newark Museum.

Ngai, M. (2010). *The Lucky Ones: One Family and the Extraordinary Invention of Chinese America.* Boston: Houghton Mifflin Harcourt.

Nickerson, J. (1946). News of Food. *The New York Times* September 7, 1946: 12.
Nickerson, J. (1955). Food: A Touch of India in New York. *The New York Times* September 19, 1955: 20.
Nochlin, L. (1971). Why Have There Been No Great Women Artists? *Art News* 69: 22–39.
Norton, M. (2006). Tasting Empire: Chocolate and the European Internalization of Mesoamerican Aesthetics. *The American Historical Review* 111, 3: 660–91.
Norton, M. (2008). *Sacred Gifts, Profane Pleasures: A History of Tobacco and Chocolate in the Atlantic World.* Ithaca: Cornell University Press.
Nwosu, C., J. Batalova, and G. Auclair (2014). Frequently Requested Statistics on Immigration and Immigrants in the United States. *Migration Information Source* April 28, 2014. Washington DC: Migration Policy Institute. Available at http://www.migrationpolicy.org/article/frequently-requested-statistics-immigrants-and-immigration-united-states [accessed January 18, 2015].
NYC Health (n.d.). Restaurant Inspection Results (Letter Grades). The New York City Department of Health and Mental Hygiene. Available at http://www.nyc.gov/html/doh/html/services/restaurant-inspection.shtml.
OED (*Oxford English Dictionary*) (1989). Oxford: Clarendon.
Omni, M. and Winant, H. (1994). *Racial Formation in the United States: From the 1960s to the 1990s.* New York: Routledge.
Orkin. I. (2015). The 5 Ramen Shops You Should Visit in Tokyo. *Lucky Peach* (website) January 20, 2015. Available at http://luckypeach.com/the-five-ramen-shops-you-can-and-should-visit-in-tokyo/.
Orleck, A. (2013). Soviet Jews. The Continuing Russification of Jewish New York. In N. Foner, ed. *One Out of Three. Immigrant New York in the Twenty-First Century* (90–119). New York: Columbia University Press.
Osler, W. (1906). *Aequanimitas. With Other Addresses to Medical Students, Nurses and Practitioners of Medicine.* New York: McGraw-Hill, Inc.
Pais, A. J. (2011a). Floyd's the Top Chef Master. *India Abroad* June 24, 2011: A3.
Pais, A. J. (2011b). Tandoori Twist. *India Abroad* February 25, 2011: M5.
Park, K. (1997). *The Korean American Dream. Immigrants and Small Business in New York City.* Ithaca, NY: Cornell University Press.
Parry, J. (1985). Death and Digestion: The Symbolism of Food and Eating in North Indian Mortuary Rites. *Man* (new series) 20, 4: 612–30.
Parsons, R. (2013). Time's "Gods of Food": Women Chefs Talk Back. *Los Angeles Times* November 13, 2013. Available at http://www.latimes.com/food/dailydish/la-dd-times-gods-of-food-women-chefs-talk-back-20131113,0,1469036.story#axzz2kdMgGCJ6.
Parsons, T. (1968). Professions. In D. L. Sills, ed. *The International Encyclopedia of the Social Sciences* (536–46). New York: Macmillan.
Peiss, K. (1986). *Cheap Amusements: Working Women and Leisure in the Turn-of-the-Century New York.* Philadelphia: Temple University Press.
Pellegrini, A. (1971). An Italian Odyssey: From Famine to Feast. In J. P. Shenton, D. Brown, A. M. Pellegrini, I. Shenker, P. Wood, and the Editors of Time-Life Books, eds. *American Cooking: The Melting Pot* (27–47). New York: Time-Life Books.
Pépin, J. (2003). *The Apprentice: My Life in the Kitchen.* New York: Houghton Mifflin Company.

Peterson, R. A. (1997). The Rise and Fall of Highbrow Snobbery as a Status Marker. *Poetics: Journal of Empirical Research on Culture, the Media and the Arts* 25, 2: 75–92.
Peterson, R. A. and Kern, R. M. (1996). Changing Highbrow Taste: From Snob to Omnivore. *American Sociological Review* 61, 5: 900–07.
Peterson, R. A. and Simkus, A. (1992). How Musical Taste Groups Mark Occupational Status Groups. In M. Lamont and M. Fournier, eds. *Cultivating Differences: Symbolic Boundaries and the Making of Inequality* (152–68). Chicago: University of Chicago Press.
Pham, Vu H. (2006). Secret Kitchen: An Amalgam of Family, Fortune and Fusion Food in Asian American Cuisine. *Amerasia Journal* 32, 2: 21–34.
Pilcher, J. (2012). *Planet Taco. A Global History of Mexican Food.* New York: Oxford University Press.
Piore, M. J. (1980). *Migrant Labor and Industrial Societies.* Cambridge: CUP.
Polanyi, K. (1944). *The Great Transformation.* Boston, MA: Beacon.
Polanyi, M. (1962). Tacit Knowing: Its Bearing on Some Problems of Philosophy. *Reviews of Modern Physics* 34, 4: 606–16.
Polanyi, M. (1966). *The Tacit Dimension.* Chicago: University of Chicago Press.
Polk, R. L. & Co. (1920–1921). *Trow General Directory of New York City.* New York: R. L. Polk & Co.
Porter, R. (1997). *The Greatest Benefit to Mankind. A Medical History of Humanity.* New York: W. W. Norton.
Portes, A., ed. (1995). *The Economic Sociology of Immigration. Essays on Networks, Ethnicity, and Entrepreneurship.* New York: Russell Sage Foundation.
Pottier, J. (2014). Savoring "The Authentic." The Emergence of a Bangladeshi Cuisine in East London. *Food, Culture & Society* 17, 1: 7–26.
Power, D. (1933). *A Short History of Surgery.* London: John Bale and Danielson.
Psilakis, M. (with Binns, B. and Shapiro, E.) (2009). *How to Roast a Lamb. New Greek Classic Cooking.* New York: Little, Brown and Company.
Rabinow, P. (1992). Artificiality and Enlightenment: From Sociobiology to Biosociality. In J. Crary and S. Kwinter, eds. *Incorporations* (234–52). New York: Zone.
Raghavan, V. 1966. *The Great Integrators: The Saint-Singers of India.* Delhi: Ministry of Information and Broadcasting.
Rana, P. (2014). How the Indian Man Leads the World in Preening. *The Wall Street Journal (India)*, March 7, 2014. Available at http://blogs.wsj.com/indiarealtime/2014/03/07/how-the-indian-man-leads-the-world-in-preening/ [accessed March 28, 2014].
Rand, McNally & Co. (1901). *Handy Guide to New York City.* New York: Rand, McNally & Co.
Rand, McNally & Co. (1909). *Handy Guide to New York City.* New York: Rand, McNally & Co.
Randolph, M. (1838). *The Virginia Housewife.* Baltimore, MD: Plaskitt, Fitt & Co.
Rao, H., Monin, P., and Durand, R. (2003). Institutional Change in Tocque Ville: Nouvelle Cuisine as an Identity Movement in French Gastronomy. *American Journal of Sociology* 108, 4: 795–843.
Rao, H., Monin, P., and Durand., R. (2005). Border Crossing: Bricolage and the Erosion of Categorical Boundaries in French Gastronomy. *The American Sociological Review* 70, 9: 868–991.

Rapp, R. (1999). *Testing Women, Testing the Fetus: The Social Impact of Amniocentesis in America*. New York: Routledge.

Ravage, M. (1917). *An American in the Making*. New York: Harper & Brothers.

Ray, K. (2004). *The Migrant's Table. Meals and Memories in Bengali-American Households*. Philadelphia: Temple University Press.

Ray, K. (2007a). Domesticating Cuisine: Food and Aesthetics on American Television. *Gastronomica* 7, 1: 50–63.

Ray, K. (2007b). Ethnic Succession and the New American Restaurant Cuisine. In D. Beriss and D. Sutton, eds. *The Restaurants Book. Ethnographies of Where We Eat* (97–114). New York: Berg.

Ray, K. (2010). A Taste for Ethnic Difference: American Gustatory Imagination in a Globalizing World. In J. Farrer, ed. *Globalization, Food and Social Identities in the Asia Pacific Region*. Tokyo: Sophia University Institute of Comparative Culture. Available at http://icc.fla.sophia.ac.jp/global%20food%20papers/html/ray.html.

Ray, K. and Srinivas, T., eds. *Curried Cultures. Globalization, Food, and South Asia*. Berkeley, CA: University of California Press.

Ray, U. (2009). *Culture of Food in Colonial Bengal*. Doctoral dissertation, Department of History, Pennsylvania State University.

Ray, U. (2010). Aestheticizing Labor? An Affective Discourse of Cooking in Colonial Bengal. *South Asian History and Culture* 1,1:60–70.

Reardon, J. (1994). *M. F. K. Fisher, Julia Child, and Alice Waters: Celebrating the Pleasures of the Table*. New York: Harmony.

Redzepi, R. (2010). *NOMA. Time and Place in Nordic Cuisine*. New York: Phaidon.

Reinitz, B. (1925). Chop Suey's New Role. *The New York Times* December 27, 1925: XX2.

Relman, A. S. (1980). The Medical-Industrial Complex. *New England Journal of Medicine* 303: 963–70.

Richman, A. (2014). The Rise of Egotarian Cuisine. *GQ* March 18, 2014. Available at http://www.gq.com/life/food/201403/alan-richman-dude-food?currentPage=1 [accessed March 27, 2014].

Ritzer, G. (1996). *The McDonaldization of Society*. Thousand Oaks, CA: Pine Forge Press.

ROC-NY. (2005). *Behind the Kitchen Door*. New York: Restaurant Opportunities Center of New York. Available at http://www.urbanjustice.org/pdf/publications/BKDFinalReport.pdf [accessed July 13, 2013].

Roediger, D. (2007). *The Wages of Whiteness: Race and the Making of the American Working Class*. New York: Verso.

Rogers, A. and Vertovec, S., eds. (1995). *The Urban Context. Ethnicity, Social Networks and Situational Analysis*. Oxford: Berg.

Romines, A. (1997). Growing Up with the Methodist Cookbooks. In A. L. Bower, ed. *Recipes for Reading. Community Cookbooks, Stories, Histories* (75–88). Amherst, MA: University of Massachusetts Press.

Roosth, S. (2013). Of Foams and Formalisms: Scientific Expertise and Craft Practice in Molecular Gastronomy. *American Anthropologist* 115, 1:4–16.

Root, W. and de Rochemont, R. (1976). *Eating in America: A History*. New York: Ecco Press.

Ross, J. P. (1968). On Teaching by Example. *Surgery, Gynecology, and Obstretics* 127: 1317–18.

Rossant, J. (2004). *Super Chef. The Making of the Great Modern Restaurant Empires.* New York: Free Press.
Roy, P. (2010). *Alimentary Tracts.* Duke University Press.
Rueschemeyer, D. (1964). Doctors and Lawyers: A Comment on the Theory of the Professions. *Canadian Review of Sociology and Anthropology* 1, 1: 17–30.
Rueschemeyer, D. (1973). *Lawyers and Their Society: A Comparative Study of the Legal Profession in Germany and the United States.* Cambridge, MA: Harvard University Press.
Ruggles, S., Alexander, J. T., Genadek, K., Goeken, R, Schroeder, M. B., and Sobek, M. (2004). *Integrated Public Use Microdata Series* [IPUMS]: Version 3.0, Machine-readable Database. Minneapolis, MN: Minnesota Population Center.
Ruhlman, M. (1997). *The Making of a Chef.* New York: Owl Books.
Rushdie, S. (1997). *The Moor's Last Sigh.* New York: Vintage.
Rushdie, S. (2009). *The Enchantress of Florence.* New York: Random House.
Ryan, M. (1981). *Cradle of the Middle Class. The Family in Onieda County, New York, 1790–1865.* New York: Cambridge University Press.
Said, E. (1979). *Orientalism.* New York: Vintage.
Salinger, S. V. (2002). *Taverns and Drinking in Early America.* Baltimore: Johns Hopkins University Press.
San Pellegrino (2010). The World's 50 Best Restaurants. Available at http://www.theworlds50best.com/ [accessed November 22, 2011].
Saran, S. and Lyness, S. (2004). *Indian Home Cooking. A Fresh Introduction to Indian Food.* New York: Clarkson Potter.
Sassen, S. (1995). Immigration and Local Labor Markets. In A. Portes, ed. *Economic Sociology of Immigration* (87–127). New York: Russell Sage.
Sassen, S. (2001). *The Global City: New York, London, Tokyo.* Princeton, NJ: Princeton University Press.
Sassen, S. (2006). *Cities in a World Economy.* Thousand Oaks, CA: Pine Forge/ Sage Publications.
Sax, D. (2014). *The Tastemakers.* New York: Public Affairs.
Schechner, R. (2007). Rasaesthetics. In S. Barnes and A. Lepecki, eds. *The Senses in Performance* (10–28). New York: Routledge.
Schelling, T. C. (1978). *Micromotives and Macrobehavior.* New York: Norton.
Schleifer, D. (2010). Reforming Food: How Trans-fats Entered and Exited the American Food System. Ph.D. Dissertation, Sociology, NYU. Paper presented at *Feast/Famine: A Food Studies Colloquia*, New York, October 15, 2010.
Schmidt, P. (1974). As If a Cookbook Had Anything to Do with Writing. *Prose* 8: 179–203.
Schwartz, V. R. (2007). *It's So French! Hollywood, Paris, and the Making of Cosmopolitan Film Culture.* Chicago: University of Chicago Press.
Scott, J. (1985). *Weapons of the Week. Everyday Forms of Resistance.* New Haven, CT: Yale University Press.
Scott, J. (1992). *Domination and the Arts of Resistance: Hidden Transcripts.* New Haven, CT: Yale University Press.
Scott, J. (1998). *Seeing Like a State. How Certain Schemes to Improve the Human Condition Have Failed.* New Haven, CT: Yale University Press.
Searle, J. (1983). *Intentionality: An Essay in the Philosophy of the Mind.* Cambridge: Cambridge University Press.

Sennett, R. (1994). *Flesh and Stone. The Body and the City in Western Civilization.* New York: Norton.
Serematakis, C. N., ed. (1994). *The Senses Still: Perception and Memory as Material Culture in Modernity.* Boulder: Westview Press.
Sertich Velie, M. (2015). Pretty in Pink: Gender and the Presentation of Professionalism in the Culinary Industry. Term paper submitted for the MA class Theoretical Perspectives in Food Studies, NYU, Spring 2015.
Shapin, S. (2012). The Sciences of Subjectivity. *Social Studies of Science* 42, 2: 170–84.
Shapiro, L. (2008). Where Are the Women? *Gourmet* (website) June 12, 2008. Available at http://www.gourmet.com/restaurants/2008/06/womenchefs18ff.html?currentPage=1 [accessed June 21, 2015].
Shierholz, H. (2014). *Low Wages and Few Benefits Mean Many Restaurant Workers Can't Make Ends Meet.* Briefing Paper 383. Washington, DC: Economic Policy Institute. Available at http://www.epi.org/publication/restaurant-workers/.
Shulman, R. (2012). *Eat the City: A Tale of the Fishers, Trappers, Foragers, Slaughterers, Butchers, Farmers, Poultry Minders, Sugar Refiners, Cane Cutters, Bee-keepers, Winemakers, and Brewers Who Built New York.* New York: Crown.
Shusterman, R. (2003). Definition, Dramatization and Rasa. *The Journal of Aesthetics and Art Criticism* 61, 3: 295–8.
Sifton, S. (2011). Crosstown Tour of India. *The New York Times* March 29, 2011. Available at http://www.nytimes.com/2011/03/30/dining/reviews/30rest.html?pagewanted=all [accessed June 16, 2011].
Silberman, L. (2013). Famous Italian Chef Gives some Sage Advice to Young People in the Restaurant Industry. *Business Insider* (website) October 21, 2013. Available at http://www.businessinsider.com/life-lessons-from-massimo-bottura-2013-10 [accessed October 22, 2013].
Simmel, G. (1990). *The Philosophy of Money.* London: Routledge.
Small, M. L. (2009). *Unanticipated Gains: Origins of Network Inequality in Everyday Life.* New York: Oxford University Press.
Smith, A. F. (2005). The French Culinary Influence in America Since World War II. Unpublished manuscript.
Smith, A. F. (2014). *New York City. A Food Biography.* New York: Rowan & Littlefield.
Smith, M. (2007). *Sensing the Past.* Berkeley, CA: University of California Press.
Snow, C. P. (1959). *The Two Cultures and the Scientific Revolution.* New York: Random House.
Snyder, G. (1995). *A Place in Space: Ethics, Aesthetics and Watersheds.* New York: Counterpoint.
Sollors, W., ed. (1997). *Theories of Ethnicity.* New York: NYU Press.
Sombert, W. (1922). *Luxury and Capitalism.* Ann Arbor, MI: University of Michigan Press.
Spang, R. (2000). *The Invention of the Restaurant: Paris and Modern Gastronomic Culture.* Cambridge, MA: Harvard University Press.
Spivak, G. C. (1988). Can the Subaltern Speak? In C. Nelson and L. Grossberg, eds. *Marxism and the Interpretation of Culture* (271–313). Basingstoke, UK: Macmillan.

Stanley, T. J. and Danko, W. D. (1996). *The Millionaire Next Door. The Surprising Secrets of America's Wealthy*. New York: Pocket Books.
Starr, P. (1982). *The Social Transformation of American Medicine*. New York: Basic Books.
Stein, G. (1973). *Everybody's Autobiography*. New York: Vintage.
Steinberg, S. (1989). *The Ethnic Myth. Race, Ethnicity, and Class in America*. Boston, MA: Beacon Press.
Stoller, P. (2002). *Money Has No Smell. The Africanization of New York City*. Chicago: University of Chicago Press.
Street Vendor Project. (2006) *Peddling Uphill*. NY: Urban Justice Center. Available at http://www.scribd.com/doc/18948529/Peddling-Uphill.
Suleri, S. (1992). Woman Skin Deep: Feminism and the Postcolonial Condition. *Critical Inquiry* 18, 4: 756–69.
Sullivan, O., and Katz-Gero, T. (2007). The Omnivorousness Thesis Revisited: Voracious Cultural Consumers. *European Sociological Review* 23, 2: 123–37.
Sutton, D. (2001). *Remembrance of Repasts*. London: Bloomsbury Academic.
Swash, M., ed. (1995). *Hutchinson's Clinical Methods*. New York: W. B. Saunders.
Swidler, A. (2001). What Anchors Cultural Practices? In Schatzki, T. R., Knott Cetina, K., and Von Savigny, E., eds. *The Practice Turn in Contemporary Theory* (74–92). London & New York: Routledge.
Taussig, M. (1992/2007). Tactility and Distraction. In M. Lock and J. Farquhar, eds. *Beyond the Body Proper. Reading The Anthropology of Material Life* (259–65). Durham, NC: Duke University Press.
Terrio, S. (2000). *Crafting the Culture and History of French Chocolate*. Berkeley, CA: University of California Press.
Tharu, S. and Lalita, K., eds. (1991). *Women Writing in India*. Volume 1. New York: Feminist Press.
Thompson, E. P. (1964). *The Making of the English Working Class*. New York: Pantheon Books.
Thompson, E. P. (1971). The Moral Economy of the English Crowd in the Eighteenth Century. *Past and Present* 50: 76–136.
Tierney, J. (2013). What is Nostalgia Good For? Quite a Bit, Research Shows. *The New York Times* July 9, 2013: D1. Available at http://www.nytimes.com/2013/07/09/science/what-is-nostalgia-good-for-quite-a-bit-research-shows.html?pagewanted=all&_r=0 [accessed July 13, 2013].
Time (1966). Everyone's in the Kitchen. *Time* November 25, 1966.
Time (2013). The Gods of Food. *Time* November 18, 2013.
Tishgart, S. (2013). "Goddesses of Food: 10 World-class Chefs Who—Believe It or Not—Are Women. *Grubstreet* (website) November 8, 2013. Available at http://www.grubstreet.com/2013/11/time-gods-of-food-women.html [accessed November 9, 2013].
Toner, R. (2003). Weapon in Health Wars: Frist's Role as a Doctor. *The New York Times* January 11, 2003: A12.
Tosh, J. (1999). *A Man's Place: Masculinity and the Middle-Class Home in Victorian England*. New Haven, CT: Yale University Press.
Tower, J. (2003). *California Dish: What I Saw (and Cooked) at the American Culinary Revolution*. New York: Free Press.
Trillin, C. (1994). *The Tummy Trilogy*. New York: Farrar Strauss and Giroux.
Trubek, A. (2004). *Haute Cuisine: How the French Invented the Culinary Profession*. State College, PA: Pennsylvania State University.

Tuchman, G. and Levine, H. G. (1993). New York Jews and Chinese Food. The Social Construction of an Ethnic Pattern. *Journal of Contemporary Ethnography* 22, 3: 382–407.

Turner, B. S. (1984). *The Body & Society*. London: Sage.

Urban, G. (2001). *Metaculture. How Culture Moves Through the World*. Minneapolis, MN: University of Minnesota Press.

US Census Bureau. (2004). Mini-Historical Statistics. *Statistical Abstract of the United States*, 2003. Available at http://www.census.gov [accessed August 21, 2004].

van Eijck, K. (2001). Social Differentiation in Musical Taste Patterns. *Social Forces* 79, 3: 1163–84.

van Gelder, R. (1944). Introducing the "I Got a Song" Man. *The New York Times* October 22, 1944: X1.

Vander Stichele, A. and Laermans, R. (2006). Cultural Participation in Flanders: Testing the Cultural Omnivore Thesis with Population Data. *Poetics: Journal of Empirical Research on Culture, the Media and the Arts* 34, 1: 45–64.

Vasari, G. (1568). *Lives of the Artists*. 1998 edition. Oxford: Oxford University Press.

Victor (1852). Philadelphia. *The New York Times* October 27, 1852: 2.

Wacquant, L. (2004). *Body & Soul. Notebooks of an Apprentice Boxer*. New York: Oxford University Press.

Waldinger, R. (1986). *Through the Eye of the Needle: Immigrants and Enterprise in the New York Garment Industry*. New York: New York University Press.

Waldinger, R. (1990). Immigrant Enterprise in the United States. In S. Zukin and P. DiMaggio, eds. *Structures of Capital: The Social Organization of the Economy* (395–424). Cambridge: Cambridge University Press.

Waldinger, R. (1992). Taking Care of the Guests: The Impact of Immigrants on Services—An Industry Case Study. *International Journal of Urban and Regional Research* 16, 1: 97–113.

Waldinger, R. (1993). Immigrant Enterprise in the United States. In S. Zukin, and P. DiMaggio, eds. *Structures of Capital. The Social Organization of the Economy* (395–424). Cambridge: Cambridge University Press.

Waldinger, R., ed. (2001). *Strangers at the Gates*. Berkeley, CA: University of California Press.

Waldinger, R. (2015). *The Cross-Border Connection. Immigrants, Emigrants, and Their Homelands*. Cambridge, MA: Harvard University Press.

Wall Street Journal (2013). Scene's Top Food Stories of 2013. *The Wall Street Journal* December 27, 2013. Available at http://blogs.wsj.com/scene/2013/12/27/scenes-top-food-stories-of-2013/ [accessed December 27, 2013].

Wallach, J. J. (2013). *How America Eats. A Social History of U.S. Food and Culture*. New York: Rowan & Littlefield.

Wallerstein, I. (2003). *Decline of American Power: The U.S. in a Chaotic World*. New York: New Press.

Walsh, J. (2004). *Domesticity in Colonial India. What Women Learned When Men Gave Them Advice*. Oxford: Oxford University Press.

Walsh, M. R. (1976). *Doctors Wanted: No Women Need Apply. Sexual Barriers in the Medical Profession, 1835–1875*. New Haven, CT: Yale University Press.

Wangensteen, O. H. (1975). The Surgical Amphitheatre: History of the Origins, Functions, and Fate. *Surgery* 77, 3: 403–18.

Wangensteen, O. H. and Wangensteen, S. D. (1978). *The Rise of Surgery: From Empiric Craft to Scientific Discipline*. Minneapolis: University of Minnesota Press.

Warde, A. (1997). *Consumption, Food & Taste*. London: Sage.

Warde, A. (2009). Imagining British Cuisine. *Food, Culture & Society* 12,2: 151–71.

Warde, A. and Martens, L. (2000). *Eating Out. Social Differentiation Consumption and Pleasure*. Cambridge: Cambridge University Press.

Warde, A., Martens, L., and Olsen, W. (1999). Consumption and the Problems of Variety: Cultural Omnivorousness, Social Distinction and Dining Out. *Sociology* 33,1: 105–27.

Watson, James L. 1997. *Golden Arches East. McDonald's in East Asia*. Stanford, CA: Stanford University Press.

Weber, M. (1968). *Economy and Society*. New York: Bedminster Press.

Weir, R. (1999). Not for the Faint of Palate. Guinea Pig, Cow's Spleen, All Part of City's Diet. *The New York Times* May 16, 1999: CY3.

Westfall, R. S. (1983). *Never at Rest*. Cambridge: Cambridge University Press.

Westwood, S. and Bhachu, P., eds. (1988). *Enterprising Women. Ethnicity, Economy and Gender Relations*. London: Routledge.

Wilensky, H. (1964). The Professionalisation of Everyone? *American Journal of Sociology* 70, 2: 137–58.

Willis, C. (1995). *Form Follows Finance: Skyscrapers and Skylines in New York and Chicago*. Princeton, NJ: Princeton Architectural Press.

Witz, A. (1992). *Professions and Patriarchy*. London: Routledge.

Woolf, V. (1929). *A Room of One's Own*. London: Harcourt.

Xu, W. (2007). *Eating Identities*. Hawaii: University of Hawaii Press.

Yates, J. and Van Maanen, J., eds. (2001). *Information Technology and Organizational Transformation: History, Rhetoric, and Practice*. Thousand Oaks, CA: Sage.

Yee, S. J. (2012). *An Immigrant Neighborhood: Interethnic and Interracial Encounters in New York before 1930*. Philadelphia: Temple University Press.

Yee, V. and Singer, J. E. (2013). The Death of a Family, and an American Dream. *The New York Times* December 30, 2013: A1.

Yelp.com (n.d.). Tulsi (reviews). *Yelp.com* (website). Available at http://www.yelp.com/biz/tulsi-new-york [accessed June 19, 2015].

Zagat (1989). *1990 New York City Restaurants*. New York: Zagat.

Zagat (1992). *America's Top Restaurants*. New York: Zagat.

Zagat (1999). *2000 New York City Restaurants*. New York: Zagat.

Zagat (2000). *America's Top Restaurants*. New York: Zagat.

Zagat (2003). *2004 New York City Restaurants*. New York: Zagat.

Zagat (2004). *America's Top Restaurants*. New York: Zagat.

Zagat (2010). *2011 New York City Restaurants*. New York: Zagat.

Zagat (2013). *2014 New York City Restaurants*. New York: Zagat.

Zardini, M., ed. (2005). *Sense of the City. An Alternative Approach to Urbanism*. Montréal: Canadian Center for Architecture and Lars Müller Publishers.

Zavisca, J. (2005). The Status of Cultural Omnivorousness: A Case Study of Reading in Russia. *Social Forces* 84, 2: 1233–55.

Zelinsky, W. (1985). The Roving Palate: North America's Ethnic Restaurant Cuisines. *Geoforum* 16, 1: 51–72.

Zhang, J. (1999). *Transplanting Identity: A Study of Chinese Immigrants and the Chinese Restaurant Business*. Doctoral dissertation, Southern Illinois University at Carbondale.

Zhao, J. (1996). *Strangers in the City: The Atlanta Chinese, Their Community, and Stories of their Lives*. Doctoral dissertation, Emory University.

Zhou, M. (2004). Revisiting Ethnic Entrepreneurship: Convergences, Controversies, and Conceptual Advancements. *International Migration Review* 38, 3: 1040–74.

Ziegelman, J. (2010). *97 Orchard. An Edible History of Five Immigrant Families in One New York Tenement*. New York: Harper Collins.

Zimmer, C. (2015) How Singapore Transformed Itself into a Food Lover's Destination. *The Salt* (blog), February 15, 2015.

Zukin, S. (1982). *Loft Living. Culture and Capital in Urban Change*. Baltimore, ML: Johns Hopkins Press.

Zukin, S. (1991). *Landscapes of Power*. Berkeley, CA: University of California Press.

Zukin, S. (1995). *The Cultures of Cities*. Cambridge, MA: Blackwell.

Zukin, S. (2010). *Naked City. The Death and Life of Authentic Urban Places*. Oxford: Oxford University Press.

Index